Lesbians, Gays, & the Empowerment Perspective

EMPOWERING THE POWERLESS
Alex Gitterman, Series Editor

EMPOWERING THE POWERLESS: A SOCIAL WORK SERIES
Alex Gitterman, Series Editor

The Empowerment Tradition in American Social Work: A History
Barbara Levy Simon

Organizing for Power and Empowerment
Jacqueline B. Mondros and Scott W. Wilson

Empowering Women of Color
Lorraine M. Gutiérrez and Edith A. Lewis

This series provides perspectives on empowerment strategy in social work, which seeks to help clients draw on personal, interpersonal, and political power to enable them to gain greater control over their environments and attain their aspirations.

Lesbians, Gays & the Empowerment Perspective

Carol T. Tully

Columbia University Press
New York

Columbia University Press
Publishers Since 1893
New York   Chichester, West Sussex
Copyright © 2000 Columbia University Press

Library of Congress Cataloging-in-Publication Data

Tully, Carol Thorpe
    Lesbians, gays, and the empowerment perspective / Carol T. Tully.
        p. cm. — (Empowering the powerless)
    Includes bibliographical references and index.
    ISBN 0-231-10958-X (cloth) — ISBN 0-231-10959-8 (pbk.)
    1. Social work with gays. 2. Social work with lesbians. 3. Gays—Social
    conditions. 4. Homosexuality. 5. Homophobia. I. Title. II. Series.

HV1449.T86 2000
362.8—dc21   99-087520

∞
Printed in the United States of America
c 10 9 8 7 6 5 4 3 2 1
p 10 9 8 7 6 5 4 3 2 1

For E. Jean Walker My Best Friend

Contents

Editor's Note

Lesbians, Gays, and the Empowering Perspective is the fourth book in the social work series, Empowering the Powerless, published by Columbia University Press. Historically, lesbian and gay persons have been severely victimized. Despite some modest advances, they continue to be an oppressed and disenfranchised minority with limited protection under the law. Religious, political, and legal forces institutionalize social homophobia, discrimination, and stigmatization.

When I practiced with adolescents, I was struck by how alone gay and lesbian youngsters were with their pain—alone in charting the transition as a gay/lesbian adolescent to becoming a gay/lesbian young adult. They confronted a painful dilemma in deciding to remain in or out of the closet with their family members and peers, to be true to themselves, or to hurt and threaten those they cared most about. Those few who disclosed often experienced reactions of hurt, disappointment, rejection, and abandonment. Understandably. most kept their "secret" to themselves.

I wondered how to help these youngsters struggle with the existential question of "Who am I?" if the people they care most about did not know, accept, ignored, or rejected their sexual orientation. They lacked family and peer supporters and adult gay and lesbian role models and I lacked sufficient knowledge and skills. I would have greatly benefited from reading *Lesbians, Gays, and the Empowerment Perspective*. Hence I am pleased that the current generation of social workers will be able to make use of this wonderful resource.

Professor Tully places homosexuality in a comprehensive historical perspective. She traces the institutional nature of homophobia over thousands of years and identifies the antecedent roots of oppression and discrimination. Then, she applies the empowerment perspective to gay and lesbian persons. Based on the empowerment perspective, she presents a model for macro and micro interventions. The assumption that heterosexuality is better than homosexuality (heterosexism) has a profound impact on service delivery and social work practice. Professor Tully instructs us on how to counteract these powerful social forces, and how to develop sensitive assessments and effective interventions.

I present the series' fourth book, *Lesbians, Gays, and the Empowerment Perspective* with particular pleasure. Professor Tully's eloquent writing and rich substance makes an irrefutable contribution to the literature of our profession.

ALEX GITTERMAN, GENERAL EDITOR

Preface

The concept of empowerment is one that has evolved from a variety of philosophical perspectives and has been embraced by social work professionals as a pragmatic method of operationalizing many social work constructs related to the profession's commitment to working with people and the environments in which they live ("person-in-environment"). While the term "empowerment" is of recent historical vintage, the principles that underlie the term and the applications of its principles are not. Since its inception in the late nineteenth century, social work has been dedicated to the empowerment of disenfranchised persons and minority groups. These include individuals and groups that have historically faced broad-based discrimination related to individual and collective legal and civil liberties and rights because of their ethnicity, race, age, physical ability, religion, political affiliation, or sexual orientation.

Because social workers traditionally have worked with disenfranchised and marginalized individuals and groups that have suffered discrimination, it is not surprising that the empowerment perspective should find its way into the social work practitioner's tool kit. Many social work texts now include concepts related to the use of the empowerment perspective (or the strengths perspective) in a general fashion but fail to explore how this dynamic perspective can be utilized with specific populations. The purpose of this book is to explore the empowerment perspective and its application with lesbian women and gay men.

The book first presents a three-chapter overview of the evolution of concepts related to gay men and lesbian women, the political realities associated with homosexuality, and a conceptual framework for the development of the empowerment perspective and how this perspective can be applied to the lesbian and gay subculture.

Chapter 1 explores, from a historical perspective, realities of gays and lesbians in the Premodern Era (before 1700 c.e.), the Modern Era (1700–1969), and the Postmodern Era (1969 to date) and the evolution of the construct of homosexuality from simply a behavior to an integral part of the personality and identity and from homosexuality as a sin, a crime, and a mental illness to a minority group worthy of legal protections. The political realities associated with lesbians and gays are detailed in the second chapter, where a political continuum is presented. Views about gays and lesbians are presented from the far right of the continuum (e.g., Aryan Nation, Ku Klux Klan) through the middle (American Civil Liberties Union, National Association of Social Workers) to the far left of the continuum (Queer Nation, Lesbian Avengers). The third chapter describes the evolution of the empowerment perspective and its application to the lesbian and gay community. The concepts of homophobia are delineated and the conceptual framework for the application of the empowerment perspective with gays and lesbians is provided.

With the first three chapters serving as theoretical background, chapters 4, 5, and 6 discuss how the empowerment perspective can be used with various populations of lesbians and gays. Using the life cycle approach, chapter 4 explores empowerment with gay and lesbian adolescents, chapter 5 uses the concepts with lesbian and gay adults, and chapter 6 deals with older gays and lesbians. Each chapter focuses on micro-, mezzo-, and macro-levels of social work intervention and brief case examples at each level are found at the end of each chapter. Finally, chapter 7 looks at empowerment through the current lens of social work, politics, and past and possible future trends.

Throughout, issues related to bisexuality and transgender identity are included only incidentally. While some may see this as a shortcoming, the sociopolitical dilemmas associated with both groups deserve their own study. The book has been written in gender neutral language as far as is possible, and generally uses the terms "lesbian" and "gay." The term "homosexual" is used somewhat throughout the text and the term "queer," while having its current advocates, has been used sparingly. "Nongay" is frequently used to describe what others call "heterosexual."

Acknowledgments

The creation of a book-length manuscript is not a solitary journey. Rather, it is an adventure of mythic proportion filled with a wide array of wonderfully interesting people. To each of the persons involved with my journey I owe a great debt of thanks. First, I would like to thank Alex Gitterman, the editor of the series on empowerment, of which this book is a part. His thoughtful and thorough critiques of each chapter were extraordinarily helpful. His insights about organization were on target and he helped me craft the manuscript into one that is less convoluted than my original ideas.

Of my colleagues at the Tulane University School of Social Work, I especially want to thank Betty Torre Reck, whose keen intellect helped me sort out some of the mysteries of philosophy, and Lynn Pearlmutter, who answered my many questions about practice. My dear friend Gary Lloyd is to be thanked for getting me involved in this project in the first place, and while there were times I was less than grateful for the opportunity he gave me, I owe him more than I can say. My master's and doctoral students were, and continue to be, a source of support, inspiration, and information. Many conversations have been held about whether or not the empowerment perspective and the strength perspective are the same. Jeanne LeBlanc, a doctoral student, read and critiqued parts of the manuscript and she, like all of my students, has watched the three-year evolution of the manuscript with eager anticipation.

The staff at Columbia University Press has been terrific—John Michel and Alexander Thorp (who has now moved on to other adventures) provided funny stories, kind words, and even the names of persons to index the volume. Mary Swigonski and John Longres were the readers who read the final draft of the manuscript and provided extremely thoughtful and detailed critiques of my work. Most of their comments have been incorporated into the final draft and I sincerely thank them for all the time and effort they put forth on my behalf. I also owe Georgia DeLabarre, a whiz with computer graphics, who helped with the figures a big thank-you. Gary Mallon and Barbara Simon were always supportive, and knowing they were there really helped.

On a more personal note, there are many more people who need to be thanked. I have been fortunate in my professional career to have been supported and encouraged by Natalie Woodman, Hilda Hidalgo, Travis Peterson, Bernice Goodman, Ray Berger, Jim Kelly, and Diane Bernard all of whom have provided me with opportunities to write various manuscripts for various publications or serve on editorial boards. To these and countless others who helped me learn my craft, thanks so much. My late parents, Francis and Laura Tully provided me with every possible opportunity and supported me with love and understanding, and my first parents, Harold and Patricia Stauffer, provided me with great genes. But, mostly my thanks goes to E. Jean Walker, my life partner without whose help and constant friendship, love, support, and editorial critique this manuscript would be far less than it is. The first chapter is primarily hers, and in its creation she learned more about herself than she had known.

Lesbians, Gays, & the Empowerment Perspective

1

Homosexuality in Historical Perspective

Descriptions of the Greeks, the berdaches, and the Sambia should make us a little unsure about our categories homosexual *and* heterosexual—*at least, they should make us think more carefully about what we mean by these words. But if we are now a little confused about categories, perhaps we can agree on a few simple facts about human sexuality: (1) same-sex eroticism has existed for thousands of years in vastly different times and cultures; (2) in some cultures, same-sex eroticism was accepted as a normal aspect of human sexuality, practiced by nearly all individuals some of the time; and (3) in nearly every culture that has been examined in any detail, a few individuals seem to experience a compelling and abiding sexual orientation toward their own sex.*
Mondimore 1996:20.

One of the difficulties inherent in attempting to place any concept in historical perspective is that circumstances and terminology change over time and across cultures. This is certainly the case in dealing with the concept of homosexuality. While significant data exist which demonstrate that same-sex practices have been present in all historical periods since human life on earth began, the word *homosexuality* did not exist prior to 1869. The term first appeared in a pamphlet authored by Karl Maria Kertbeny, a German-Hungarian writer, translator, and journalist. While same-sex eroticism was condemned in some places and times, it was considered quite acceptable and even expected in others (Mondimore 1996). Even to use the term "homosexuality" in this chapter title (and as used throughout the book) presents some problems since, for reasons which will become clear, this word has fallen out of favor in postmodern gay society and has been replaced by other terms, such as "gay persons," "lesbians," "gay men," and "queer."

Drawing from the historical work done in the field (Adams 1987; Boswell 1980, 1994; Brooten 1996; Bullough 1976, 1979: Bullough and Bullough 1995; Faderman 1981, 1991; Greenberg 1988; Mondimore 1996), this chapter examines the antecedent roots of homosexuality by exploring the societal context of gays and lesbians across time. Providing a comprehensive, worldwide perspective is outside the scope of this chapter; rather, the focus will be on those historical periods and events that have contributed most directly to the American gay and lesbian movement. My purpose is to introduce the reader to the realities of gay and lesbian persons by providing a general overview demonstrating the existence of such persons throughout history, identifying periods of intense persecution and relative tolerance, and recognizing the resilience and persistence of persons of same-sex orientation across time. For purposes of this discussion, history will be divided into three periods: the Premodern Era (before 1700); the Modern Era (1700–1969); and the Postmodern Era (1969 to the present).

The Premodern Era: Before 1700

Prehistoric: Before 3700 B.C.E.

Two primary methods of gaining information about this vast period of history are available. Obviously, one method is the study of artifacts (graves, tools, cities, etc.); sources of such information are relatively few and very fragmented. Thus, historians, anthropologists, sociologists, and other scholars have turned to the second method-the study of existing tribal societies whose lifestyles closely resemble what prehistoric life was believed to be like. While many of the results of such cross-cultural and cross-historical study are suspect (largely because of the unevenness of the data collected and the conscious or unconscious biases of the observers), researchers have been able to make some general observations regarding prehistoric lifestyle, religious practices, family structure, and sexual behavior patterns, including those involving same-sex practices (Bullough 1976; Dynes and Donaldson 1992b; Ford and Beach 1951; Greenberg 1988; Mondimore 1996).

How prehistoric and primitive people viewed sexuality in general is important to understand before looking specifically at same-sex practices. Mondimore (1996) describes this attitude as relaxed and accepting. Sex was generally seen as a gift from the spirit world, a pleasure to be enjoyed. Sexual play among children and adolescents was not forbidden or discouraged. Same-sex bonding was almost an expectation between male and female adolescents, although such bonding among adults apparently was often discouraged. Generally, people appear to have accepted diversity in gender and sexual expression.

One of the early and most comprehensive of the cross-cultural and cross-historical studies was conducted by Ford and Beach (1951). They studied some 190 cultural groups or peoples from around the world, all of which had been the subject of firsthand observations. Even after acknowledging the limitations imposed by the nature and extent of the evidence, the authors found that in 49 of the 76 (64%) societies for which records were available to them, "homosexual activities of one sort or another are considered normal and socially acceptable for certain members of the community" (Ford and Beach 1951: 130). Partly because data regarding female homosexuality was not available (specific information for women was available for only 17 of the 190 peoples included in the sample), the authors concluded that homosexual behavior appeared to be generally more common in men than in women.

In a more recent study that explored primitive cultures, Greenberg (1988) devotes an entire chapter to "Homosexual Relations in Kinship-Structured Societies." He discusses three types of same-sex relations—transgenerational (in which the partners are of disparate ages); transgenderal (in which one of the partners relinquishes the gender/sexual identity ordinarily associated with his or her anatomical sex and lays claim to the gender associated with the opposite sex); and egalitarian (in which the partners are socially similar)—and finds evidence of the existence of all three in prehistoric and primitive cultures. He further finds that, in the setting of the prehistoric/primitive cultures, there was neither social conflict nor stigma over same-sex relationships or practices (Greenberg 1988).

Transgenerational homosexual activities are usually described in the context of boys' initiation rites in primitive cultures, and represent perhaps the most prevalent form of same-sex activity in the prehistoric period. Ritual pederasty is an extraordinarily old practice and has been traced, along with cannibalism and headhunting, to the Paleolithic period (Greenberg 1988). Male children were separated from their mothers at an early age (from about eight to twelve or thirteen) and went to live in the men's house, where they underwent extensive preparation for manhood. As part of the initiation ritual a boy entered into a homosexual relationship with an older man; in many cultures this man was his mother's brother. This practice was based upon the belief that, in order to achieve manhood, young males had to be implanted with the semen of an adult male. The relationship lasted for roughly seven years, generally until the boy married. However, in some cultures, the practice appears to have continued for some years before marriage or even after marriage. As the boys became young men they were expected to serve as initiators for other boys. All males were obliged to participate. Although most of the young men married and became exclusively heterosexual, some few did not and became true homosexuals (Dynes and Donaldson 1992b; Ford and Beach 1951; Greenberg 1988; Mondimore 1996).

While transgenerational homosexuality appeared to be an almost universal practice among males, there exist very few accounts of transgenerational lesbianism. There were puberty rites for girls; however, for the most part, these were associated with periods of forced seclusion and marked the young women as being in a "tabooed" condition. For girls, there was no elaborate initiation ceremony in which they learned the clan's secrets or accomplishments; such ceremonies were reserved for males (Stephenson 1981). Greenberg reports finding "hints of ritualized lesbianism" in a few Melanesian cultures but found few details. What was reported was the practice whereby lactating mothers nourished pre-pubescent girls who were not their daughters by offering them their breasts. This practice was based on a belief that the mother's milk derived from her husband's semen would strengthen the child.

Transgenderal same-sex practice in kinship-structured societies is probably best illustrated by the *berdache,* found among the Indians of North America. These were men who dressed as women, performed the tasks usually assigned to women, and often, though not invariably, engaged in same-sex relations. In parallel fashion, there were female berdaches who adopted male social roles, although this practice does not appear to have been as widespread as that of the male (Dynes and Donaldson 1992b; Ford and Beach 1951; Greenberg 1988; Mondimore 1996).

Roles analogous to that of the berdache (that of the shaman, medicine man, healer, or prophet) have been reported in many other parts of the world. Generally, these individuals held positions of power and prestige among their tribes or clans. They were believed to have undergone gender transformation by a supernatural power; in many cultures, some male children were apparently reared from infancy to assume the female role of shaman or berdache.

Experts differ in assigning the designation of "homosexual" to these individuals. Greenberg (1988) feels that the role was more one of gender transformation than that of homosexuality per se; Mondimore (1996) describes them as primarily homosexual, while agreeing that they were not exclusively so among all people. Whatever the case, the berdache phenomenon serves to illustrate that transgenderal homosexuality represents a practice which existed/exists in many primitive cultures and which could well have existed during the prehistoric period.

Some forms of what Greenberg refers to as egalitarian homosexuality (in which the partners are socially similar) also existed in primitive/prehistoric societies. The most common form was probably that practiced among prepubescent youth. As has been previously observed, prehistoric and primitive cultures tended to have relaxed and accepting attitudes toward sexuality. There is much evidence to suggest that same-sex activities among children and young boys and girls were not discouraged, indeed often encouraged. Since such relations did not jeopardize marriage alliances or risk pregnancy, they were sometimes preferred over youthful heterosexual affairs (Greenberg 1988).

The practice of egalitarian homosexuality was not generally institutionalized among adults, although there is evidence of its existence in certain cultures. Bullough (1970) and Greenberg (1988) both found an important variable in determining the presence or absence of significant same-sex activity to be the availability of partners of the opposite sex. Polygamous practices and forced segregation were included as other variables. The hunting-gathering lifestyle of prehistoric cultures dictated periods of time in which the men of the tribe were away and the women were left to care for the children and maintain the family structure. In such circumstances, both groups likely participated in sexual liaisons.

Greenberg identified a number of kinship-structured societies in which lesbian affairs were virtually universal among unmarried women, sometimes continuing after marriage. Likewise, among many such societies, single men who had lovers often continued to take boy lovers after marriage. These patterns differed greatly from society to society. Where such same-sex patterns existed, they were usually not recognized publicly, but occurred on an individual, temporary, and covert basis, and they tended to exist along with heterosexual relationships or marriage (Greenberg 1988).

Three general conclusions are offered from this brief and somewhat sketchy review of the prehistoric period. First, same-sex practices in various forms were present in prehistoric cultures and in many, if not all, primitive cultures. While many of these practices applied predominantly to male members (especially with regard to the transgenerational practices associated with the rites of passage), female-female practices also occurred (especially as related to transgenderal and egalitarian same-sex activities).

Second, within the social context of kinship-structured societies, no conflict existed over same-sex practices. No stigma was attached; instead, these practices were considered to fall within the acceptable range of sexual activity. Finally, the provided examples illustrate the difficulty inherent in applying the word "homosexual" to all forms of same-sex relations. While there is ample evidence that various forms of same-sex practice were present in many primitive cultures as well as in the period we call prehistoric, one would probably not describe most of these practices as "homosexuality" in the modern sense. At the same time, at least some of the men and women who assumed the role of berdache or shaman, and some of the men and women who sought out the company of same-sex partners in what has been referred to as egalitarian homosexual relations were indeed similar to those we today refer to as gay men and lesbians.

Ancient Civilizations: 3700 B.C.E. to 500 C.E.

The beginning of the history of Western civilization is generally recorded as having occurred in lower Mesopotamia. By 3700 B.C.E. civilization had developed on the plain of Sumer, in the valley of the Tigris and Euphrates rivers. From this time to about 60 B.C.E., this region was the site of several civilizations, chief among them Sumeria (3000–1750 B.C.E.); Babylonia (1900–1600 B.C.E.); Assyria (900–600 B.C.E.); and Judea (1300–60 B.C.E.). From Mesopotamia, civilization spread to Egypt and, somewhat later, to the Aegean and the Indus, and to China. This section will provide a brief description of same-sex practices as they are known to have existed in the ancient Mesopotamian civilizations as well as those of Egypt (3000–332 B.C.E.); Greece (800–146 B.C.E.); and Rome (800 B.C.E. to 500 C.E., all considered to be lineal ancestors of Western civilization. Also included will be information concerning the advent of the Christian era (30–500 C.E.).

The Mesopotamian Civilizations

In many ways, the nature of same-sex practices in Sumeria and Babylonia represented a gradual evolution of patterns that had been established during the prehistoric period. The remaining two civilizations under discussion in this section, those of Assyria and Judea, represent a more dramatic departure from these patterns. Dynes and Donaldson (1992a) observe that "the ancient patterns of same-sex behavior did not, for the most part, conform to the androphile model of modern industrial societies—a model that involves pairs of adults, both considered to be of the same gender, of roughly equal social status, and reciprocal in their behavior" (vii). Instead, they generally adhered to gender- and age-differentiated patterns noted in the prehistoric period.

Generally speaking, much less information is available regarding same-sex practices in the ancient Mesopotamian and Egyptian civilizations than for those of Greece and Rome. However, we do know that, with the possible exception of the Assyrians and the Hebrews, none of the Mesopotamian civilizations prohibited same-sex activity as such (Bullough 1976; Greenberg 1988). Bullough (1976) provides several examples from later Middle Assyrian law tablets that contain specific references to unproved allegations of same-sex conduct as libelous or slanderous. Since allegations of same-sex behavior had not previously been regarded as slander, Bullough suggests that a change of attitude toward same-sex intercourse had taken place. Although Hebrew positions regarding same-sex behavior were to become more negative during the period following the Babylonian exile in 586 B.C.E., there is little evidence to suggest that the early Hebrews viewed same-sex practices any differently than other Mesopotamian civilizations (Bullough 1976; Greenberg 1988).

Available information suggests that same-sex practices were far from unknown in the Sumerian and Babylonian civilizations. Some patterns remained essentially the same as they were in kinship-structured society, although some new patterns emerged during this period (Greenberg 1988). For much of Mesopotamian civilization, attitudes toward sex exhibited the same tolerance which was characteristic of the prehistoric period. Sex was accepted as a way of life and there are clear indications of the existence and acceptance of same-sex practices (Bullough 1976).

The most prominent form of institutionalized same-sex practice in the Mesopotamian civilizations has been referred to as temple prostitution, male and female (Dynes and Donaldson 1992a) or male cult prostitution (Greenberg 1988). This practice evolved from the worship of gods and goddesses, in which a female priesthood developed to serve male gods and a male priesthood to serve female gods. As time passed this practice evolved into a system in which effeminized males (often eunuchs) replaced women in serving temple worshipers. No doubt this practice grew out of the berdache phenomenon, with which there were strong similarities. Interestingly, such gender-defined, institutionalized homosexuality that used male temple prostitutes flourished among the ancient Hebrews (Dynes and Donaldson 1992).

Another type of same-sex practice present to some extent in the ancient Mesopotamian societies was that which has been referred to as the "love of warriors"(Greenberg 1988). Since early civilizations were often at war, there were frequent periods of separation of warriors from their wives and families. Such periods of separation were often conducive to same-sex activities. Such activities typically involved individuals of different age and social status so as to pose no threat of competition. Extensive male homosexuality in these conditions was completely accepted (Greenberg 1988).

As societies became increasingly stratified socially and economically, class-structured same-sex practices, in which the wealthier partner commanded the service of the poorer, also appeared. Two forms of class-structured homosexuality began to be observed in the Mesopotamian civilizations and became even more prominent later in those of Greece and Rome: prostitution and master-slave relations (Greenberg 1988). They will be discussed in more detail later.

The extent to which female same-sex activities occurred within the Mesopotamian societies is difficult to determine. As in the case of kinship-structured societies, we can only surmise. Several authors have suggested that in polygamous societies, and at least some of the Mesopotamian societies were polygamous, and in circumstances where women are deprived for periods of time of their husbands' attention, there is a tendency for them to turn to each other for sexual satisfaction. Where harems existed, for example, they were known for lesbianism (Bullough 1976; Greenberg 1988).

The restrictions placed on women that accompanied the rise of early civilizations may have prevented them from engaging in some of the behaviors available to them in kinship-structured societies. Yet, even with these restrictions, there must have been opportunities for them to establish close friendships, if not sexual relationships, with one another. The extent to which such relationships developed is, and will perhaps remain, unknown.

In sum, male homosexuality in the Mesopotamian civilizations was accepted and even institutionalized. While little is known about lesbianism during that era, no doubt same-sex relationships between women existed and were not prohibited.

The Egyptian Civilization

Egyptians settled along the Nile for much the same reasons the Mesopotamians settled around the Tigris and Euphrates river valleys: mild climate, abundance of water, rich soil for the cultivation of crops. In the case of Egypt, more than Mesopotamia, relative security from foreign invasion was an additional factor. Within this favorable environment Egyptian civilization developed and prospered for over 2,000 years, from about 3200 to 300 B.C.E. (Stephenson 1981).

The limited evidence available regarding ancient Egyptian views of acceptable or nonacceptable sexual behavior yields somewhat confusing and contradictory findings. Regarding same-sex activities, Manniche (1987) found few examples that such activities were indulged in for pleasure. He cites a passage from *The Book of the Dead*, from one of the wisdom texts, and a list of prohibitions valid in various cities, which suggest that it was considered a virtue not to have committed a homosexual act. He found pictorial evidence ambiguous, even though several appear to depict same-sex activities.

The negative confessions found in the *Book of the Dead*, along with cited statements from the wisdom texts, have been used by some authors as evidence of Egyptian opposition to certain kinds of same-sex behavior (Bullough 1976). However, as Greenberg (1988) observed, care should be taken in drawing conclusions based on this information because of the problems involved in obtaining accurate translations as well as because of so few references. What is clear is that available Egyptian artifacts do not contain the abundance of visual representations of same-sex practices that are found in the case of later Greek and Roman civilizations. This, in itself, is not proof of the absence of same-sex activity or of disapproval of same. Rather, it may suggest that this type of activity was simply not of primary interest to the Egyptians.

Given the limited information available, we can conclude that temple prostitution or male cult prostitution apparently was not widely practiced, if at all (Greenberg 1988). When male prostitution occurred it was not in connection with temple worship (Dynes and Donaldson 1992a). Likewise, the type of "initiation rites" so common in prehistoric cultures and in Greek civilization apparently were not practiced. Relics of the tribal ritual remained; however, they seem to have been mostly symbolic and applied only to the rulers (Greenberg 1988). Pederasty appears to have been condemned by the Egyptians (Bullough 1976; Manniche 1992).

On the other hand, several authors refer to the fact that out of the Old Kingdom (2355–2261 B.C.E.) came the oldest documented pair of homosexual lovers—the pharaoh Neferkere (Pepy II) and his general Sisene (Bullough 1976; Dynes and Donaldson 1992a). Greenberg (1988) cites evidence that, even without a specific ritual, Egyptians believed homosexual intercourse with a god to be propitious.

Anal intercourse, both heterosexual and homosexual, was common. At the same time, Egyptian society generally frowned upon same-sex activity between adult males, at least for the passive partner, probably because submissive behavior was implied (Bullough 1976; Greenberg 1988). Indeed, the available sources documenting the presence of same-sex activity primarily refer to that performed as an act of violence against an enemy. Manniche (1992) noted that phallic aggression was humiliating as the implanting semen in the body of another man meant gaining power over him. To what extent this dominant-submissive type of same-sex activity was practiced in ancient Egypt is unclear; however, apparently it was not regarded with favor.

Same-sex activities among women is even more sparsely documented than that among men. Both Dynes and Donaldson (1992a) and Manniche (1992) suggest that some forms of same-sex activity among women existed. However, few details are known. Manniche (1987) cites a passage from *The Book of the Dead* written for a woman which contains the following statement: "I have not had intercourse with any woman in the sacred places of my city god" (22). However, he does not accept this as evidence of same-sex activity; rather, he believes that this statement represented an uncorrected passage from a text which had been intended for a male.

Manniche (1987, 1992) and Brooten (1996) found passages in ancient Egyptian dream books which they feel demonstrate that at least the Egyptians recognized the possibility of intercourse between women. Manniche (1992) observed from the pictorial evidence that, while not conclusively establishing same-sex activity between women, it seemed obvious that women enjoyed the physical touch of other women. He also cited the existence of dildoes and suggested that their use was probably not uncommon in a country where harems flourished.

In summary, all that can be said from the evidence is that same-sex relationships did not appear to occupy a prominent place in Egyptian culture, and that they appear to have been viewed somewhat negatively. Especially scorned were the passive partners in same-sex relations involving two adult males. When an adult male and a young boy were involved, such activity appears to have been strongly condemned. As was the case in the Mesopotamian civilizations, same-sex activities were regarded with more hostility later in the civilization than earlier (Bullough 1976; Greenberg 1988).

The Greek Civilization

Greece, a peninsula bounded by the Ionian, Mediterranean, and Aegean Seas, became the site of one of the greatest civilizations of Antiquity and the birthplace of European civilization. In one of history's most remarkable achievements the Greeks, from about 900 to 500 B.C.E., evolved from barbarism to the height of civilization. Concepts of political freedom, great works of literature, and the foundations of modern science emerged (Smith and Smith 1980).

In classical Greek civilization we find a clear example of a society that not only accepted but also actively encouraged patterns of same-sex activity, at least among males of the ruling classes. The Greeks, like most of the civilizations of antiquity, had no word for homosexual or heterosexual persons. Rather, they felt that people were capable of responding erotically to persons of both sexes. As a matter of fact, classical literature tended to accept same-sex desire as entirely natural; with some authors identifying same-sex practices as superior to those between men and women (Boswell 1980; Greenberg 1988; Mondimore 1996). From about the sixth century B.C.E., secularized male homosexuality flourished in many of the Greek city-states. The most common form of same-sex activity is described by the Greek word *paiderasty* (anglicized as "pederasty") and took the form of intimate relationships between older men and young boys (Bullough 1976; Dynes and Donaldson 1992a).

As demonstrated in the section on prehistoric societies, the origins of institutionalized pederasty are much older than the Greeks. In fact, Greek pederasty bears striking resemblance to the ritualized transgenerational male homosexuality common in tribal societies (Greenberg 1988). These practices may have come to the Greek city-states through the influence of the Dorians who entered Greece with bands of warriors around the eleventh century B.C. The Dorians tended to settle in Crete and Sparta, both very conservative, almost fossilized states where past or primitive attitudes were much in evidence. From Crete and Sparta, patterns of transgenerational same-sex practice spread to other Greek city-states (Bullough 1976). They became institutionalized through both the military and the educational systems. Bullough (1976) holds that the very organization of the city-state encouraged close and intimate relationships between males.

In Sparta, ritualized same-sex practices appear to have been universal among male citizens; such practices were encouraged by the military organization of its society. Indeed, they represented the initiation and integration of Spartan boys into the adult male community. There, as in Crete and elsewhere, the custom was for an adolescent male between twelve and sixteen years of age to pair with an honorable man of his tribe. The older man became the teacher/lover; the young boy the learner/ beloved. In Crete, this custom was solemnized by an actual "abduction" ceremony. The man and boy stayed together, sometimes sharing the same bed; however, sexual play was forbidden. The purpose was to teach the boy by precept and example, to bring about valor and to provide a good education (Bullough 1976).

In Athens and other city-states, institutionalized pederasty became an integral part of the educational system. At the age of six or seven boys were removed from their mothers and families. For the most part fathers, in turn, left their upbringing to an adult male who became lover/teacher of the son. In the idealized sexual partnership that ensued, the older man was known as the *erastes* (lover); the young boy/man as the *eromenos* (beloved). This form of pederasty was considered the most beautiful, the most perfect form of education (Bullough 1976; Mondimore 1996). As in Sparta, the purpose of the system was to inculcate manliness and to provide the young boy/man with the proper education. In Athens, education extended well beyond military discipline to include artistic and literary subjects.

Classical pederasty as described above was essentially an upper-class male institution, although there is some evidence that the Spartan system also included adult women and girls (Greenberg 1988). Mondimore (1996) makes the point that the system described as classical pederasty, while admittedly containing some form of same-sex practice, should not be described as homosexuality, at least as we know it today. Rather, it is more clearly described as a form of bisexuality, since many males engaged in both homosexual and heterosexual activities throughout their adulthood. Other authors have observed that the Greeks tolerated (and even encouraged) same-sex relations as long as they did not threaten the family (Boswell 1980; Bullough 1976; Greenberg 1988). Exclusive homosexuality tended to be discouraged, because it was essential that the Greek citizen marry and have children.

The social acceptability of same-sex practices was determined not by the gender of the partners but rather by the balance of power between them. Acceptable same-sex affairs usually emphasized superior/inferior roles (such as the adult lover and the adolescent beloved). Same-sex relations between two adult male citizens were not as universally acceptable, although they did exist (Bullough 1976; Greenberg 1988; Mondimore

1996). Some long-term relationships were solemnized in ceremonies not unlike that found in heterosexual marriages (Boswell 1994).

Male homosexual prostitution was a feature of everyday life in ancient civilizations. Yet, because of the importance placed on the power relationship, Greek citizens attempted to monitor and control this industry. For a Greek citizen to prostitute himself for money was shameful. Moreover, no matter how much the Greeks might have approved of man-youth relationships, they frowned upon the practice of young men and boys selling their services. In practice, many of the male prostitutes were slaves or prisoners of war who had been sold into slavery. Castration of such individuals for nonreligious purposes was not uncommon, and eunuchs were often used as male prostitutes for same-sex purposes (Bullough 1976; Greenberg 1988).

Evidence of same-sex relationships among women remains sparse, even with the outpouring of literary and artistic works that characterized classical Greece. Early Greek civilization may have seen ritualized initiation rites for young women similar to that reported to have existed in Sparta. On the other hand, increasingly severe restrictions placed upon women's social, political, and religious roles may well have prevented such practices from occurring. If such practices existed, evidence has been lost (Greenberg 1988).

If males in Greek societies formed a close, autonomous fellowship, then women presumably also sought similar companionship with other women. It is true that, especially in the classical period, women were far more restricted than men. Confined to their homes, citizen women had little or no opportunity to meet with women of their own social status outside their family group. Most of their time was spent with their immediate families and with female slaves. How they spent the many hours in such environments is largely a matter of conjecture. Some form of same-sex activity might well have occurred among the secluded upper-class women as well as between them and slaves and/or other socially acceptable companions (Dynes and Donaldson 1992a; Bullough 1976).

Convincing evidence has been provided that women could and did engage in same-sex activities during the Greek and Roman periods. Based on a detailed analysis of astrological texts, Greek love spells, Greek medical writings, ancient dream interpretations, and other sources, Brooten (1996) reveals that such activities existed and were generally known although not generally favorably viewed by Greek society.

One of the few surviving literary examples of same-sex practices among women is that of Sappho of Lesbos (about sixth century B.C.E.).

Sappho, a poet who was openly read and admired by Plato and other scholars and writers of the late Greek and Roman periods, was also the head of a school for girls. Surviving fragments of her poetry reveal feelings for and suggest intimacy with other women. Several literary references in the later Greek and Roman periods referred to her as a woman who loved other women; the term *lesbian* was used to describe her and, subsequently, came to be used to describe female homosexuals (the terms *sapphic* or *sapphist* have also been applied).

Further evidence of same-sex relationships among women lies in the fact that the Greeks had terms, apart from lesbian and sapphist, to describe female-female relationships. The word *tribades* (from *tribein*, "to rub") was generally used in Greek literature to describe the women who took the active sexual role with women and performed male functions. The term implied that women so designated derived their sexual pleasure from friction against one another's bodies (Brooten 1996). Preserved by the texts of classical authors whose manuscripts survived into the Renaissance, the word *tribade* found its way into the modern languages, where it remained the usual term for female same-sex practices and activities well into the nineteenth century (Johansson 1990; Mondimore 1996).

The Roman Civilization

The seeds of the Roman civilization were planted long before they developed into the most widespread empire the world had ever known. Men and women inhabited the plains of Italy some 30,000 years before Christ. Three original tribes—Romans (or Latins), Sabines, and Etruscans—emerged from this early period and formed the basis of Rome's social and political organization. In 509 B.C.E., leaders of these tribes joined together to form the Senate and establish the Roman republic.

During the period of the republic, Rome saw great territorial expansion. In 509 B.C.E., Rome controlled only 300 square miles of territory; by 275 B.C.E., they ruled southern Italy and some 10,000 square miles. Between 265 and 146 B.C.E., the Romans conquered the western Mediterranean. The conquest of the eastern Mediterranean region (including Macedonia, Greece, Asia Minor, Syria, Judea, and Egypt) began in 200 B.C.E. and was complete by 30 B.C.E. Almost all of what is now western Europe was later added to what was to become the Roman Empire.

The very vastness of the empire caused ever more serious problems of administration. Eventually, the empire was divided into four prefectures:

Gaul, Italy, Illyrium, and the East. Increasingly, civil wars and rebellions erupted in various parts of the empire. There was a gradual decline of Italy and its Roman center as the eastern provinces grew in importance. Already weakened from within, the empire finally fell to invasions of Germanic tribes. In 47d C.E., the Roman Empire in the West was defeated; that in the East continued for another one thousand years, until 1450. Western civilization, born in Sumer about 4000 B.C.E., was halted, at least temporarily, with the collapse of the Roman Empire.

Initially, the Romans tended to adopt Greek attitudes toward same-sex practices, possibly because the two civilizations shared the same Indo-European heritage. There is some evidence that these pre-Roman settlers, such as the Celts, brought with them same-sex tribal initiation rites as well as warrior cults in which homosexual intimacy was widely accepted. The Etruscans—from whom the Romans borrowed heavily in areas such as religion, art, and architecture—enjoyed the reputation among Greek writers of having loose morals and of engaging in many types of same-sex practices. Thus, while Etruscan-style orgies might not have been widespread throughout pre-Roman civilization, it has been established that various forms of same-sex practice occurred (Greenberg 1988; Mondimore 1996).

While notable similarities between Greeks and Romans in attitudes toward same-sex practices existed, there were also notable differences, prompting some writers, such as Bullough (1976, 1979), to conclude that the Romans had a negative view of homosexuality. Indeed, the Romans of the early republic tended to be more conservative than the Greeks. While proud of their material success, they nevertheless tended to idealize a past in which all Romans were courageous and virtuous. Roman institutions such as family and educational system did not view with favor the pattern of pederasty practiced by the Greeks. Furthermore, the Romans were never quite comfortable with public nudity, nor did they tend to idealize the male body as did the Greeks. While they recognized the existence of various forms of same-sex practice and, indeed, freely engaged in them, many Romans tended to attribute such practices to the Greeks. In fact, much of the Roman vocabulary of homosexuality consisted of adopted Greek words (Bullough 1976; Greenberg 1988).

Though not as institutionalized a practice in Roman life as in that of the Greeks, at least under the republic, same-sex practices were by no means uncommon. Abundant evidence exists that the Romans, as the Greeks, accepted male same-sex activity as a normal part of life (Boswell 1980, 1994). In fact, four types of same-sex relationships existed in the

Greco-Roman world: (1) use, the exploitation of males owned or controlled by other males; (2) concubinage, the use of certain male slaves to meet the sexual needs of the masters; (3) same-sex lovers, a more egalitarian type relationship in which two men or two women were united by affection, passion, or desire; and (4) formal unions, publicly recognized relationships entailing some change in status for one or both parties (Boswell 1994).

Boswell makes a strong case that same-sex practices dealing with more egalitarian love relationships existed in Rome of the republic and of the empire although they were less well documented and idealized than similar relationships were in Greece. Many of these relationships were long lasting, similar to heterosexual marriage, although they tended to be more fluid and less legalistic. He cites evidence of the widespread acceptance of a deeper and more spiritual love between members of the same sex. Moreover, Boswell cites several examples of formal unions (i.e., publicly recognized relationships entailing some change in status for one or both parties). The same-sex "marriages," while not possible under the republic, occurred during the period of the empire when such alliances were more commonly accepted. Such unions became less common as the empire waned; Boswell reports that, in 342 C.E., a law was passed forbidding same-sex marriage (Boswell 1980, 1994).

To the extent negative attitudes existed toward same-sex activity in Roman society, the bias was not against the activity per se, but against passive sexual behavior. For most Romans, the social status of the partner made a same-sex act unacceptable. As in Greece, the passive (or receptive) role was considered incompatible with the honor and dignity of a free man, especially when such behavior continued into adulthood. Conquered soldiers, foreigners, slaves, and freedmen who remained dependent on former masters were expected to be passive and subordinate. Even when socially inappropriate, homosexual desire was not considered abnormal as long as it took the active form. This type of prejudice declined significantly under the empire, possibly because some of the emperors were themselves known to be passive (Boswell 1980; Dynes and Donaldson 1992a; Greenberg 1988).

Within this active/passive (ruler/slave) environment the Romans developed a type of same-sex relationship, called dominance-enforcement homosexuality, which divided roles not on the basis of age or effeminacy but on political or power relationships. Roman soldiers were allowed to rape enemy soldiers after victory in battle. Slaves played an important role as sex objects for the Romans, who saw the act of sexual penetration as analogous to political and military conquest. Male prostitution flourished. Not only was such activity lawful; it was taxed, and a legal holiday declared for the prostitutes. Some of the very rich had seraglios of boys, called *paedagogia*, most of whom were slaves (Boswell 1980; Dynes and Donaldson 1992a; Greenberg 1988).

As with the other ancient civilizations under discussion, most authors describe a paucity of information in looking at same-sex practices among women. Generally, same-sex practices among women were acknowledged. Yet, most of the premodern historical and literary accounts that survived were by men and about men. Most of these male writers apparently did not consider female homoeroticism worthy of note. When same-sex activities between women were mentioned, it was usually with indications of disapproval and distaste. Attitudes were more hostile toward female same-sex relationships than toward those involving males (Boswell 1980, 1994; Bullough 1976; Greenberg 1988).

Brooten (1996), in a pioneering study of female homoeroticism during the period preceding the rise of Christianity, reaches a somewhat different conclusion. Drawing upon a broad range of sources—astrological texts, Greek love spells, ancient medical writings, and dream interpretations, Booten demonstrates that the Roman world was one in which people from all walks of life acknowledged that women could have sexual contacts with other women, and provides evidence that more was known about female same-sex activities than previous scholars have assumed. Indeed, she found that awareness of sexual relations between women increased dramatically in the Roman period, and illustrated that early Christian views of female homoeroticism closely resembled those of their non-Christian contemporaries.

In the final analysis, Brooten agrees with the other writers that attitudes toward female homoerotic relationships tended to be more hostile than those toward same-sex activities among males. She ascribed the hostility primarily to the strict distinction drawn in Roman society between active and passive sexual roles. For her, gender role transgression emerges as the primary reason for the rejection of female romantic friendship. Free, adult male citizens ought never to be passive and women should never be active; to do so was considered to be "contrary to nature." Since every sexual pairing was viewed as including one active and one passive partner, regardless of gender, the "active" partner in female same-sex relationships was viewed along with the "passive" male with disdain and disapproval. Brooten (1996) describes the prevailing attitude of male authors toward female homoeroticism as follows:

Monstrous, lawless, licentious, unnatural, and shameful—with these terms male authors throughout the Roman Empire expressed their disgust for sexual love between women. They often represented women who actively sought the love of another woman as physically phallic and culturally masculine. They sometimes classified *tribades* with prostitutes. In short, authors in that period demonstrated both awareness of sexual love between women and disgust for it (29).

Brooten further found that in spite of widespread disgust for and opposition to female romantic friendship, the sources she reviewed testified to the presence of sexual love between women throughout the Roman Empire. Indeed, she discovered that, in spite of this opposition, there was some evidence of social tolerance of female same-sex relationships, apparently extending to woman-woman marriage.

The growth of the empire, accompanied by long periods of relative peace, gave rise to a life of conspicuous luxury for the Roman ruling class. The rich increasingly filled their days and nights with revelry and entertainment. Extensive extramarital affairs, both heterosexual and homosexual, became part of the social scene, and same-sex practices of all kinds became more openly tolerated. During this period same-sex marriages were recognized (Boswell 1980).

This type of lifestyle came under greater criticism as the empire neared collapse. Beginning with the Emperor Augustus, probably as a backlash to this atmosphere of great permissiveness, strict laws were passed in an attempt to reestablish a sense of order in the increasingly disorderly sexual behavior of Roman citizens. Between 18 and 16 B.C.E., Augustus issued the *Lex Julia de adulteriis coercendis*, attempting to regulate extramarital sexual relationships and ensure the propagation of future generations of Roman soldiers. Adultery, which had previously been considered a private family matter, came under the state's jurisdiction. This legislation was bitterly resented and never widely enforced. Same-sex relations continued to be practiced in public without interference during the first two centuries of empire, often by the emperors themselves (Greenberg 1988).

We have seen that, with several possible exceptions (Assyrians, Hebrews, Egyptians), male same-sex relationships were accepted by all of the ancient civilizations under discussion within the broader acceptance of human sexuality as a positive good (much less is known about female same-sex practices). There remains a paucity of information that looks at same-sex practices among women. Generally speaking, such relationships were acknowledged, but most of the historical and literary accounts that have survived were written by men about men. Apparently these writers did not consider female homoeroticism worthy of note, but when such were mentioned it was usually with indications of disapproval or distaste as attitudes tended to be more openly hostile toward female same-sex relationships than to male (Boswell 1980, 1984; Bullough 1976; Greenberg 1988). But this level of acceptance toward male homoeroticism was to come to an end during the last years of the Roman Empire largely as the result of the spread of asceticism, hostile to all forms of sexual pleasure, and the advent of the Christian era (30–500). We will now turn to that period and attempt to understand more of the reasons for this drastic change of attitude and its impact on modern European and American history.

The Early Christian Era

The introduction of Christianity to the Roman world coincided generally with the beginning of the Roman Empire. Initially, Christianity was considered as part of Judaism and was protected by Roman law, which had allowed the Jews to live in relative peace and religious freedom. The followers of Jesus of Nazareth were treated as nothing more than another cult and an irritant to the Romans. However, as their strength grew and influence spread, they posed a more serious threat to the empire. Christianity appealed to many people in the Roman Empire because, among other things, it represented an alternative to the worst side of what had become the Roman way of life. First ignored, then persecuted, Christians found themselves in a powerful position when, in 323 Emperor Constantine converted to Christianity and made it the state religion. Christianity became one of the few Roman institutions to survive the collapse of the empire. As the invading barbarians converted to the faith, church bishops solidified a prominent place in municipal administration. By the end of the sixth century, the pope had become the virtual ruler of Rome. In about 400 years, Christianity had grown from a small, unpopular sect to a massive, sustained movement (Smith and Smith 1980; Stephenson 1981).

While writers covering this period of history somewhat disagree regarding the role of the early Christian church in the process, all agree that profound changes in public attitudes toward sex and morality took place between the time of the later Roman Empire (476 C.E.) and the end of the Middle Ages (1500) (Boswell 1980; Bullough 1976; Greenberg 1988).

With the advent of Christianity came a slowly developing conservative reaction to the almost limitless tolerance of the earlier Roman era. This conservative backlash resulted in increased violence and hostilities toward Jews, heretics, political dissidents, and other nonconformists-including those engaged in same-sex activities (Boswell 1980). While this antigay feeling was beginning to emerge during the early Christian era, same-sex behaviors were generally not stigmatized (Boswell 1980; Greenberg 1988) although there were some church leaders that condemned homosexual behaviors from the beginnings of Christianity (Bullough 1976).

Overall, when Christianity, a monotheistic system, replaced the poly-theistic system of the ancient civilizations, attitudes toward what had been acceptable behaviors in the old system (e.g., same-sex behaviors) became less and less tolerated. This pattern of increasing intolerance would continue as same-sex behaviors would move from being mildly rebuked sins to intolerable behavior in the fourth century, and what Canon Law, in the eleventh century, described as one of the most despised forms of behavior (Goodrich 1979).

The Medieval Period: 500–1500

The medieval era is generally divided into three distinct periods-the "Dark Ages" (500–1000), the "Mini-Renaissance" (1000–1300), and the "Late Middle Ages" (1300–1500). The Dark Ages were characterized by the dissolution of the Roman Empire and organized society. The resulting societal chaos had little effect on Christianity, which continued to flour-ish and became the cultural cornerstone of medieval society (Smith and Smith 1980). As one attempt to reestablish the once powerful empire, the church crowned Charlemagne emperor in 800. While Charlemagne's rule did achieve a certain degree of unity, it was not to last, and by the tenth century the church had become a fragmented entity of Christian and pagan rituals housed in various localities (Smith and Smith 1980). These local groupings would become the antecedent roots of the feudal system of the later medieval era. The feudal system reinforced the ideology of the Christian church where the church was a major landholder, art and drama were concerned with matters of faith, and the clergy were consid-ered a privileged class. Attitudes toward same-sex behaviors during the Dark Ages seemed similar to the attitudes expressed in the early Christian era-namely, little evidence exists to substantiate the view that early Chris-tians and Christians of the feudal era held differing opinions on same-sex practices than their pagan counterparts. Same-sex behaviors were deemed of little importance until the end of the later Middle Ages when the Bible was written and became part of church dogma.

An increased social openness and tolerance for all minority groups characterized the Mini-Renaissance of the era, including gays. This cultural acceptance of same-sex practices and the development of what could be called a gay subculture, was centered in the church and monastic societies (Boswell 1980). As it would be in the twentieth century, during this period of acceptance within the church, there was, too, a small minority of clerics, theologians, and church officials who condemned same-sex practices by equating them with such other sins as murder. However, these dissenting voices were largely ignored by the majority of church officials (Boswell 1980). This era of acceptance represents only one of three such historical eras in modern times where same-sex practices were generally condoned (the earlier Roman era and the latter part of the nineteenth century being the other two).

Finally, the Late Middle Ages was characterized by an increasing intolerance and repression of all nonconforming behaviors and beliefs. Rediscovering early church teachings about the unnaturalness and sinful nature of same-sex practices, writers of Canon Law from the twelfth to the sixteenth centuries increasingly condemned same-sex practices. All forms of homoerotic activity were labeled as sodomy; sodomy, in turn, was seen in Canon Law and theology as the most "heinous of sins" (Goodrich 1979:ix). During this time theologians developed a specific theory of sodomy as a sin. Under Roman law, sodomy was raised to the status of a crime during the thirteenth century (Goodrich 1979). This stricter interpretation of the law, condemning sodomy as a sin and a crime, replaced the earlier views of sodomy as simply a sin that was frequently overlooked.

The Gregorian reform movement of the thirteenth century, no doubt an effort to add stability to a fragmented church system and to consolidate the power of the church, was the period in which condemnation of homosexuality became institutionalized. In a similar way and at about the same time, secular laws evolved that declared war on heresy and all forms of sexual nonconformity (Goodrich 1979). In sum, this period was one of increasing intolerance for all minorities (Boswell 1980). A resulting consequence of this increased hostility was the Inquisition in which heretics and nonconformists were condemned to torture or death. However, in spite of heightened rhetoric, there is little evidence that homosexuals were actually prosecuted or burned, as prescribed by law, until the fourteenth century (Goodrich 1979).

The crime of homosexuality became politicized insofar as it was used by those in power to discredit and defeat political enemies. During this period, various groups—clergy, nobility, university students, heretics—were all accused of nonconformist sexual behaviors. Celibacy became a prerequisite for being ordained as a member of the clergy, but priests and university students were forced into same-sex living situations that undoubtedly fostered same-sex practices. The nobility was accused of bringing back unnatural sexual behaviors from the Crusades (Goodrich 1979).

Overall, the Medieval period was one where same-sex practices were largely ignored during the Dark Ages, and where such behaviors were not only tolerated but openly accepted by the church during the Mini-Renaissance of the period. Such tolerance and acceptance was viewed as hedonism and blasphemy by the clerics of the Late Middle Ages who condemned same-sex practices, as did their secular counterparts. This condemnation would last well into the nineteenth century and would reemerge in the latter part of the twentieth century.

The Renaissance and the Reformation: 1500–1700

The start of modern civilization is generally referred to as the Renaissance, a period characterized by the end of feudalism and the beginnings of the development of cities and states. Regional societies, increasingly ruled by monarchs rather than local barons, evolved as towns freed themselves from the control of feudal lords. The power and authority of the church was steadily diminished as nation-states arose and as trade, exploration, and colonization occurred (Smith and Smith 1980). During this period of rebirth, a cultural explosion of literature, art, music, and science swept across Europe. Greek and Roman traditions reasserted themselves with a renewed interest in the classical past. This revival, which became known as humanism, had appeal for scholars and the emerging urban middle class. Humanism was primarily a non-religiously oriented philosophy—a digression from the highly religious and church-dominated Middle Ages.

While the resurgence of Greek and Roman thought included an acceptance of same-sex practices among some, this acceptance was far from universal. The church had already institutionalized its position on same-sex practices, and the increasingly powerful nation-states continued earlier legal proscriptions that condemned such behaviors. Although same-sex practices continued to exist, the punishment for such behavior could be death. This death penalty however, was rarely applied, and the usual punishment for sodomy was a fine (Boswell 1980).

During the Renaissance there was an increasing shift in power from the once all-powerful church to the newly emerging nation-states. The Protestant Reformation of the early sixteenth century further weakened the power of the Catholic church. Protestants were perhaps more condemning than Catholics of same-sex practices because of their non-procreative nature and viewed sodomy as a sin against nature. Generally, all forms of sexual activity that did not lead to procreation were believed to be unnatural by the Protestants (Bullough 1976). In both Catholic and Protestant countries, the state was becoming more directly involved with the definitions and control of morality and behavior. The church's sins against nature became the state's crimes against nature and same-sex practices became generally illegal. In England, the first laws condemning homosexuality emerged in 1533 under King Henry VIII (Bullough 1976). These laws, as with church law, did not include same-sex practices between women. Women were generally viewed as a sexually invisible entity until well into the twentieth century.

Overall, the attitude toward same-sex behaviors during the period of the Renaissance and Reformation was one of intolerance and condemnation. Although some humanists favored the idea of the acceptance of homosexuality, the prevailing view was that such behaviors were not to be tolerated. The sin of sodomy yielded to the crime of sodomy and the Protestant Reformation more strictly enforced the institutionalization of this belief. Not unsurprisingly, this attitude of intolerance and disapproval of same-sex practices was transported to the colonies of the New World and remained in place, in American society, generally unchallenged until the nineteenth century. Because of the newly emerging American society, the focus of this chapter will now turn to how the construct of homosexuality evolved in the colonies and later in the United States.

The Modern Era: 1700–1969

What has been defined as the Modern Era covers roughly 150 years from the start of the eighteenth century to about the middle of the twentieth century. During this time great changes occurred in American society and these had a significant impact on the social construction of the concept of homosexuality as it is currently known. This section details changes in the American view of homosexuality from the colonial era to the Stonewall riots, an era in which the focus of sexuality in general shifted from the idea of sex only for procreation to the idea of sex for personal pleasure.

From Reproductive Responsibility to Personal Pleasure: 1700–1900

The early settlers brought with them religious values and beliefs from the Protestant Reformation and these are reflected in mores, customs, and laws that had been developed in colonial America. Rejecting the more Catholic views on celibacy, lust could be dealt with in the context of marriage. Thus, through marital love and procreation that necessitated sexual intercourse, sexual sins were prevented (D'Emilio and Freedman 1988). The family was considered the basic unit of society; only sexual acts inside the marital union were considered "proper." Other sexual acts (for example, those for pleasure, those outside the marital union, or those not used for the sole purpose of having children) were deemed sexual transgressions—sins for which one could atone. Such sins might include adultery, rape, sodomy, or buggery (D'Emilio and Freedman 1988; Katz 1976). Since the normal sexual expression was within the family unit between a man and a woman for the purpose of bearing children, sodomy as a form of sexual expression was considered taboo and sinful. But, because it was thought that the sinner could be forgiven for the sin and reclaimed by the church through repentance, the person was not stigmatized or given a lifelong identity as a sodomite.

The term "sodomy" in both the seventeenth and eighteenth centuries referred to sexual activity that was not designed to produce children and therefore included sex between men, sex between a man and an animal (buggery), or sex for pleasure between a man and a woman. The term was not applied to sexual acts between women, but one colony called such activity "acts against nature" (Altman 1982; D'Emilio and Freedman 1988).

For the two million people that inhabited what would become the United States in late 1600s and early 1700s (Smith and Smith 1980), the family-centered social structure encouraged sexual expression for the sole purpose of procreation. Citing such biblical passages as Genesis 38:1–11, where Onan fails to fulfill his familial responsibilities; Genesis 19: 1–29, which cites the Sodom and Gomorrah story; and Leviticus 18:22; 20:13, the Holiness Code (Swigonski 1998), the penalty for the crimes of sodomy, bestiality, and buggery was death (D'Emilio and Freedman 1988). During the seventeenth century at least five men (the laws were silent as to same-sex sexual behavior between women) were executed for what had been sins earlier in the century but were now crimes against the state (D'Emilio and Freedman 1988). Sodomy and buggery had been seen as such fundamental challenges to the family system that only the death penalty could ensure the extinction of the behavior.

However, sexual expression outside the marital bed did not die and same-sex sexual activity continued throughout the remainder of the eighteenth century. As the colonies developed there was a decline in the puritanical views of the earlier part of the century, and there was a movement toward the creation of an independent nation. The Revolutionary War, with its emphasis on independence, also contributed to a decline in the regulation of morality by parents and the state (D'Emilio and Freedman 1988; Smith and Smith 1980). No one was put to death in the eighteenth century for the sexual crimes of sodomy or buggery; rather men convicted of these crimes were given repeated whippings, were burned with a hot iron, or were simply banished (D'Emilio and Freedman 1988; Katz 1976). Fewer persons were convicted of sexual crimes and the punishments were becoming less harsh.

Perhaps one reason for the reduction in the punishment of such crimes was an evolving philosophy away from the idea that sex should be only for procreation and toward the idea that personal pleasure in the form of sexual expression was gaining acceptance. Sexuality was being viewed more as a personal choice and no longer just as a reproductive responsibility. Personal choice and not state control became an important philosophical view that would shape social views on dating and courtship, marriage, and sexual deviance (D'Emilio and Freedman 1988).

That is not to say that, suddenly, same-sex liaisons were acceptable forms of sexual expression. The late eighteenth- and early nineteenth-century citizen still viewed sodomy (which was now defined as anal sex between men, oral sex, and masturbation) as an unacceptable form of behavior. What was clear was that same-sex love was freely willed and therefore able to be controlled (Bayer 1981). But, the nineteenth century brought with it great social changes that questioned the sanctity of the family unit as it had been known and offered other forms of family life that expanded on the idea of one man and one woman. (Altman 1982; D'Emilio and Freedman 1988).

The years following the American Revolution were ones where a newly formed United States was developing its democracy with its federal government. There were the beginnings of industrialism and the population in 1783 was 3.25 million persons. The newly formed country found itself at war in 1812 and the Capitol and White House were burned by the British in 1814 (Smith and Smith 1980). This was a time of social upheaval and a time when new ideas and philosophical views were being explored.

By the middle of the nineteenth century there were thirty-six states in the union, the industrial revolution was quickly progressing, the railroad connected most of the country, and there was a great movement westward. The country was also again headed for war. This time it would be a civil war sparked by differences in the North and South with regard to their geographic adaptations to the industrial revolution and slavery. Once the war was over one-fifth of the South's male population had been killed, the slaves had been freed, and the South was in economic disarray (Smith and Smith 1980; Trattner 1994). From the end of the Civil War in 1865 until the turn of the century the industrial revolution was at its peak. Industries increased threefold from the first half of the century, the value of manufactured goods increased by seven, and the number of wage earners increased four times. Formal education was expanded so that by 1899 there were 20,000 female undergraduates in colleges around the country. The population swelled to 75 million persons by 1900, the Native Americans had been driven off their land, the frontier had vanished, and reconstruction and segregation had done little to assist the African American (Smith and Smith 1988; Trattner 1994).

During the nineteenth century there seemed to be a gradual shift from the concept of reproductive responsibility to newly defined concepts of romanticism and erotic love. Because of this, new opportunities for sexual gratification outside marriage emerged. Utopian communities offering free love gave members a chance to be involved in a variety of sexual relationships from monogamy to polygamy. And, while even utopian communities considered same-sex couples as immoral, same-sex unions that patterned themselves after the ideals of romantic marriage were also evident throughout the century (D'Emilio and Freedman 1988; Faderman 1982).

The newly evolving social order provided numerous opportunities for same-sex coupling. While romantic friendships among women were considered quite a middle-class to upper-class phenomena, men in coal mining camps and newly developing western towns were often left in settings with few, if any, women. Further, young women were in equally sexually segregated settings in female academies and colleges. The ideals of the nineteenth century, where women and men could passionately express their longings for one another in spiritual, emotional, and physical ways without having the burden of reproduction (D'Emilio and Freedman 1988; Faderman 1981) no doubt allowed for the development of same-sex sexual expression.

For the nineteenth-century citizen, the concepts of heterosexuality and homosexuality as they are now socially constructed had no meaning and therefore were not ascribed to romantic friendships until the turn of the century. "Crimes against nature" were beginning to have some interest to the medical community, who viewed the behavior either as innate or learned (Bayer 1981). The end of the century brought with it the use of the terms as a label to stigmatize same-sex relations as unnatural and perverse. Terms like "congenital inversion" and "perversion" evolved and were used to define same-sex love as unnatural. The term "homosexual," while coined by the Hungarian doctor Karoly Benkert (also known as Kertbeny) in 1869, came into more current usage toward the end of the century, when it was used by psychiatrists and medical doctors who were responsible for its beginning definition as something less acceptable than heterosexual behavior (Altman 1982; D'Emilio and Freedman 1988; Herzer 1990).

In sum, from 1700 until 1900 the concept of same-sex love had undergone significant changes. Not known as a concept of personal identity or condition in the early 1700s, same-sex relationships evolved from a sin for which one could atone, to a crime against nature for which men were executed, to state sodomy statutes where punishments varied. And, although same-sex love between women was virtually never mentioned in colonial America or even during most of the nineteenth century, by the end of the 1800s the terms congenital inversion, homosexual, and perversion were being applied to same-sex romantic friendships and sexual expressions whether they occurred between two men or two women.

From Romantic Friendships to Personal Identity: 1900–1969

The period from the turn of the century to the latter part of the 1960s was one where the concept of homosexuality and homosexuals moved from being considered a sin or a criminal activity for which one could atone or be punished through being considered a mental illness and finally being thought of as an alternative lifestyle (Altman 1982; D'Emilio and Freedman 1988; Faderman 1981). These changes paralleled changes in the social and medical evolution of the country and climaxed in 1969 with the Stonewall riots.

As noted, at the end of the nineteenth century the concept of same-sex romantic friendships was beginning to be characterized as a perversion or illness. This view of homosexuality as an illness paralleled the increasing reliance on the medical establishment's ideas of scientific thought regarding sexuality that were usurping the more traditional views of the clergy. With science it was thought possible to define human behavior and therefore it was equally possible to define "normal" human behavior. Normal behavior did not include homosexuality (Altman 1982; D'Emilio and Freedman 1988). It seemed logical to equate the sociological concept of sexual deviancy (e.g., homosexuality) with medical illness, and so, the belief of homosexuality as illness has a very recent history (Altman 1982).

The early sexologists like Krafft-Ebing and Havlock Ellis, while thinking that same-sex sexuality was a tragedy (at least in women), believed that the condition was innate and used such terms as "invert," "urning," or "third sex" to describe it (D'Emilio and Freedman 1988; Faderman 1981). Between 1900 and the 1920s their ideas were being replaced by the Freudian idea that homosexuality was caused by a childhood trauma; thus it was a condition that was not inborn but rather a psychological perversion that required therapeutic intervention (Altman 1982; D'Emilio and Freedman 1988).

This era was also marked by World War I and the emergence of the United States as a world power. There was migration from the countryside into cities, and the first gay subcultures began to emerge in urban areas (Bullough and Bullough 1977; Smith and Smith 1980). There were more opportunities for women to live independently of men because of increased educational and economic opportunities, and same-sex unions flourished in both the middle class, where the concept of romantic friendships lingered, and the working class, where the idea of "Boston marriages" (one woman assuming the role of the man) took root (Faderman 1981).

The late 1920s and 1930s saw tremendous social upheaval with the Great Depression and the New Deal. In 1932 there were more than 12 million people unemployed in the country, and this number only significantly changed by 1939, when there were 10 million unemployed persons (Smith and Smith 1980). Little has been written about the challenges faced by gays and lesbians during this period, but there is evidence that the homosexual subculture did exist during this time and did survive both the depression and the country's economic recovery with little change in the general belief that homosexual behavior was now an identity and one for which the person needed medical and psychiatric treatment (Altman 1982; Bullough and Bullough 1977).

So, from the turn of the century to the end of the 1930s there was a gradual shift from the idea that homosexuality was a temporary affliction to the generalized belief that it was a lifelong condition that required intervention (D'Emilio and Freedman 1988). These beliefs, while of recent historical derivation, played an important role in how lesbian and gay persons continued to be viewed through the 1940s, 1950s, and 1960s.

The 1940s and World War II finally succeeded in bringing the country out of an economic slump and back to higher employment rates. Women were filling jobs vacated by men who went to war, Kinsey was beginning his seminal work on sexuality, more and more gay bars were emerging in urban areas, and the gay subculture was growing (D'Emilio and Freedman 1988; Kinsey, Pomeroy, and Martin 1948; Smith and Smith 1980). And, while the gay subculture was growing, it was still virtually invisible to the larger heterosexual culture and, because bars were generally hidden in rough inner-city areas, difficult to find even for gays and lesbians. Even when found, the bars were the scene of frequent police raids and considered unsafe by many (Katz 1976; Kennedy and Davis 1993). But the 1940s provided an opportunity for gays and lesbians to begin to socialize in larger groups, and this would lead to the formation of national gay and lesbian groups in the 1950s.

The 1950s were a time of contradictions for gays and lesbians. Still carrying the stigma of "mentally ill," but fortified by the growing gay community, gays and lesbians began to mobilize by forming organizations. The first, the Mattachine Society, was begun in 1950 as a secret society of gay men, many with left-wing ideologies. It was formed as a support group and met nightly. Although not a political protest group, by 1955 the organization's publication, *Mattachine Review*, became one of the first to grapple with the idea of gay rights (Streitmatter 1995). The Daughters of Bilitis, a similar organization for lesbians, emerged in 1955 and met three times weekly. Their publication *The Ladder* was published from 1956 until 1972 and provided a feminine view on issues impacting the gay community.

On a parallel course with the emergence of a more formalized gay community came the conservative views of Joseph McCarthy, the Cold War, and Eisenhower's now infamous Executive Order Number 10450. While McCarthy hunted Communists, there was a generalized fear of homosexuals and homosexuality that led, in June 1950, to a U.S. Senate federal inquiry into the employment of homosexuals by the federal government. By 1953 Eisenhower had issued an executive order stating that no known homosexual would be employed by the federal government where the interests of national security were concerned (D'Emilio and Freedman 1988; *U.S. Code* 1953). The effect on the gay community was for lesbians and gays to hide and not disclose their sexual orientation. There was a growing fear, substantiated by the dismissal of known homosexual governmental employees, that were their sexual orientation discovered they would lose their means of economic support and be unable to find other suitable employment (Katz 1976).

The continuing themes of gay emergence and acceptance on one side and conservatism and gay bashing on the other, begun at the turn of the century, became focused with the Cold War in a way not previously seen. The 1960s with its radical social changes would see the conservative element briefly eclipsed, only to reappear renewed in the 1970s.

By the 1960s there was a growing militant feeling in ethnic minority groups, students, women, and even in the gay community. And, while the gay community would not find its own voice until 1969, the militancy and subsequent victories and struggles in the social and legal arenas by African Americans, students, and women during this decade provided the gay community with needed courage to confront the heterosexual establishment by the end of the decade. Throughout the decade, gay groups followed the lead of other minority groups by mailing publications to elected officials that supported gay rights, publicly demonstrating in Washington, D.C., and daring to confront the still popular idea that homosexuals were mentally ill (*The Ladder* 1965; Streitmatter 1995).

Similar strategies when used by other groups were fairly successful, as the 1964 passage of the Civil Rights Act will demonstrate. But, perhaps because of the continuing legal, psychiatric, and social stigmas attached to homosexuals and homosexuality, often when gays and lesbians held demonstrations in the 1960s the African Americans and women, who had included gays and lesbians as supporters in their fights for civil rights, failed to support the gay community and were generally absent from gay civil rights rallies. The civil rights movement for gays and lesbians floundered, as there seemed to be no one unifying theme other than sexual orientation that bound the group together. The newly defined lesbian feminists of the 1960s struggled with their role in not only the women's movement, which wanted to distance itself from them, but also the gay rights movement which, at times, seemed focused only on the issues of gay men.

For the moment, the conservative political right wing was a distant memory as gays and lesbians became energized by a growing belief that the self-loathing they had been taught to accept was something unnecessary and that perhaps the concept of normalcy could be expanded. To this end there was a growing movement dedicated to gay liberation, whose roots can be traced from the early part of the century, in those that did not succumb to the ideology of either the early sexologists or Freud, but with "dignity in the face of oppression" (the meaning of the lambda sign) survived.

Although few social movements can trace their beginnings to a singular event, the gay rights movement in this country is generally said to have begun on the early morning of June 28, 1969. Judy Garland, a favorite of many gay men, had been buried the day before in New York and on that Friday night the gay bars were full. The Stonewall Inn, a favorite bar for drag queens, gay men, and lesbians in Greenwich Village, was doing a brisk business that weekend. A not-unusual police raid on the bar precipitated the riots. What was different that night was that the patrons, rather than willingly being arrested and herded into the police wagons, decided to fight back. After decades of abuse and misunderstanding the riots ebbed and flowed throughout the entire week, eventually involving more than 2,000 gays and lesbians and 300 police officers (Streitmatter 1995). This singular series of riots heralded the start of the gay rights movement and gave voice to the decades of silence and secrecy that had gone before.

In sum, from the turn of the century until the Stonewall riots the socially constructed concept of homosexuality had evolved from one of acceptable romantic friendships that were only one part of an individual's identity to one that defined the individual's identity as being homosexual necessitating psychiatric intervention. The idea of the mentally ill homosexual who would remain hidden in fear of losing a job or facing other social and legal stigmatization began to be publicly challenged in the 1950s and 1960s and culminated in the birth of the post-modern era of gay and lesbian history that followed the Stonewall riots in June of 1969.

The Postmodern Era: From 1969

For the gay male and lesbian community, the postmodern era began with the Stonewall riots in New York City and continues through the 1990s. The postmodern era reflects a time of contradictions where great strides toward the acceptance of homosexuality are juxtaposed against a time of increasing political and religious conservatism condemning homosexuality as a sin and a behavioral choice. This section explores the postmodern era in the lesbian and gay community and traces the evolution of views related to that community. From 1969 to the end of the century there has been a gradual move away from the prevailing view of homosexuality as a mental illness to one that holds the behavior as innate and normal. The result has been the increasing homosexualization of the United States that is occurring in the context of an extremely conservative national philosophy.

From Mentally Ill Perverts to Gay Liberation: 1969–1980

In the Stonewall riots, gay men, drag queens, and lesbians fought back against routine police raids for the first time, heralding the beginning of the movement to ensure equal rights for lesbians and gays (Altman 1982; D'Emilio and Freedman 1988; Faderman 1981; Mondimore 1996; Streitmatter 1995). The actions of this group of enraged bar patrons were the culmination of years of police harassment, hate crimes, religious and political disenfranchisement, societal condemnation, and general frustration with living in a homophobic society where gay organizations existed in secret and difficult-to-find gay bars acted as churches, family gathering spots, and sources of support (Altman 1982; Perry 1998).

Unlike any activity before, the Stonewall riots mobilized the entire lesbian and gay community toward social, political, and religious actions that still have meaning thirty years following the actual event. The decade of the 1970s was one characterized by the rapid development of an identifiable gay and lesbian community throughout the country and was one of reaction, increased visibility, redefinition of gender roles, the rise of the gay press, and sexual promiscuity evolving side by side with an increasingly conservative religious and political agenda.

The war in Vietnam was ebbing in the early 1970s and would be ended by the end of the decade. The era of the Great Society had passed and the women's movement was gaining strength. Encouraged by the empowerment felt following the riots, gays and lesbians entered into the 1970s with a spirit of radicalism that propelled them into the streets and into the boards of such groups as the American Psychiatric Association (APA). Such action, unheard of prior to 1969, would, in the 1970s, result in the development of annual Gay Pride marches and the elimination of homosexuality as a mental disorder in the third edition of the APA's diagnostic manual of mental disorders.

The 1970s also saw the development of thousands of organizations devoted solely to the gay community. By 1974 some 800 organizations existed, and that number would increase into the thousands by the decade's end (D'Emilio and Freeman 1988). Such organizations included social clubs, restaurants, bathhouses, bars, churches, travel agencies, and bookstores. The increasing visibility of the gay and lesbian culture had both empowering and damaging effects. Increased visibility meant publicly coming out, which was seen both as a personal affirmation of the self and a political statement against an oppressive society (D'Emilio and Freedman 1988). Within the gay community debates were held as to whether or not those gays and lesbians who were in public positions but not forthright about their sexual orientation should be "outted." In an effort to claim the gay community's own, many such individuals' sexual orientation was made known during the 1970s through long published lists in the gay press (Streitmatter 1995).

While this philosophical debate occurred in the gay community, increased visibility also meant that more of those in the homophobic society were aware of who comprised the gay community, where they met, and their growing activism and radicalism in their demands for equal rights. This new knowledge resulted in an increase in hate crimes against lesbian and gay persons during the 1970s. Probably the most noted hate crime during this decade was that of the murder of San Francisco's Mayor George Moscone and Board of Supervisors member Harvey Milk by another Board of Supervisors member, Dan White. Harvey Milk, the only openly gay board member and Mayor Moscone were brutally murdered in Milk's office following a vote related to a gay rights law where Mr. White had cast the only dissenting vote. Claiming that his ingestion of junk food had made him act irresponsibly, White was found guilty not of first degree murder, but of manslaughter. With this verdict, as with the Stonewall riots of almost a decade before, gays and lesbians again resorted to violence (Streitmatter 1995).

The violence evolving from the Milk murder and other oppression in the decade yielded to an increased determination to struggle forward with the fight for equality that resulted in the nomination of many openly lesbian or gay candidates and the actual election of several. Mel Boozer, an African-American openly gay man, was nominated for Vice President of the United States at the 1980 National Democratic Convention and Elaine Nobel won a seat in the Massachusetts state legislature in 1974.

These small, but notable events gained larger stature when coupled with the elimination of sodomy statutes in half the states, the passage of civil rights protections in several cities and municipalities during the 1970s, and the first national gay and lesbian march on Washington in

1979. While national progress was being made incrementally, women were struggling with the new ideas of feminism and what role, if any, lesbians were to play in the women's movement.

The fledgling women's movement of the early 1970s faced a dilemma—what to do with the often radical lesbian feminists who had so enthusiastically embraced such organizations as the National Organization for Women. Lesbians, now empowered to be visible, were dismayed to discover that the feminist movement was not as enthusiastic about their membership as they were to be part of the movement. Debates among the leadership of women's groups reflected difficulty including the lesbian agenda with the more tolerated nongay woman's needs.

Lesbians of the 1970s were beginning to define for themselves what it meant to be lesbian. Having the freedom no longer to be defined as mentally ill, these women broke away from using the all-inclusive term "gay," and began to call themselves "lesbian," "lesbian womyn," "lesbian feminists," "lesbian separatists," "dykes," "political lesbians," or "women identified women." In doing so they began to also define for themselves the family units in which they chose to live.

These new definitions for lesbians caused a split between the gay male community and the lesbian community. The gay and lesbian community as a whole had difficulty uniting simply because sexual orientation alone was not enough to cement an otherwise heterogeneous group. The women's movement and its feminist ideals further separated lesbian women from their gay male counterparts. Primary issues around which lesbians and gay men could not agree included concerns of pornography, pederasty, equal rights for women, sexism, and public sex. The early gay liberation movement was run almost exclusively by gay men who paid little attention to the issues of their lesbian sisters. This further alienated lesbians from gay men. Twenty years later, this division has yet to be equitably addressed.

And, while lesbians were struggling to give voice to their own stories, so, too, were gay men redefining themselves. The theme of the decade was that of extreme sexual promiscuity; the male bathhouses became synonymous with gay male culture. Gay men, too, began moving back into inner-city neighborhoods now all but abandoned by the white community. A surge of renovation and revitalization of blighted properties began that encouraged other gays and lesbians to move into what would become gay ghettos.

Coupled with the sexual promiscuity in the gay male community of the 1970s was a resurgence of gay male and lesbian spirituality. In the mid

1970s, books such as Reverend Troy Perry's *The Lord Is My Shepherd and He Knows I'm Gay* (1971) and Scanzoni and Mollenkott's *Is the Homosexual My Neighbor: Another Christian View* (1978) were published and the Metropolitan Community Church had congregations in many U.S. cities. Having grown up with religious proscriptions against them, gays and lesbians began to believe that a religious system that had once disowned and despised their existence could embrace them as whole. This was still twenty years before the idea of same-sex marriage and almost ten before the lesbian baby boom of the mid 1980s.

Even as some positive steps for lesbian and gay male equality were emerging and the gay community was becoming more visible and viable, the 1970s also brought with it a newly defined political and religious conservatism that argued against homosexual rights. Noted spokesperson for this view was Anita Bryant, whose Save the Children campaign of the late 1970s, when coupled with Reverend Jerry Falwell's Moral Majority, created formidable opposition to the floundering gay liberation movement. A painful example of this homophobia was demonstrated when, in 1973, 32 mostly gay men were burned to death in the Upstairs Lounge Fire in New Orleans. Trying to find a church where a memorial service for the victims could be held became an almost impossible task; church after church and denomination after denomination refused to allow the Reverend Troy Perry access. Only one small church with a brave pastor, in the French Quarter of New Orleans, agreed to allow such a service. The pastor's decision was not met with unanimous approval from his board, who questioned his judgment in allowing such a group to use the church. The pastor simply stated that he believed his church was there to serve those in need (Perry 1998).

Overall, the 1970s was a time of growth for the lesbian and gay male community who, while defining for themselves what it meant to be a gay or lesbian person and making significant inroads into the social, political, and religious arenas, had to struggle with virulent homophobia resulting from increasing religious and political conservatism. As we shall see, the juxtaposition of these seemingly oppositional philosophies was to continue through the 1980s and the 1990s.

AIDS and Its Impact: The 1980s

Still riding the wave of gains from the 1970s and reacting to the campaigns of Anita Bryant and Jerry Falwell, the start of the 1980s promised to be a continuation of the good and bad times of the previous decade.

The split in the lesbian and gay male community still existed, but no one paid much attention to it. The organizations and businesses begun in the 1970s that served the gay and lesbian community were thriving, and few people noticed the first small news articles describing a new cancer that was showing up in the gay male population. Even when it was thought that the disease was sexually transmitted, there was no rush to close the male bathhouses, and the promiscuity of the 1970s continued. When, in 1984 a test became available for what had first been called Gay Related Immunodeficiency (GRID) or the gay plague, and came to be known as the Human Immunodeficiency Virus (HIV) (believed to cause Acquired Immunodeficiency Syndrome (AIDS), it became clear that the disease was a significant public health issue. By the end of the decade more than 100,000 persons had been diagnosed with HIV/AIDS and 90 percent of them were gay men (Houser 1990; Lloyd 1995; Streitmatter 1995).

HIV/AIDS had an immediate and significant impact on all aspects of both the gay male and lesbian communities as well as in the larger non-gay society. There was an initial denial of the severity of HIV/AIDS in the gay male community. When hundreds and then thousands of young, previously healthy gay men began dying, gay men and lesbians joined forces not only to provide caregiving services to those who were sick, but also to challenge the political and social forces that were keeping promising drugs from being developed and made available. Social support networks created by lesbians and gay men emerged in the mid 1980s; from them were created the now institutionalized social service organizations (like AID Atlanta or the NOAIDS Task Force of New Orleans) for persons with HIV/AIDS. As a corollary to the HIV/AIDS health crisis, which impacted mostly gay men at the time, there was also a beginning interest in the unique health issues of lesbians. For example, it was learned that lesbians risked contracting breast cancer more than their heterosexual counterparts. This reality, coupled with other uniquely lesbian health issues, also helped bring the gay and lesbian communities together. Sadly, the gay and lesbian community now had an issue about which they could mostly agree.

The conservative religious and political communities viewed HIV/AIDS as God's wrath being demonstrated on a population of sinners and used it as proof that God did not approve of a homosexual lifestyle. Those who were discovered to be HIV+ or to have AIDS risked the loss of their jobs, health insurance, homes, and families. Legal protections were still some years away and those with HIV/AIDS often hid that fact out of fear. To further enforce the conservatism of the 1980s, the U.S. Supreme

Court, in a 5 to 4 vote, upheld the right of states to outlaw certain sexual acts between consenting adults committed in the privacy of personal bed-rooms (*Bowers v. Hardwick* 1986). HIV/AIDS had caused an antigay backlash and a public health pandemic. The sexual promiscuity of the bathhouses gave way to male telephone sex, gay men appeared to assume a manly man's look by wearing leather and denim, lesbians no longer felt the need to look like the guys, and neither lesbians nor gay men felt a need to adopt the previously accepted cross-gender roles of earlier decades (Altman 1982; D'Emilio and Freedman 1988; Streitmatter 1995). The strides of the 1970s seemed far distant and shrouded.

Additionally, the 1980s produced another, much larger gay and lesbian march on Washington, D.C. Vice-President Walter Mondale spoke at a gay rights dinner, films depicting lesbians and gay men as normal attracted gay and nongay audiences, bumper stickers with gay themes began appearing, more localities and larger companies were recognizing domestic partners, and laws supporting gay and lesbian civil rights were passed in many areas (Altman 1982; Streitmatter 1995). The gay and les-bian liberation movement continued to move forward and such national organizations as the National Gay and Lesbian Task Force (NGLTF) and Human Rights Campaign (HRC) assumed a major role in the develop-ment and implementation of gay and lesbian friendly public policies. Fur-ther, the 1980s saw the emergence of visible family units composed of gay male and lesbian couples who may or may not have children. The lesbian and gay male baby boom, generally thought to have been made openly visible in the late 1980s, and the idea of same-sex marriage, also openly discussed in the late 1980s, have challenged traditional family values.

Overall, the 1980s were a mixture of emotional lows and highs. The HIV/AIDS pandemic provided the gay and lesbian community with its most significant challenges and yet it, too, brought the community together to fight for a common cause. National organizations such as NGLTF and HRC appealed to a range of political approaches to equal rights, and laws providing some protections for gay and lesbian lifestyles became more common. Gay men and lesbians became more visible, viewed by many as a disenfranchised minority who, because of genetics, is condemned by some. Lesbians and gay men in elected public office were no longer unique, and health issues related to gay men and lesbians were becoming important to the medical profession. The loss of thousands of gay men to AIDS and the recurring themes of the right wing that homo-sexuality is a mental illness and a sin haunts the collective memory of all gay and lesbian persons who, in the name of therapeutic intervention,

have had to endure "cures" ranging from institutionalization to elec-
troshock treatments in the name of treatment. These dual themes of
growing acceptance of gay men and lesbians on one hand and the antigay
conservative backlash on the other continue into the 1990s.

Radicalism and Conservatism—A Curious Mix: The 1990s

The 1990s have been characterized by Vaid (1995) as being a time of "virtual equality," where there seems to be the perception of lesbian and gay
equality; however, that perception is not borne out in unified legal protections, equal political representation, general religious acceptance, or
social protections. While it would be in error to say that the lesbian and
gay community has not made steady and significant inroads into each of
these four areas, the accomplishments that have been made are tempered
by increased antigay legislation, hate crimes, and damnation by the radical right.

In the legal and political arenas lesbians and gay men were becoming
more and more visible. By 1998, 10 states had passed legislation that
included sexual orientation in their nondiscrimination laws and another
7 states were considering similar legislation (Birch 1998). A total of 29
states and the District of Columbia have no sodomy laws, 19 states have
hate crimes legislation that includes hate crimes based on sexual orientation, and 27 states have elected openly gay or lesbian persons to public
office (Bond 1998; National Gay and Lesbian Task Force 1998c). Scores
of municipalities, companies, and universities include sexual orientation
in nondiscrimination policies, and the American public generally supports nondiscrimination on the basis of sexual orientation in the workplace (NGLTF 1998c). In the next months, Hawaii, Vermont, and Utah
will grapple with the issue of allowing same sex marriages (St. Pierre
1998) and the 1997 U.S. Congress narrowly defeated the Employment
Non-Discrimination Act (ENDA) that would have ended discrimination
on the basis of sexual orientation in the workplace (Stachelberg 1997).
Bills to ban lesbian and gay male couples from adopting children, to cut
funding for HIV/AIDS, and to repeal the Washington, D.C., domestic
partner law have been defeated (HRC 1996). Organizations that serve the
gay community continue to thrive and expand. The National Gay and
Lesbian Task Force and Lambda Legal Defense and Education Fund both
celebrated their twenty-fifth anniversaries in 1998, Gay, Lesbian, and
Straight Educational Network (GLSEN) began in 1990, and the Gay and

Lesbian Victory Fund and Human Rights Campaign have helped ensure gay rights during the 1990s. The Hetrick-Martin Institute, founded in 1980, provides services to gay, lesbian, bisexual, and transgender youth; the Astrea National Lesbian Action Foundation provides funding for projects that empower and enrich lesbian lives. Groups devoted solely to transgendered persons emerged and members of the transgendered community were accepted into the gay and lesbian sexual continuum (Goldberg 1998). A popular television show, *Ellen,* had a lesbian protagonist and gay and lesbian characters were common in mainstream television and films. The 1990s also saw the development of the Internet where now thousands of websites devoted to lesbian and gay issues can be found.

Yet with all these advances that seem to favor and support gay rights, the 1990s also brought a significant antigay backlash. For example, in 1996, while there were 60 pro-gay legislative initiatives in 26 states, there were 100 antigay legislative initiatives passed in 40 states (NGLTF 1998c). In 1997 state legislatures were introducing an average of two new antigay laws per day (NGLTF 1998b), and while not all of those passed, the fact that such legislation is introduced seems to demonstrate a conservative thrust. Twenty-one states still have sodomy laws that make homosexual behavior illegal and 30 states do not include sexual orientation as being protected by hate crimes (NGLTF 1998b, 1998c). There are 474 active hate groups in the Unites States that are found in every state (Southern Poverty Law Center 1998). In a rush to protect themselves in the event Hawaii passes its same-sex marriage law, by 1998, 17 states had already passed legislation ensuring that same-sex couples could not wed in their state (NGLTF 1998b, 1998c), and a study in early 1998 showed that suburban Americans were exceptionally tolerant of everyone except lesbians and gay men (Wolfe 1998). The Christian right is adamant about its antigay position and conservative politicians echo that sentiment. Hate crimes against gays and lesbians increased (Abrams 1998), discharges against lesbian and gay service personnel were up 67 percent as witch hunts increased during the decade (Weiner 1998), and a coalition of right-wing Christian groups took out full-page ads in major newspapers calling for homosexuals to find heterosexuality through the Christian religion (Reisner 1998).

Overall, the 1990s continued to be a time where there was great confusion over the legal rights and social position of gay men and lesbians. Gay family structures were not as alien as they were in the 1980s, public schools had to deal with children of same-sex couples, same-sex commitment ceremonies in both the Christian and Jewish faiths are not unheard of, domestic partnership benefits were no longer nonexistent in many companies and municipalities, and the gay community continues to grow. With all these advances in the 1990s in many states it is still illegal to engage in same-sex, consensual behavior; hate crimes and organizations that condone hatred are increasing, and those condemning same-sex relationships are becoming more and more militant.

In sum, same-sex activity has been in existence since time began; however, it has only been since the end of the nineteenth century that is has been viewed as an important part of one's identity. Perhaps as a result of this new social construction of homosexuals and homosexuality and the emphasis on scientific explanations that occurred at the same time, interest in same-sex relationships remains a topic of significant interest.

This chapter has focused on the historical development of the concept of homosexuality. It is clear that same-sex behaviors have been in evidence for thousands of years and that, until the end of the nineteenth century, it was mostly considered a behavior. The societal views of the behavior have varied from era to era where some societies embraced homosexual behaviors as acceptable, while others viewed the behavior as sinful or criminal. As the views of sexuality moved from reproductive responsibility to personal pleasure (1700–1900) the ideas about same-sex sexual behaviors were somewhat modified; while still seen as a sin, such behaviors were not generally prosecuted. Same-sex romantic friendships, especially between women, considered quite acceptable in the mid to late 1800s, were redefined by the medical community as homosexual behaviors began to be viewed as an unacceptable part of personal identity that, with proper treatment, could be made "normal." Society's view of same-sex sexuality has, in the century of the 1900s, moved from being a mental illness to being considered a minority culture worthy of equal protection under the law. And, while there are still opposing views on the concept of same-sex behaviors, gay men and lesbians continue to expand the definitions and acceptance of their lifestyles. The following chapters will explore how social workers can best serve lesbians and gay men using an empowerment approach.

2

Homosexuality and the Political Continuum

The lesbian and gay community has made a lot of advances in visibility, civil liberties, and political organization in the last twenty-five years. We have also learned through hard lessons that for the most part we have to depend on ourselves to make change happen. But we have come to appreciate that we cannot achieve equality or liberation without some help. As Mahatma Gandhi said, "None of us are free until all of us are free."
Witt, Thomas, and Marcus 1995:493.

This chapter presents an analytical evaluation of the current views about homosexuality from the standpoint of a philosophical continuum ranging from conservative to liberal. Three areas of the continuum will be explored—far right, middle, and far left. In each area, philosophical views, beliefs, and values are explored in terms of social, legal, and political activities that impact the lesbian and gay community.

As was evident in chapter 1, lesbians and gays find themselves interwoven with the historical era in which they live. The situation of the late 1990s finds gays and lesbians enjoying more freedoms and equalities than in recent times, yet facing the continuing burden of institutional, individual, and internalized homophobia.

The Philosophical and Political Continuum

In the United States there are a variety of philosophical views that are buttressed by beliefs and values. One end of this continuum is generally referred to as conservative (often called "the right"), while the other is referred to as liberal (or "the left") (see figure 2.1). Where individuals' beliefs fall along this continuum influences their philosophical views on the welfare state and governmental involvement with social welfare pro-

Figure 2.1

The Philosophical and Political Continuum

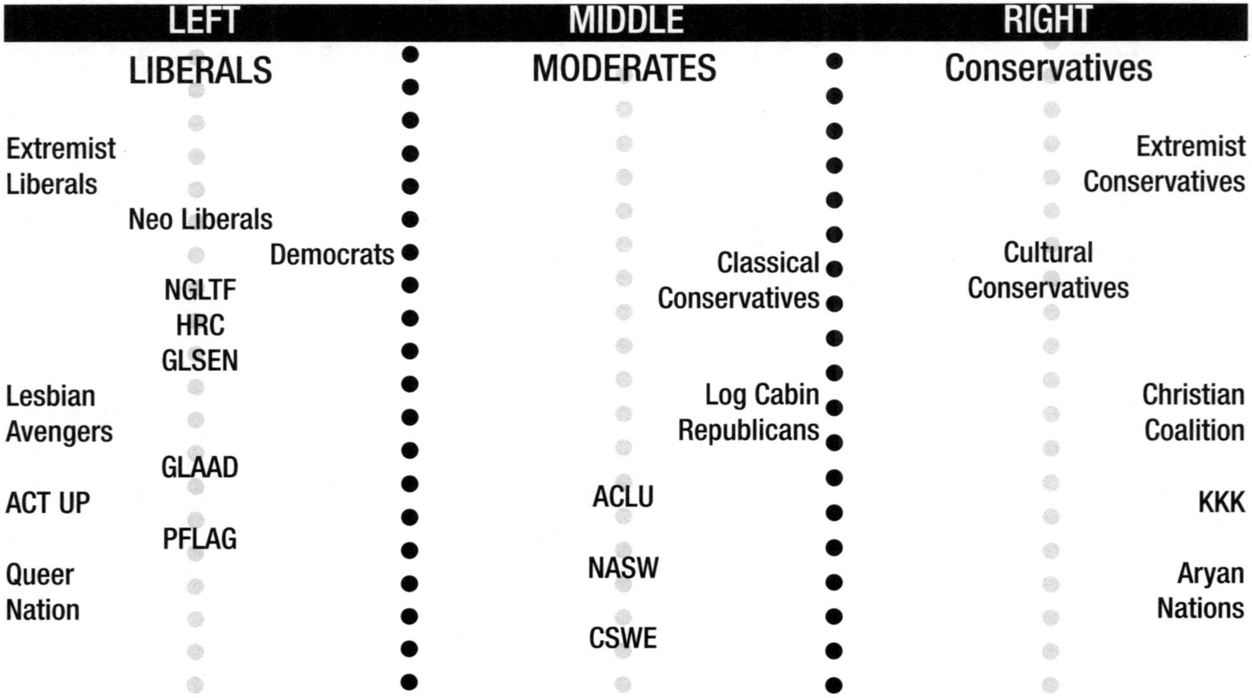
LEFT
MIDDLE
RIGHT
LIBERALS
MODERATES
Conservatives
Extremist Liberals
Neo Liberals
Democrats
NGLTF
HRC
GLSEN
Lesbian Avengers
GLAAD
ACT UP
PFLAG
Queer Nation
Classical Conservatives
Log Cabin Republicans
ACLU
NASW
CSWE
Extremist Conservatives
Cultural Conservatives
Christian Coalition
KKK
Aryan Nations

grams. In politics, conservatism generally refers to a desire to maintain traditional values and to conserve the existing order. Emerging during the nineteenth century, political conservatism sought to limit government and preserve links between church and state. Reemerging in the twentieth century, conservatives advocate limited government intervention and oppose the expansion of the welfare state (*AHD* 1992; *CCE* 1995). Conservatives of the late twentieth century believe private sector intervention, not governmental, is the best means by which the social welfare can be achieved. Essentially, government's role in providing a welfare safety net should be minimal (Karger and Stoesz 1998). They further favor the abolition of abortion laws, applaud traditional family values, and see homosexuality as sinful (CCW 1998b, 1998c; Ku Klux Klan 1998).

At the other end of the political continuum are the liberals. Political liberalism refers to a worldview that is not bound by tradition or authoritarian attitudes but rather one that is progressive and free from bigotry. The political approach has its basis in the goodness of humanity and individual autonomy that is open to new ideas for development and progress and tolerant of the behaviors of others (*AHD* 1995; *CCE* 1992). Emerging in the nineteenth century as a Protestant movement, liberalism favored intellectual inquiry and de-emphasized dogmatic theological teachings. This Protestant movement was met with a Roman Catholic liberalism in the nineteenth century that stressed political democracy coupled with an orthodox theology (*CCE* 1992).

In the latter part of the twentieth century, liberalism maintains the values of a democratic government with its basis in laws and the consent of those governed, but with protections from arbitrary governmental authority and a separation between church and state (Karger and Stoesz 1998). Liberals believe that government, not the private sector, is the only way to ensure an adequate safety net for social welfare and therefore favor government intervention into social welfare programs that provide the greatest good for the greatest number of people (Karger and Stoesz 1998).

Not surprisingly, political parties in the United States cluster around this philosophical continuum. Traditionally, the Republican Party is characterized as being conservative and defending more traditional values, whereas the Democratic Party is seen as defending those values that are more liberal. However, along the continuum lie infinite varieties of philosophical views, each supported by various political parties. On the conservative side there are classical conservatives and cultural conservatives; on the liberal side there are neo-liberals and traditional liberals.

Each philosophical perspective brings with it varying perceptions on major issues, and each of the more than 15 registered political parties in the United States (National Political Index 1998) has specific attitudes, values, and beliefs about the concept of homosexuality. While it is beyond the scope of this chapter to explore the views of each political party, general themes associated with conservative and liberal philosophies around the concept of homosexuality will be analyzed.

A Conservative Conundrum: Gays and Lesbians

As noted, the conservative philosophy allows for a perspective that includes little separation between church and state where there is an emphasis on traditional values and family life. There has been a curious merger between fundamentalism, the conservative religious movement whose main aims are to maintain the traditional views of the Bible and oppose liberalism, and political conservatives. It is therefore not difficult to see why what has come to be known as the "radical right," "the New Christian Right," or the "Christian Coalition" found congruence between their strict religious dogma and the philosophy of conservatism.

One of the first modern religious groups to equate morality with Christianity, Jerry Falwell's Moral Majority of the 1970s, quickly moved from being solely a Christian organization to being a political group that lobbied on behalf of those who favored their philosophy of "traditional moral values" (eventually shortened to "family values")(De Mar 1998). Eventually eclipsed by the Christian Coalition, founded by Pat Robertson in 1989, the Moral Majority's fundamentalist views provided the foundation for the Christian Coalition's development.

Boasting more than 2 million members, with more than 2,000 local chapters, the Christian Coalition moved away from the Moral Majority's nondenominational view by providing only "Christians" a voice in government. Their philosophy stems from a belief that people of the Christian faith have both a right and a responsibility to be involved with community, state, and national social and political action. Their 8 major goals are:

- The protection of religious freedom;
- The strengthening of family life;
- The protection of innocent human life;
- The return of public education to localities and parents;

- The defense of marriage;
- The reduction of taxes on families;
- The punishment of criminals and the defense of victims' rights; and,
- The protection of communities from pornography (CCW 1998b).

These goals, broad-based in their appeal, define the political mission of the Christian Coalition, and have specific operational definitions that have been socially constructed by the leaders of the coalition. For example, the protection of innocent human life has been defined as the protection of the unborn fetus; that is translated into the pro-life political movement that wants to prevent abortion. More germane are the goals that relate to strengthening family life and defending marriage, for it is these two that are used by the Christian Coalition to define homosexuality as not only a sin, but also a curable mental illness (De Mar 1998; CCW 1998; McAllister 1998; Miller 1998).

Some of the rhetoric about homosexuality has changed from the vitriolic attacks of Pat Robertson, who equated homosexuals with Satanists and noted that AIDS was an effective vehicle to move the homosexual agenda into every facet of society (People for the American Way 1998) to a language of moderation and tolerance where Ralph Reed chastises the previous methods of the Christian Coalition and urges its members to adopt a spirit of charity and Christian mercy (People for the American Way 1998). Although the rhetoric may have softened, the message remains the same—homosexuality is not acceptable. Others within the Christian right still believe that the Bible views homosexuality as equal to other forms of sexual temptations not used within marriage for procreation (such as adultery, incest, bestiality, and masturbation) and that the biblical sanctions for homosexuality should be enforced—namely gays and lesbians should be put to death (De Mar 1998). No doubt bolstered by the Christian ideal of "loving the sinner but hating the sin," most conservatives choose not to condemn homosexuals to death, but rather provide a means by which the unfortunate homosexual's natural inclination toward heterosexuality can be discovered and practiced (CCW 1998).

The Institute of Religion and Democracy monitors mainstream churches and centers on media campaigns that highlight differing opinions in the church in an effort to exploit the internal conflicts by bringing them to national attention. Issues within the Methodist, Episcopal, and Presbyterian churches have centered on such things as homosexuality, feminism, abortion, and sexual morality (Stan 1996). Further monitory by the religious right is seen on its crusade against the National Endowment for the Arts (NEA) which supports what the Christian Coalition views as the production of plays funded by taxpayers that are considered blasphemous to Christians (CCW 1998c). Additionally, the Christian Coalition condemned Vice President Al Gore for his support of positive gay and lesbian lifestyles as portrayed on television citing that he was merely courting the Hollywood left for their support in his 2000 campaign (CCW 1998b).

This belief in the sinful nature of homosexuality and the further belief that homosexuality is an acquired rather than an innate trait is supported by some in the psychiatric community, who believe that homosexual behaviors can be replaced by heterosexual ones using conversion or reparative therapy (Bieber 1965; Bieber et al. 1962; Nicolosi 1991; Socarides 1978). This psychoanalytically founded viewpoint seemed to have merit during the early and middle part of the twentieth century when, by common definition, homosexuality was considered a mental illness and so identified in the American Psychiatric Association's (APA) first two editions of its diagnostic manual (Lloyd and Tully 1996). However, even with the APA's removal of homosexuality as a mental illness in the 1970s, certain psychiatrists failed to accept increasing scientific data refuting their beliefs. As recently as 1998, the APA was still struggling with the reality that reparative therapy to cure homosexuals was still being practiced (Lloyd and Tully 1996). And, while even the most ardent reparative therapists believe that not all homosexuals can be cured, they seek to treat and cure only those who have a strong desire to extinguish their homosexual behaviors in favor of heterosexual behaviors (Bieber et al. 1962; Nicolosi 1991). Even with this highly motivated group, of those treated only about one-third convert to heterosexuality (Bieber et al. 1962; Miller 1998; Nicolosi 1991). This low success rate does not deter reparative therapists from insisting their therapeutic interventions, which can include electroconvulsive therapy (ECT), aversion therapy, and drug therapy in addition to more traditional therapeutic activities, are beneficial.

The Christian right has seized on the belief that homosexuality can be cured as this would support biblical scripture as well as some schools of scientific thought. To that end, organizations such as Exodus have been founded. Exodus is an organization supported by the Christian right that comprises 85 agencies and ministries that blend counseling with religious teachings to change lesbians and gays into heterosexual people. Members believe that through faith in Jesus Christ as Savior and Lord and repentance, freedom from the sin of homosexuality is possible (Exodus International 1998). Exodus boasts that since its founding in 1976, more than 200,000 gays and lesbians have sought help to change their sexual orientations. Since no follow-up records are kept, there is no estimate as to the total number of conversions that have occurred, but the estimate is that only about one-third were converted from homosexual to heterosexual (Miller 1998).

In support of the belief that sexual orientation is a choice, on July 13, 1998, 15 national ministries ran a full-page advertisement in the *New York Times* (at a cost of almost $75,000) that featured a photograph of a large group of people who had been saved from their homosexuality by their faith in God. The caption under the picture read, "We're standing for the truth that homosexuals can change" (Miller 1998). The ad also contains testimony from one former lesbian who is now married to a former gay man about her spiritual journey from lesbianism to heterosexual motherhood. Other similar "Truth in Love Campaign" advertisements appeared the same week in *USA Today* and the *Washington Post*, but were more strongly worded and cited the nongenetic roots of homosexuality, the recruitment of students in public schools by gays and lesbians, and the sinfulness of the homosexual lifestyle (Miller 1998; Reisner 1998). Additionally, to call attention to the contradictions between the beliefs of homosexuals and the beliefs of most Americans, annually on October 11 (to coincide with the pro-gay National Coming Out Day), Coming Out of Homosexuality Day is held (Marantha Newswatch 1997).

The visibility of the attack on all things lesbian or gay is a fairly recent phenomenon in the Christian right. Although the Christian Coalition's Pat Robertson noted in the 1980s that he would do everything in his power to restrict the freedom of homosexuals (People for the American Way 1998), the press releases of the Christian Coalition have had an interesting evolution in regard to gays and lesbians. In 1996 the Christian Coalition issued only 6 press releases, none of which dealt with homosexuality. In the following year there were 36 news releases; 2 (5.5%) dealt with homosexuality. However, by July 1998, the Christian Coalition had already issued 52 news releases where homosexuality was the topic of 6 (11.5%) of them (CCW 1996, 1997, 1998c). The topic of homosexuality was not one of major concern in the Christian Coalition's magazine, *Christian American* in 1995, 1996, or 1997, but gained some prominence in 1998 (CCW 1996, 1997, 1998c). Likewise, other Christian right organizations that paid little attention to gays and lesbians during the early part of the 1990s began to see homosexuality as a threat to the natural family order that will lead to the ultimate destruction of the nation (People for the American Way 1998). One possible explanation for this increased emphasis on homosexuals and gay issues as a target may be that the Republican Party identified gay rights as a major emphasis for the 1998 elections (Goodman 1998).

The Ethics and Religious Liberty Commission of the Southern Baptist Church (1998) identified 16 current issues associated with homosexuality about which all Christians should be concerned. Of these 16, 4 centered on the idea that homosexuality was sinful, 9 dealt with issues of homosexuals trying to gain legal and civil rights, while the other 3 chastised politicians for courting the gay vote. The John Birch Society's magazine, *The New American*, had no major articles related to homosexuality in 1995, 1996, or 1997, but on June 8, 1998, homosexuality became a topic for the magazine's cover story where the major themes were the deterioration of American morals, the perversion of the American political system, and the encouragement of young Americans to adopt the gay lifestyle (*The New American* 1998). The only other major article on homosexuality appeared in the magazine in 1994 when the theme was how traditional values were being undermined by the lavender left (Grigg 1994).

The Family Research Council provides an excellent perspective on the political views of the Christian right and has the "homosexual culture" listed among its 8 major issues (the other 7 being crime and drugs, cultural renewal, education, family issues, military readiness, and pro-life issues) as members believe homosexuality to be immoral and unhealthy. Further, homosexuality is seen to be destructive not only to individuals and families, but to society as well. Any attempt to provide homosexuals with legal or civil rights or to equate homosexuality with race or other innate characteristics is opposed by the Family Research Council, whose members "lovingly" support only the healing of homosexuals who wish to be changed (FRC 1998).

The political agenda of the Christian right strongly supports tradition and is thus firmly opposed to legislation that would protect gays and lesbians from discrimination. Such includes legislation that would protect lesbians and gays from employment discrimination on the basis of sexual orientation, or general nondiscrimination legislation on the basis of sexual origin to legislation that would permit same-sex couples to marry (CCW 1998; FRC 1998a; John Birch Society 1998). As a grassroots movement, the Christian right is well funded and politically savvy.

The rhetoric of the religious right has fluctuated between the open hostility of Pat Robertson to the "more compassionate" views of Ralph Reed (People for the American Way 1998). There has been a shift in how the religious right views its interactions with the gay community. With the more compassionate tone of the religious right has come the contention that it is its supporters who are being discriminated against—and that it is not discriminating against the gay community (Goodman 1998; Grigg 1994). Grigg (1994) asserts in an article in *The New American* that the gay agenda requires the media to view homosexuals as an oppressed minority and victim. He further asserts that this is not reality, but that gays and lesbians are the oppressors of the rights of the Christian right. He notes that the tactics of the gay movement are similar to those used in Nazi Germany and that radical homosexual groups such as ACT-UP conduct campaigns of intolerance using such tactics as intimidation, violence, and harassment and liken all traditionalists to ranting homophobes who want to ensure that God's will is carried out by killing all homosexuals.

Both Grigg (1994) and Goodman (1998) note that fundamentalist Christians are being targeted by the pro-gay movement as being intolerant and homophobic bigots. Grigg explores the idea that the media view anti-gay intolerance from the Christian right as intolerable, but largely ignores anti-Christian intolerance from the pro-gay movement. Goodman (1998) notes that the Christian right seems to want those who are pro-gay to be tolerant of anti-gay intolerance and says the religious right has usurped the word "tolerance" just as it did the word "family." The real argument, Goodman postulates, is between those who see gays and lesbians as mentally ill sinners and those who view them as productive members of society.

That argument seems acceptable even to the most ardent of anti-homosexual groups. The web-site of the Christian Anti-Homosexuals (*http://www.antihomosexual.com*) is devoted to the condemnation of homosexuality on the basis of theological scripture and proclaims that no homosexual could be a Christian because homosexuality is contrary to the natural laws of God. However, the creator of the site notes, in an article entitled "Living on the Edge" (1998), that homosexuals are betting their souls on the reality that God does not condemn their lifestyle. The author is betting her or his soul on the belief that homosexuality is an unacceptable lifestyle. If the author is in error about her or his beliefs he or she is willing to accept the fact that the Bible was wrong.

Knight (1995) explores a study conducted by the National Institute of Health that demonstrated that homosexuality in male fruit flies is a learned behavior. The study, which was touted by pro-gays as indicating a definitive link between homosexuality and genetics, did find that chemically altered male fruit flies engaged in homosexual mating patterns and that, when placed in the environment, unaltered male flies, too, succumbed to same-sex behaviors. Knight concludes that homosexual behavior is learned and that it occurs in environments that permit it to exist. He moves from the research findings to note "that homosexuality is not only universally discouraged as learned behavior but can also be temporary, controlled, or even changed" (Knight 1995:3). He supports this statement on the basis of scientific research data from the start of the twentieth century and the entire history of mankind. But, Knight does acknowledge that it seems the causes for homosexuality are multivariate and that more scientific data are needed.

This seeming willingness to be somewhat open-minded about homosexuality is not universally acceptable to the religious right. Seen as a visible threat to the family and the nation (Goodman 1998; Grigg 1994; Sullivan 1998), homosexuality has been referred to as being like alcoholism and kleptomania by Senate Majority Leader Trent Lott (Goodman 1998), a sinful free choice not worthy of civil rights protections (Sullivan 1998), a pathological disease that Jesus Christ can cure (Walker 1997), a destructive lifestyle (Heritage 1997), and as presenting unnecessary health and security risks in the military (Maginnis 1995b). Such views were championed by numbers of persons running for office in the 1994 elections, and the Christian right succeeded in playing a major role in that election. However, even with the major drive of the radical right in the early 1990s, the campaign of 1996, that was to further their major electoral victory and accomplishments of the 1994 election, brought mixed results. The major political issues of the religious right (abortion, school prayer, and homosexuality) were largely overlooked by the major presidential candidates in 1996 and several religious right candidates lost their campaigns. However, the religious right still has a significant hold on the Republican Party and in the United States House of Representatives and Senate and is anxious to control both houses and the presidency in the 2000 election. To ensure success the Christian Coalition has developed a grassroots initiative called Family 2000.

The Christian Coalition's Family 2000 initiative seeks to enlist the aid of more than 100,000 volunteers nationwide to link them with Christian Coalition chapters (located in every state) for the purpose of mobilizing hundreds of thousands of pro-family activists by November 2000—the date of the next presidential election. Two of the goals of Family 2000 are the repeal of all legislation that gives special rights based on sexual orientation and to defeat state laws that allow gays and lesbians to adopt children (CCW 1998c).

As testimony to the political power of the Christian right, in 1995 Maine voters, with a 44 percent voter turnout, passed gay rights legislation that was eventually signed into law. When in 1997, a move to repeal the law was introduced, the Christian Coalition distributed 240,000 voter guides in 900 churches and mailed 100,000 "get out to vote" postcards stressing the importance of repealing the law that gave special legal rights on the basis of sexual orientation. In February 1998, with a 31 percent voter turnout, Maine voters repealed the gay rights legislation. The Christian Coalition credits its new Family 2000 strategy with the victory in Maine (CCW 1998b, 1998c; Porter 1998).

More extremist organizations like the Ku Klux Klan, Aryan Nations, or ALPHA would certainly not accept any argument that homosexuality was anything but sinful and unnatural but would easily support and accept antigay legislation. It has been estimated that there are 25,000 Americans who identify themselves as hardcore white separatists and that in the late 1990s, there were almost 500 such groups in the United States (Racial Supremacy and Neo-Nazi Groups 1998; SPLC 1998). While some of these organizations are relatively benign religious sects, others are openly militant and hostile (Racial Supremacy and Neo-Nazi Groups 1998). But, irrespective of their mandate and tactics, the thread that is common to all of the extreme rightwing groups is a strong identification with Christianity and the Bible.

Perhaps the two most well-known extremist organizations on the right side of the philosophical and political continuum are the Ku Klux Klan (KKK) and Aryan Nations. The KKK is by far the older of the two, having been established in 1866 by Confederate veterans who wanted to return to the prewar plantation aristocracy. In an effort to do so they traumatized recently freed slaves and their white supporters by kidnappings, murders, and burning of crops and homes. Wearing what has become to be viewed as the Klan's symbol, white robes and hoods concealed the identity of the perpetrators. The Klan's acts of violence became so intolerable that, in 1871, a federal law, the Ku Klux Klan Act, caused the Klan to significantly diminish. Reemerging in 1915, the KKK has ebbed and flowed during subsequent decades. It reached a peak in the 1920s when it had a membership of more than 2 million members. Conceptualized as one organization until the 1970s, the KKK became fragmented into several different Klan organizations. Some are more extremist than others, but all claim a Christian base. The total number of KKK members (in all the various Klan organizations) is estimated to be some-where between 6,000 and 10,000 (Compton's Encyclopedia Online 1997; Knights of the Ku Klux Klan 1998; Ku Klux Klan).

Although there is not currently one national organization that repre-sents all factions of the KKK, all groups generally see themselves as being part of the oldest white, Christian fraternal organization (although women are now allowed to join) in existence. And, they use the Bible to support their beliefs. Referred to as the "Invisible Empire" the KKK states that it does not condone violence, but does encourage self-defense and does not hate nonwhites, but loves the white race (Knights of the Ku Klux Klan 1998; Ku Klux Klan 1998).

With its Christian ideology and literal belief in biblical scripture, mem-bers of the KKK view homosexuality as undermining the values of Amer-ica. The oldest surviving KKK group, the Knights of the Ku Klux Klan, is the only group that wishes to form a nationally recognized political party—the Knights Party. To achieve its goal of attaining national politi-cal power, the Knights Party has developed a political agenda for the con-servative right. Its political agenda, as noted in its party platform, has two planks that relate to gays and lesbians. One plank states that there should be specific laws that oppose the practice of homosexuality. The basis for this platform plank comes from the belief that homosexuality is con-demned by God. The other platform plank states that all persons who are HIV+ should be placed in national hospitals. This is based on the belief that the persons most likely to contract HIV/AIDS are homosexuals and those of non-European descent and they should be quarantined for their protection and for the protection of others as well (Knights of the Ku Klux Klan 1998). Thus, to further a Christian revival and foster the ideals of white Christians, things related to homosexuality are not acceptable. Other extremist groups would agree with this viewpoint.

Another relatively well-known right-wing white extremist group is Aryan Nations. Founded in 1974, its members believe Europeans to be the lost tribe of Israel and, as such, embrace the ideology that Jesus Christ died for the white race. They fervently believe Jews to be satanic and African Americans to be subhuman. The federal government, which they renamed the Zionist Occupational Government (ZOG), is viewed as ille-gal and, following what they call Christian identity and philosophy, they advocate for the elimination of all minority groups in the United States, but especially Jews. Tactics to achieve their goals include murdering those who oppose them, and they are particularly active in prisons where white men are recruited into the Aryan Nations (Office of International Crimi-nal Justice 1998).

Members of the Aryan Nations condemn homosexuality on the basis of Christian ideology as do members of other, less well known extremist groups such as ALPHA. ALPHA was founded in 1993 and sees as its central mission the securing of the existence of white people to ensure a future for white children. Although it proclaims itself as not being a KKK, neo-Nazi, or religiously based organization it is supportive of the Nazi position and does follow a similar philosophy. It identifies itself as a racial, political, and parliamentary organization that is committed to positive Christian values. As such, it strongly opposes homosexual rights of any kind and states that its membership will not include homosexuals, liars, drug users, criminals, thieves, or those who are unable to function under a command structure (ALPHA 1998). ALPHA is not pro-Jewish, but does not identify homosexuality as being a mechanism of Jewish mind control as does White Pride Worldwide, another right wing extremist perspective interested primarily in the elimination of the Jewish people (White Pride Worldwide 1998).

Groups like the KKK, Aryan Nations, ALPHA, and others that include such organizations as the American Nazi Party, the Holy Order, the Silent Brotherhood, American Knights, Church of the Creator, New Christian Crusade Church, and countless more may have as many as 50,000 members nationwide (Racial Supremacy and Neo-Nazi Groups 1998; SPLC 1998). They all are fervent in their beliefs and, between 1996 and 1997, there was a 20 percent increase in the number of such extremist groups (SPLC 1998). Interestingly, the type of organizations that have emerged since 1996 are less like the Knights of the Ku Klux Klan that identifies itself as a "professional organization" that middle Americans can be proud to join and more like the neo-Nazi, Hitler-like militant action groups such as ALPHA.

Overall, the religious right has gained legitimacy and political clout since its emergence in the late 1970s. It appears to a number of political observers that the Christian right has even taken over the Republican Party. Concerned with the traditional values of American society, the religious right has, since the middle of the 1990s, targeted homosexuals and pro-gay legislation in a systematic campaign. Homosexuality, while not a popular topic until the late 1990s, has emerged as a major part of the agenda of the Christian right, where it is now viewed as sinful and capable of destroying the very core of American society—the family. To ensure the survival of the American way of life members of the religious right have mounted sophisticated legal and spiritual campaigns based on the word of God. The religious right is a well-funded, well-organized, and politically savvy group whose influence will be felt well into the next century.

The Liberal Left's Response to Lesbians and Gays

While the right side of the philosophical and political continuum tends to value tradition and strict adherence to traditional Christian values and family structures, the left side of the continuum has traditionally philosophically been more tolerant of diversity. As noted at the start of the chapter, liberals are generally characterized as being free of bigotry, not bound by traditional or authoritarian views, and being open to new ideas and tolerant of the behavior of others (*AHD* 1992). Stemming from a nineteenth-century Protestant movement that de-emphasized dogmatic theology, liberals emphasized intellectual inquiry while espousing the ethically humanitarian nature of Christianity. The Roman Catholic movement of the same century, while favoring ecclesiastical and political reform, remained steadfast in its orthodox theology (*CCE* 1995). The liberal philosophy of the late 1990s is represented by a number of organizations just as dedicated to assuring social, political, and legal rights for gays and lesbians as are those on the other side of the continuum set on assuring the elimination of all things homosexual.

Such groups include two nationally recognized organizations, the National Gay and Lesbian Task Force and the Human Rights Campaign, both of which actively pursue the challenge of ensuring gay rights at all levels of society. Coupled with these relatively mainstream, by some standards, organizations are the more militant groups like ACT UP, Queer Nation, and the Lesbian Avengers which, as will be discussed, take a more militant approach to gaining gay rights.

Founded in 1973, the National Gay and Lesbian Task Force (NGLTF), initially called the National Gay Task Force, celebrated twenty-five years of activities in 1998. The goal of this grassroots politically oriented organization is to provide the lesbian, gay, bisexual, and transgender communities support in their quest for social justice at the local, state, and national levels (NGLTF 1996a, 1996b, 1998b, 1998c). To provide voice to the gay community, it promotes public advocacy, holds national conferences, maintains its own public policy institute, and actively creates linkages in various localities to further gay rights. Housed in Washington, D.C., the organization has been responsible for encouraging the American Psychiatric Association to remove homosexuality from its list of mental illnesses in 1973, organizing the first White House meeting with gay activists in 1977, winning a 1985 Supreme Court decision that overturned a law prohibiting teachers from discussing gay rights, and persuading Attorney General Janet Reno to have the Department of Justice's

Community Service unit mediate an antigay conflict in Ovett, Mississippi, during 1994. More recently, in 1997 and 1998, NGLTF has been coordinating grassroots demonstrations and media coverage to make middle America more aware of the realities of the gay and lesbian world and holding town-hall meetings in major cities across the nation (NGLTF 1998b).

By being at the forefront of initiatives designed to strengthen the lesbian, gay, bisexual, and transgender communities, NGLTF has a broad appeal to those wishing to fight the radical right, antigay legislative actions, and sodomy laws. NGLTF also has appeal to anyone with interest in reforming the health care system to be more responsive to the needs of gays and lesbians or who wants to change the federal government's approach to gays in the military. As a grassroots organizing and advocacy movement, it seeks to create change from the bottom up and is particularly interested in the activities of the radical right, committing significant resources nationwide to fight what is perceived as an increasingly dangerous ideology (NGLTF 1998a). The Human Rights Campaign (HRC), which was begun in 1980, has an almost identical mandate—that of ensuring civil rights for lesbians and gays—but seeks to create change from the top down by being a political lobbying force at the federal, state, and local levels (HRC 1998). With more than 200,000 gay and nongay members nationwide, the HRC lobbies Congress, contributes to and engages in political campaigns, sponsors National Coming Out Day on October 11, and mobilizes national training and action (HRC 1998a). Housed in Washington, D.C., HRC's mission is designed to secure equal rights and equal treatment under the law for lesbian and gay people. To accomplish this goal, the HRC employs the largest team of full-time lobbyists in the nation whose task is devoted solely to gay and lesbian issues (HRC 1998a).

In 1996–97 HRC had revenues of more than $11 million, of which its donors contributed 37 percent: 33 percent of its revenues came from membership dues, and the remainder of its budget was from monies raised from events (HRC 1997). Although similar to NGLTF in mandate, the HRC seems to attract those in the middle to upper end of the socioeconomic continuum. While the HRC maintains a grassroots "action network" designed to impact state and local legislative issues of importance to the gay community, much of its political efforts are at the federal level. Its political action committee's campaign contributions are targeted primarily at federal level candidates. For example, when, in 1994, Chuck Robb (Democratic Senator from Virginia) was running against conservative, antigay candidate Oliver North, the HRC deemed it vital to provide dollars and volunteers to counter the millions of dollars Mr. North's campaign had received from the religious right. Mr. Robb won by a 29 percent margin—the HRC credits itself with securing that victory (HRC 1995a).

Another indication that the HRC may be viewed as slightly more conservative than the NGLTF is the HRC's position on transgendered individuals. The NGLTF has a statement of purpose that includes persons who are bisexual and transgendered as well as those who are gay or lesbian; the HRC refuses to include transgendered individuals as part of its mandate. This seemingly intransigent position on the part of the HRC has tended to cause a slight organizational dilemma within the HRC between those more liberal and inclusive members and those more conservative members.

Like the NGLTF (and the religious right), the HRC uses the news media to inform the general population of positive and negative legal, political, and social issues impacting the gay and lesbian community. And, like the religious right, the news releases during the 1990s have increased rather dramatically in both the NGLTF and the HRC. In 1995, the HRC produced 68 news releases and NGLTF created 21. By 1996, the NGLTF created 71 news releases perceived by many as a result of the religious right's increased condemnation of homosexuality. But, that year also saw the pro-gay organizations support such measures as the Employment Nondiscrimination Act (ENDA) and condemn state and federal legislation aimed at banning same-sex marriage. The news releases of both the HRC and the NGLTF on these two issues soared the following year. In 1997, the HRC's news releases numbered 89 while the NGLTF's numbered 66. By August 1998, the NGLTF and HRC had produced a total of 25 news releases where the major topics were aimed at continuing skirmishes between the antigay agenda of the religious right and the pro-gay agenda of the liberal left. Central to this was the religious right's declaration through its ad campaign in several major newspapers that homosexuality was curable and that through a program of Christian counseling and acceptance of Jesus Christ, homosexual behaviors and desires would be erased. As noted above, it supports that belief on literal interpretations of certain translations of Hebrew and Christian scripture.

Groups such as NGLTF and HRC seem conservative when compared to the more radical pro-gay activist groups such as the Lesbian Avengers, ACT-UP, or Queer Nation. Found at the extreme left of the political continuum, as might be assumed, these groups are not as different in tactics from those found on the extreme right. The two best-known extremist pro-gay groups are the Lesbian Avengers and ACT-UP.

Formed in 1992 in New York City, the Lesbian Avengers is a grassroots, nonviolent, activist organization dedicated to lesbian visibility and survival (DC Lesbian Avengers 1998). There is no one national organization, but rather several chapters located in major cities throughout the country. Each chapter shares a common heritage and purpose. Its rallying cry, "Get Mad! Get Even! Join the Lesbian Avengers and join the riot. We Recruit" and its Dyke Manifesto that urges all lesbians to fight are seemingly common to each chapter. Lesbian Avenger activities have included holding a torchlight parade down Fifth Avenue in New York City during rush hour without a permit; giving out balloons that read "Ask About Lesbian Lives" to elementary school children in an antigay area; invading antigay establishments, and chanting, "We recruit! We want your children!" at a church where an antigay member of the religious right was giving a speech denouncing homosexuality (Lesbian Avengers Handbook 1998; CCW 1998c). The Lesbian Avengers see sit-ins, chanting, or picketing as no longer useful and tend toward dramatic presentations to convey their message (Lesbian Avengers Handbook 1998).

An example of the creative efforts on the part of the Lesbian Avengers includes its actions to counter the religious right's ad campaign. In August 1998, the DC Lesbian Avengers held a "Thank God I'm a Lesbian Rally" across the street from the Family Research Council's main office in Washington, D.C., and later that day attended the Women's National Basketball Association game where its name was flashed across the stadium scoreboard and pro-lesbian banners were unfurled (Romesburg 1998). No doubt such creativity would be appreciated by ACT UP.

The AIDS Coalition to Unleash Power, more commonly known by its acronym, ACT UP, agrees that the time for picketing and passive demonstrating has passed. And, as the most extremist confederacy of grassroots, local organizations dedicated to issues associated with HIV/AIDS, ACT UP encourages its member organizations to be familiar with all forms of civil disobedience and provides protesters with information about being arrested and jailhouse solidarity (ACT UP 1998). Their main form of protest has been that of throwing the cremated remains of a person with AIDS on the lawn of the White House, disrupting traffic during rush hour on Wall Street in New York City by lying in the middle of the street, or holding the funeral (complete with the deceased) of an AIDS activist in front of the White House (ACT UP New York 1998; Kim 1998). Formed in the 1980s, ACT UP, like the Lesbian Avengers, is a coalition of groups comprised mainly of gays and lesbians who protest, demonstrate, and are interested in research, medical advances, legal issues, and social consequences related to HIV/AIDS.

One of the lesser known, but perhaps the most radical and aggressive, of the lesbian and gay rights organizations is called Queer Nation. Known primarily for its slogan, "We're here. We're queer. Get Used to It," Queer Nation was founded in 1990 as an offshoot to ACT UP. Its confrontational tactics include such activities as outing "celebrities," staging a public queer kiss-in to protest the Boy Scouts ban on gay leaders, and, dressed as nuns or wearing dresses, disrupting religious services being held by the religious right. Queer Nation redefined the word "queer" as a complimentary term and has been met, by some members of HRC and NGLTF, with criticism of its tactics (alt.culture 1998; Information About the Queer Nation 1998).

While their tactics for meeting their goals may differ, what each of these groups has in common is a genuine concern for the rights of gays and lesbians and a deeply rooted anxiety about the legal, political, and social issues and accusations emerging from the religious right. The issues, since the beginning of 1990, tend to center around the themes of homosexuality as a sin, homosexuality as a disease, and legal rights for gays. These broad categories get narrowed by specific issues related to religious conversion cures, reparative therapy, same-sex marriage, hate crimes, sodomy statutes, gays in the military, and employment discrimination.

Homosexuality Is Not a Sin

Just as the religious right cites the Bible as its source of the condemnation of homosexuality, those who are less antagonistic about same-sex relations, too, cite the Bible as a source of support. Overlooked by the religious right is the loving story of the relationship between Ruth and Naomi as recounted in the Book of Ruth, and the Book of Judith, which describes Judith's rejection of male suitors and her decision to live her life with her female servants.

The Bible also recounts the story of David and Jonathan, who make a public display of love, make a lifetime commitment, and where one acknowledges his love as surpassing what he feels for women (1 Samuel 18–20; 2 Samuel 1:26) (Swigonski 1998). Further, to counter allegations that human sexuality is something that can be "cured" by God, more open-minded and moderate organizations, including religious groups like the Metropolitan Community Church (MCC); social action groups like Parents, Families, and Friends of Lesbians and Gays (PFLAG); public school oriented groups like the Gay, Lesbian, and Straight Educational Network (GLSEN); and media watchdog organizations like the Gay and Lesbian Alliance Against Defamation (GLAAD) all condemn the religious right's latest maneuvers (GLAAD 1998b; GLSEN 1998; PFLAG 1991; 1998b, 1998c). Like the HRC and the NGLTF these organizations view homosexuality as something to be accepted, not condemned, and sexuality as something that neither God nor reparative therapy can cure.

Homosexuality Is Not a Disease

Those on the more liberal side of the continuum tend to view sexuality as immutable and reparative therapy as unethical and dangerous. They cite the American Psychiatric Association's position that homosexuality is not a mental disorder and laud recent research that tends to demonstrate that sexuality is innate (LeVay 1991). They further cite reparative therapists who themselves note that even with those persons who want desperately to have their sexual orientation changed from homosexual to heterosexual, the success rate is extremely low (Nicolosi 1991). In an effort to convince those less tolerant, pro-gay researchers have, since the late 1960s, gathered countless data supporting the psychological health of gays and lesbians and have put forth endless scientific evidence that homosexuality is, for some percentage of the population, normal.

Legal Rights for Gays

While the radical right continues to promulgate bills that would deny same-sex couples the right to legally marry, or the right to be equally protected under the law in such areas as hate crimes, sexual expression, or employment benefits, those on the pro-gay liberal side continue to draft their own bills and lobby for more tolerant views on gay issues. In November 1998 Hawaii voted on whether to allow same-sex couples the legal right to marry. Even though the measure was defeated, that there even was such a vote in this era of radical religious right thinking is, in and of itself, somewhat incredible.

Impressive, too, are the many localities, businesses, and organizations that no longer discriminate on the basis of sexual orientation and include domestic partners in benefits' packages. Sodomy laws, while still on the books in many states, are increasingly the target of pro-gay activities and are gradually disappearing even in the face of the religious right's rabid opposition. Perhaps one of the most impressive near victories for gay activists was the Senate defeat, by one vote, of the Employment Nondiscrimination Act (ENDA) in 1996. ENDA would provide federal legislation to protect gays and lesbians from workplace discrimination on the basis of sexual orientation. The hopes are that the 105th Congress will pass this legislation.

The issue of gays serving in the military has been one of longstanding duration. When Clinton's "Don't Ask, Don't Tell" policy went into effect in the early 1990s the number of gays and lesbians who were dishonorably discharged rose dramatically. Gay activists see this trend as an issue to be dealt with as the military continues to see lesbian and gay members as unwelcome. Although not likely to occur in the very near future, pro-gay organizations believe that equal rights for lesbians and gays is not only possible at some point, but probable (GLAA 1998a; GLSEN 1998; HRC 1997, 1998a; NGLTF 1998a; PFLAG 1998d).

Both the religious, conservative right and the more tolerant, liberal left have extremist groups that, on both far ends of the continuum may use civil disobedience or, in some groups of the far right, even violence to get their message heard. Both have more moderate groups that advocate a quieter dialogue to ensure change. Those at either end of the philosophical and political continuum by no means constitute the majority needed to win any political race. The great numbers of persons in the middle-of-the-road or the moderates hold the key to the most widely accepted philosophy in this country and who decide whether the political pendulum swings to the left or to the right.

The Moderates and Homosexuality

If the number of persons reported to be at the far ends of the right and left sides of the continuum are accurately represented, one can conclude that the majority of U.S. citizens have philosophical and political views that lie between the ends—in the middle somewhere. Granted, persons can be slightly left or right of center or lean more toward one end or the other but, generally, most people are an interesting mix of contradictory ideologies. For example, members of the Log Cabin Republicans are gays and lesbians who support a traditionally conservative political and philosophical agenda.

The term "moderate" has been defined as one who is neither extreme nor excessive or given to radical views in religion or politics—in short, one who assumes a centrist posture with regard to these issues (*AHD* 1992). Moderates of both the Republican and Democratic parties tend to share a pragmatic approach and a willingness to compromise that is generally unseen on the far sides of the continuum (Turn Left 1998). The word "centrist" has also been used to describe this middle-of-the-road position. A centrist has been defined as one favoring pragmatic solutions to current issues and limited government intervention. Centrists tend to keep an open mind about new situations and see governmental checks and balances as good (Centrist 1998). Organizations that assume a more moderate or centrist position with regard to lesbian and gay issues would be those that try to honestly and without bias represent both sides of an issue and make a decision on the basis of sound, nonprejudiced reasoning. Such organizations tend to make those on either side of an issue unhappy some of the time, but not all of the time. One such centrist organization, although generally identified as left wing, is the American Civil Liberties Union (ACLU).

The ACLU was founded in 1920 with a mission to assure that the Constitution's Bill of Rights is protected for every generation and in doing so is a staunch defender of the civil rights of all individuals (ACLU 1997). The ACLU, currently with a 50-state organizational network and 300 local chapters, more than 60 staff attorneys and over 2,000 volunteer attorneys, handles approximately 6,000 legal challenges to civil liberties per year. Historically, some of its more interesting cases have included issues such as the anti-evolution law of the Scopes Trial in 1921, the move to impeach President Richard Nixon in 1973, and the defense of such groups as the KKK, the neo-Nazis, and the Black Panthers (ACLU 1997). The ACLU does follow its mandate to defend the right of the individual to express her or his opinion irrespective of the views expressed. This flows from a belief that once the government denies rights to one group, the rights of other groups are also at risk (ACLU 1997).

The ACLU and its protections of the rights of lesbians and gays are viewed as radical to the religious right, but its beliefs about the protections of free speech are viewed as conservative by the liberal left. Seen from either end of the continuum, those organizations that tend to support one side or the other are viewed as being supportive. And, while those on either side of the middle tend to characterize their groups and philosophies as being centrist (for example the Christian Coalition or the Human Rights Campaign), there are few organizations that are truly in the middle of the continuum.

The religious right tends to view those with even moderate to slight congruence with any of their positions as being allies; gay organizations tend to accept as allies those nongay organizations whose platform includes a plank dedicated to gay and lesbian rights. For example, the Democratic Party embraced the gay community in its 1996 presidential campaign; the Republicans denounced it. Classical conservatives, unlike their neoconservative counterparts, support the separation of church and state while being open-minded about gays and lesbians; neoliberals are more likely to be more conservative than classical liberals (Karger and Stoesz 1998). Members of the religious right tend to align themselves with the Republican Party and those who are neoconservative and perhaps even neoliberal. Because of their views on personal freedom, many lesbians and gays may edge toward being Democrats, classical liberals, or classical conservatives (HRC 1997).

Moderate organizations that support gay rights include the Gay, Lesbian, and Straight Education Network (formerly the Gay, Lesbian, and Straight Teachers' Network) or GLSEN, and the older more established Parents, Families, and Friends of Lesbians and Gays (PFLAG). Whereas the membership of the National Gay and Lesbian Task Force and the Human Rights Campaign are almost exclusively gay, lesbian, bisexual, or transgender persons, both GLSEN and PFLAG have a more diverse membership because many members are nongay. PFLAG, based in Washington, D.C., has over 400 affiliates with membership of more than 69,000 households and sees itself as a grassroots organization. Its mission of supporting the well-being and health of lesbians, gays, and bisexuals is carried out through a well-organized series of activities designed to enlighten and educate an inadequately informed public about issues of homosexuality and to secure equality under the law for gays, lesbians, and bisexuals. PFLAG encourages ongoing dialogue between adversarial groups and works toward the development of a society that respects and embraces human diversity (PFLAG 1998a, 1998b, 1998c, 1998d).

Issues affecting the lesbian, gay, and bisexual community are the focus of policy incentives by PFLAG. In the late 1990s, the policy issues of importance to PFLAG are similar to those addressed by HRC and NGLTF. For example, policy issues in late 1998 included such topics as family values, the radical right, ENDA, parenting, and discrimination (PFLAG 1998d). PFLAG's response to the religious right's advertising campaign to cure gays was one of vigorous condemnation and it reacts with equal indignation when confronted with what it views as intolerance or hate (PFLAG 1998a, 1998b, 1998c).

One of PFLAG's initiatives is Project Open Mind (POM). Begun in

1995, POM's primary objective is to tell the public about lesbian and gay Americans. Begun as a reaction to the expanding attacks, intolerance, and hatred directed at the gay and lesbian community, POM seeks to provide factual information to counter widespread misinformation and ignorance found in antigay groups. POM is a multimedia public awareness campaign centered on eradicating discrimination based on sexual orientation. Cities such as Atlanta, Seattle, Houston, and Tulsa support the initiative as do several national organizations including NGLTF, HRC, Nordstrom, and US Bank. The campaign is also supported by various chapters of the conservative Log Cabin Republicans (PFLAG 1998e).

Media campaigns such as POM increase the visibility of the gay community in the nongay world. With increased visibility comes the reality that lesbians and gays are found across the social structure and in every segment of society. According to the religious right, one profession from which gays and lesbians should be banned is that of teaching. The Gay, Lesbian, and Straight Education Network (GLSEN) began in Boston in 1990 and claims to be the largest national organization that works with teachers, students, parents, and concerned citizens to end homophobia in the school setting. GLSEN's membership is primarily lesbian or gay, but one third of its members are nongay. With over 40 local groups in 1998, GLSEN participates in curriculum development for in-school programs, community organizing, and advocacy designed to work with and create change in the beliefs of those educational leaders and policy makers who control the public schools (GLSEN 1998).

One interesting initiative in which GLSEN was involved during 1998 involved legislation passed by the U.S. Senate promoting Internet censorship to public schools by denying teenage children Internet access to gay- and lesbian-oriented materials through school access networks. The argument on the religious right's side is that such materials are inappropriate for minors, and the public schools have a moral responsibility to protect children from illegal, immoral, sinful, and unhealthy activities and information. The argument on the liberal side is that all teenagers are isolated and confused anyway, but gay or lesbian teenagers are particularly at-risk for problems. To deny them access to honest, helpful materials that could reduce the possibility of suicides and lead to better self-esteem is immoral and psychologically damaging (Einhorn 1998). GLSEN was joined in this challenge by a watchdog organization designed to keep the public aware of gay and lesbian issues in the national media—the Gay and Lesbian Alliance Against Defamation (GLAAD).

GLAAD founded in 1985 and has had a wide-reaching effect on how gays and lesbians are portrayed in the media. GLAAD's beginning is traced to offensive and sensationalistic stories in the *New York Times* in 1985. GLAAD protested them and began to fulfill its mission of ending discrimination and violence toward gays and lesbians by improving the public's image of them. This was to be accomplished through more realistic portrayals of lesbians and gays as depicted in film, cartoons, newspaper stories, soap operas, advertisements, and television. GLAAD's successes in these areas have been, in the face of the increasingly homophobic religious right, impressive. GLAAD has been involved with such initiatives as having Hallmark Cards withdraw the word lesbian from its list of banned words, the installation of gay positive images in subway posters, and even getting 60 Minutes commentator, Andy Rooney, suspended and reprimanded for his homophobic statements (GLAAD 1998a).

These more moderate pro-gay organizations, while being on the left side of the center of the philosophical and political continuum, are still in that great middle sphere of influence and have their counterparts on the right-of-center side. While more difficult to identify organizations that are moderately right of center, Log Cabin Republicans seems to be one such group. Begun in 1978 as a group dedicated to fighting the nation's first antigay ballot measure (California's Proposition 6), Log Cabin Republicans provide a political alternative for gays and lesbians who support traditional Republican values and positions. Like other Grand Old Party (GOP) members, it favors limited government and individual rights. It sees its role as one of educating more conservative Republicans about the issues and concerns relevant to lesbians and gays and acts as a liaison between the Republican Party and the gay community. The organization is located in Washington, D.C., and claims to have more than 50 chapters across the nation that support the work of its national staff (LCR 1998).

In an effort to have its voice heard, Log Cabin Republicans raises $100,000 per election cycle for Republican candidates that support gay and lesbian causes. Its donations are not without controversy in some sectors of the GOP. For example, in 1995 Log Cabin Republicans donated $1,000 to the Dole for President campaign fund. The money was returned to the organization when it was announced that the Dole campaign fund was the first Republican campaign in history to accept a donation from a gay and lesbian political action committee. The donation was subsequently made to Arlen Specter's 1996 presidential campaign fund (Greer 1995).

Even the Republican Party itself is seen as more moderate than many of its vocal antigay minority would have the general population believe. While the extremely vocal radical right wing of the Republican Party points to homosexuality as a major policy issue, a review of the Republican National Committee's (RNC) website (*http://www.rnc.org*) indicates that issues associated with the gay and lesbian community are not a major concern. A review of the RNC's magazine, *Rising Tide*, indicates that from December 1993 through Spring 1998 not one article dealt with gay or lesbian content, issues, or problems. In examining the Committee's official newsletter, "In the LOOP," for 1998 there is not a single mention of lesbian or gay related content, nor is the topic mentioned in the RNC's 1998 Press Releases, Talk Topics, or In Case You Missed It agenda (In Case You Missed It 1998; In the LOOP 1998; Press Releases 1998; Talk Topics 1998). Further, homosexuality is not a topic mentioned in either House Speaker Gingrich's or Senate Majority Leader Lott's agenda for the second half of the 105th Congress that began in January 1999 (Gingrich 1998; Lott 1998). This moderate view of lesbians and gays is becoming more evident in recent political issues associated with the gay community.

In the philosophical and political middle, in 1998 Americans had mixed opinions about issues related to the gay and lesbian community. While a majority (84%) of citizens favor employment nondiscrimination and equal rights for lesbians and gays, most still believe homosexuality to be environmentally caused (47%), morally wrong (59%), and that same-sex couples should not raise children (56%) (Berke 1998). Most Americans agree that gays and lesbians should be protected from hate crimes, yet think they make poor military personnel (Maginnis 1995b). There seems to be mixed opinions about whether or not gays and lesbians should be allowed to teach (GLSEN 1998).

An example of the more moderate Republican view on homosexuality was seen in August 1998 when Congress voted 252–176 to reject the Hefley Amendment. The proposed amendment would have undone an Executive Order signed by President Clinton in May 1998 that added the words "sexual orientation" to an existing Executive Order signed by President Nixon in 1969 barring federal agencies from discrimination on the basis of gender, national origin, age, race, color, religion, or disability (Alvarez 1998; Attey 1998; Holland 1998). By rejecting the more conservative view that nondiscrimination on the basis of sexual orientation in federal employment would lead to affirmative action for gays and lesbians, moderate Republicans showed an increasing sense of discomfort with the radical right's attacks on gay and lesbian citizens (Alvarez 1998;

Attey 1998). This vote supports the general view of the nation that equality in the workplace is an acceptable position.

The vote taken by that same House of Representatives one day later also represents the national perceptions about whether or not lesbians or gays should raise children. With a vote of 227–192 Congress approved an antigay amendment that banned dual party adoptions (adoption of a child by two unrelated persons or by an unrelated partner) in Washington, D.C. (Besen 1998). These policy issues are being debated at the same time the Congressional Human Rights Caucus (for the first time in history) agreed to host a briefing on sexual orientation with representatives from Amnesty International and the International Gay and Lesbian Human Rights Commission (Canning 1998). The late 1990s was an active time for those in the moderate camp.

In sum, those in the middle-of-the-road are the target of both ends of the continuum, for it is in the middle where the true power seems to exist. The major thrust of the antigay religious right may be dwindling as the more moderate members of both the traditional political parties seem to be more willing to accept lesbians and gays as law-abiding, productive, tax-paying citizens who are not the mentally ill, sinful, child molesters as depicted by the religious right.

The idea of a philosophical and political continuum is an old one. It originated in the 1790s when the French Assembly seated its members by party to calm disturbances. The Republicans were seated on the left, the monarchists on the right. Soldiers were placed in the center to avoid bloodshed (Fritz 1988). The continuum from extremist conservative to extremist liberal allows for a variety of approaches to thought and action. Where one happens to fall on the continuum plays a role in the personal, political, and professional choices she or he makes. That is not to say that one's position on this continuum is static. More realistically an individual's beliefs, values, and attitudes change on the basis of any number of variables, including education, age, sex, etc. The philosophical and political views of Generation X will undoubtedly change as it approaches its middle and later years. If you have ever wondered about your personal orientation on the liberal to conservative continuum, perhaps you would like to take the "World's Smallest Political Quiz" (see figure 2.2. Based on the work by Nolan (1971) and modified by Fritz (1988), this Diamond Chart provides a more three-dimensional view of the generally viewed as two-dimensional conservative-liberal continuum. If you find your scores to be in the Libertarian quadrant and feel the test to be perhaps biased, you are urged to ask those congressional representatives, senators, or other political aspirants to take the quiz.

FIGURE 2.2
World's Smallest Political Quiz

Please decide how you feel about the following 10 questions and then circle "Yes" when you agree, "No" when you do not agree, and "Maybe" if you are uncertain.

Are you a self-governor in personal issues?

1. Military service should be voluntary – no draft.	YES MAYBE NO
2. Government should not control radio, television, the press, or the Internet.	YES MAYBE NO
3. Regulations/laws on sexual acts between consenting adults should be repealed.	YES MAYBE NO
4. Drug laws should be repealed as they do more harm than good.	YES MAYBE NO
5. Peaceful people should be able to cross borders freely.	YES MAYBE NO

Personal self-governor score:
Score 20 for every "YES," 10 for every "MAYBE, " and 0 for every "NO."

Your Score: _____

Are you a self-governor in economic issues?

6. Businesses and farms should operate without government subsidies.	YES MAYBE NO
7. People are better off with free trade than with tariffs.	YES MAYBE NO
8. Minimum wage laws cause unemployment and should be repealed.	YES MAYBE NO
9. Taxes should be ended and services paid for by user fees.	YES MAYBE NO
10. All foreign aid should be privately funded.	YES MAYBE NO

Economic self-governor score:
Score 20 for every "YES," 10 for every "MAYBE," and 0 for every "NO."

Your Score: _____

On each scale, your score can range from 0 to 100. On the diamond following, circle your total score on each axis and draw a line across the chart. Where the two lines intersect is your current political position.

Adapted from Fritz, M. 1988. Hope for the Politically Homeless (On-line).
Available: http://www.self-gov.org/hope.html

FIGURE 2.2 *(continued)*
World's Smallest Political Quiz

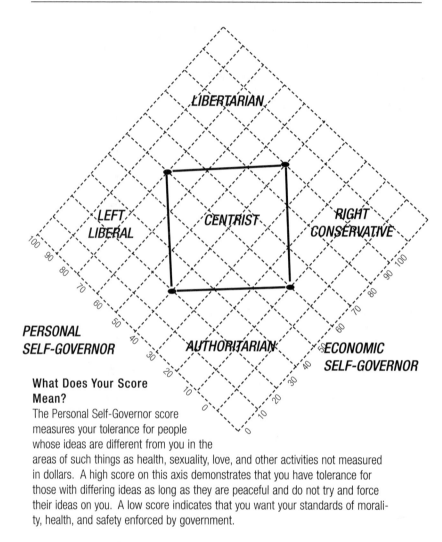

What Does Your Score Mean?

The Personal Self-Governor score measures your tolerance for people whose ideas are different from you in the areas of such things as health, sexuality, love, and other activities not measured in dollars. A high score on this axis demonstrates that you have tolerance for those with differing ideas as long as they are peaceful and do not try and force their ideas on you. A low score indicates that you want your standards of morality, health, and safety enforced by government.

The Economic Self-Governor score measures your responsibility as a consumer and producer of goods and services, how you support your family and spend your money. A high score on this axis shows that you value free trade, competition, and responsibility more than government intervention and that you tolerate variation in economic success as long as wealth is gained by honest means and not theft, cheating, or political means. A low score indicates that you believe society's success depends on governmental distribution of wealth.

In sum, the philosophical and political continuum encompasses a wide diversity of political and philosophical views and beliefs. No one is immune from these concepts although many will deny their involvement in things of a political or philosophical nature. And, having discovered your current position on this liquid political continuum, it is vital to remember that every client comes to you with his or her own values, beliefs, and attitudes based on his or her philosophical and political view of the world. From sharing these values, belief, and attitudes the client and social worker will be able to best operationalize the concepts of the empowerment perspective.

This chapter has presented an overview of an existing political continuum that helps inform the societal structure in which gays and lesbians exist. Organizations are defined by philosophical beliefs that range from extremely liberal through moderate to extremely conservative. Lesbians and gays, like all members of society, have various philosophical values and beliefs and therefore can be found in all areas along the political continuum. Keeping the gay and lesbian historical perspective from these first two chapters in mind, in the following chapter I explore the development of the empowerment perspective and how this model can be applied when working with lesbian and gay persons.

3

The History and Application of the Empowerment Perspective

Social workers of the empowerment tradition do not encourage clients to place their faith in the judgment of experts. Instead, they prompt clients to develop trust in their own capacities to discern, through dialogue and reflection, the respective merits and pitfalls of any recommendation, whether that of a professional, a governmental official, a supervisor at work, a friend, a support group, or a family member.

(Simon 1994:187).

Since the charity organization societies, the settlement house movement and, at the start of the twentieth century what emerged as the social work profession, social workers have been assisting in the process of empowering individuals to better their lives, working with communities to determine the causes of poverty, and challenging social systems to assure equal treatment for all groups (Trattner 1994). To say that social work from an empowerment perspective (Simon 1994; Solomon 1976, 1985) or a strengths perspective (Saleebey 1992), or an externalizing perspective (White 1989) is a new phenomenon would be incorrect and would overlook the rich heritage of the philosophy that undergirds this viewpoint. To examine what has come to be called the empowerment perspective without exploring its philosophical and historic antecedents is to overlook the sociocultural influences on its development.

This chapter first provides an operational definition of the term "empowerment," and then traces the philosophical development of the concept from antiquity to postmodern thought. It also provides a conceptual framework for the remainder of the book by detailing how social work professionals can pragmatically apply an empowerment perspective when working with gay or lesbian clients, when struggling within homophobic communities, or when advocating on behalf of change within a context of institutional homophobia.

The Evolution of the Empowerment Perspective

To better understand the concept of empowerment, a working definition of the term is necessary. Notably, the latest edition of the *Social Work Dictionary* (Barker 1995) has no entry related to the term; *The American Heritage Dictionary* (1992) defines empowerment as a verb meaning to invest with legal power or official authority. That same reference defines the noun, power, as the capacity or ability to act or perform effectively. By combining these two, one could deduce that empowerment has to do with the act of providing someone or something with the ability to act or perform effectively. In the context of social services empowerment is defined somewhat differently. Rappaport (1986) said that empowerment requires a commitment to identify and create contexts for even the most incompetent persons and others who are marginalized in social settings and organizations so that they can gain understanding, voice, and influence over decisions that impact their lives. Saleebey described the act of empowerment as both "returning power to the people" and "discovering the power within the people (individually and collectively)" (1992:8). He further saw empowerment as helping individuals to discover power within themselves, their families, and their communities. The Cornell University Empowerment Group defined empowerment as "an intentional, ongoing process centered in the local community involving mutual respect, critical reflection, caring, and group participation, through which people lacking an equal share of valued resources gain greater access to and control over those resources" (1989:2). Solomon, in her seminal work on empowerment theory, views empowerment as "a process whereby persons who belong to a stigmatized social category throughout their lives can be assisted to develop and increase skills in the exercise of interpersonal influence and the performance of valued social roles" (1976:6). Solomon goes on to define empowerment as:

> a process whereby the social worker engages in a set of activities with the client or client system that aim to reduce the powerlessness that has been created by negative valuations based on membership in a stigma-

tized group. It involves identification of the power blocks that contribute to the problem as well as the development and implementation of specific strategies aimed at either the reduction of the effects from indirect power blocks or the reduction of the operations of direct power blocks (1976:19).

Inherent in each of these definitions are the following assumptions:

1. Power over one's destiny is good and should be achieved;
2. Those in disenfranchised positions want to be empowered;
3. Oppression is damaging and social workers and their clients must challenge it;
4. People, communities, and societies have intrinsic power that can be discovered and applied to oppressive situations;
5. Social workers have the ability to help tap and release internalized power.

Clearly, there are numerous definitions of empowerment, yet each incorporates the above assumptions and manifests respect for the strengths of clients, motivating change based on these strengths, viewing the helper as an equal collaborator with the client in creating change, avoiding the medical/diagnostic model, and utilizing the existing environment as the focus for beginning (Rappaport 1981, 1986; Saleebey 1992; Simon 1994; Solomon 1976; Weick 1992; White 1989).

The operational definition for empowerment used in this book synthesizes current thought related to both empowerment and strengths perspectives and is supported by a philosophy of power. Empowerment is viewed as dynamic and evolutionary as opposed to static and quick changing; it is seen as a process that utilizes personal narratives as its base; and it is perceived to have its antecedents in a rich philosophical tradition. Empowerment then is defined as the process whereby those persons or groups who are defined by themselves or others to be without power are enabled, through a collaborative process utilizing personal narratives, to increase skills necessary for acquiring and controlling resources necessary for effective and satisfying social functioning, including personal, interpersonal, and political aspects.

All of these definitions and assumptions of empowerment fit within the values and ethics defined in the National Association of Social Workers (NASW) Code of Ethics (1996), and a close reading of the Code evidences the use of a strengths emphasis throughout the document. Indeed, the basic tenets of the profession of social work that are explicated by the Code of Ethics (1996) have historically comprised a philosophy that is congruent with what has come to be termed the empowerment perspective. The mission of social work has been variously defined, but a common theme included in all of the definitions is one of the enhancement of social functioning and/or the solution of social problems and a concern with the dynamic interrelationships between people and their environments. There is a basic premise that people can only be understood in concert with the social and physical environments of which they are a part (Germain and Gitterman 1980; Hartman and Laird 1983). The empowerment perspective fits snugly within these parameters and enhances the profession's objectives by helping to strengthen individuals' innate capacity for adaptation and growth; by working toward removing environmental blocks that impede growth and adaptation; and by encouraging the environment's nutritive qualities (Germain 1979).

The empowerment perspective derives from philosophical perspectives that date back to the work of Abdel Rahman ibn-Khaldun (1332–1406), an Arab historian and early positivistic organicist, who stressed the linkages between historical observation and sociology and had a commitment to empirical research (Martindale 1981). More recent contributions are found in the philosophical thought of the later positivistic organicists (August Comte, Herbert Spencer, Ferdinand Tonnies, and Emile Durkheim) through the humanistic elementarism of Georg Hegel's idealism, Wilhelm Dilthey's neo-idealism, and Max Weber's social behaviorism. The empowerment theme winds through the phenomenology of Alfred Schutz, Arthur Schopenhauer, Søren Kierkegaard, Friedrich Nietzsche, and Theodor Herzl and through the structuralist views of Claude Lévi-Strauss (a structural anthropologist), Ferdinand de Saussure (a linguistic structuralist), and Karl Marx (a conflict theorist). It develops further with the poststructuralistic and constructivistic thought of Roland Barthes, David Fisher, Auguste Comte, and Jean Piaget whose philosophies connect to Giambattista Vico, one of the first constructivists. The empowerment perspective gains more legitimacy with the deconstructive philosophy of Jacques Derrida and the postmodern views of Michel Foucault, Jean-François Lyotard, and Martin Heidegger. And, although still a relatively new philosophical approach for social workers, those currently writing in the field of empowerment include such prominent social workers as Barbara Simon, Judith Lee, Alex Gitterman, and Barbara Solomon. As an aspect of empowerment, the explicit strengths perspective of such authors as Dennis Saleebey and the implicit one of Michael White have also gained credibility and are, for the purpose of this book, included as part of the empowerment perspective.

While it is not necessary for the reader to have an in-depth understanding of the philosophical underpinnings of the empowerment perspective, a brief review is presented to put it into proper historical context and to facilitate the understanding that, as with all things, there is an evolution of thought that brings us to current beliefs. As a caution, the evolution of thought is not linear but often circular, or spiraling, involving contributions from one philosopher to another as opposed to having one philosophy give birth to another.

From Positivistic Organicism to Empowerment

Positivistic organicism combines the philosophical ideologies of positivism—the idea that the world can be interpreted exclusively on experience and that there are certain facts or universal realities that can be known—and organicism—the idea that the world is an organic model and that the autonomous organism is responsible for its activities. Refuting classical ideas of the ancient Greeks, that cerebral processes such as logic and mathematics constituted the only rational proof, August Comte drew on Enlightenment thought and used positivism to reveal the laws and regularities of social events. For Comte, the use of scientific investigation and the gathering of empirical data overshadowed speculation of the supernatural as all things could be known through empiricism (Martindale 1981). Spencer, like Comte, believed there were identifiable laws that could be known through study. However, Herbert Spencer disputed Comte's view that experience alone could explain an individual's actions by noting that mental and social development is also affected by the capacity of the mind. As one who believed in evolution, Spencer, in his philosophy, tried to synthesize all knowledge in terms of evolutionary thought. He viewed society as an organic entity with six distinct "organs" (societal institutions)—industrial, ecclesiastical, political, ceremonial, domestic, and professional.

Ferdinand Tonnies and Emile Durkheim were contemporaries who were each influenced by positivistic organicism. Tonnies visualized social relationships, groups and societies as three types of social units. His major premise was simply that all social interactions are products of will. From Tonnies come the classic concepts of Gemeinschaft (characteristic of the feminine and ruled by sentimentality or the immediate social world) and Gesellschaft (typified by the male and characterized by inten-

FIGURE 3.1
Genesis of the Empowerment Perspective

EMPOWERMENT			
Barbara Solomon	Barbara Simon	Judith Lee	Alex Gitterman

Strengths Perspective

Dennis Saleebey   Michael White

POSTMODERNISM	
Martin Heidegger (1899-1976)	Michel Foucault (1926-1984)

POSTSTRUCTURALISM/DECONSTRUCTION		
Immanuel Kant (1724-1804)	Roland Barthes (1915-1980)	Jacques Derrida (1930-)

STRUCTURALISM		
Conflict Ideology Karl Marx (1818-1883)	Linguistic Structuralism Ferdinand de Saussure (1857-1913)	Structural Anthropology Claude Lévi-Strauss (1908-)

PHENOMENOLOGY		
Friedrich Nietzsche (1844-1900)	Edmund Husserl (1859-1938)	Alfred Schutz (1899-1959)

HUMANISTIC ELEMENTARISM	
Arthur Schopenhauer (1788-1860)	Soren Kierkegaard (1813-1855)

IDEALISM	**NEO-IDEALISM**	**SOCIAL BEHAVIORISM**
Georg Hegel (1770-1831)	Wilhelm Dilthey (1833-1911)	Max Weber (1864-1920)

POSITIVISTIC ORGANICISM			
Auguste Comte (1798-1857)	Herbert Spencer (1820-1903)	Ferdinand Tonnies (1855-1936)	Emile Durkheim (1858-1917)

tion or the broader social order) (Martindale 1981). Durkheim, most noted for his study in the area of suicide and the related concept of anomie (1897), defined social dynamics as common to all societies constituting what Durkheim calls a "collective consciousness" (Durkheim 1951). This collective consciousness generates and shapes an individual's ideals (Durkheim 1938). Considered one of the "fathers" of sociology, Durkheim applied the scientific method to the study of society and decided that individuals were products of their environment and could not be studied outside the context of the society in which they lived (Martindale 1981).

Overlapping with the positivistic organicism thought was the humanistic elementarism of such noteworthy philosophers as Georg Hegel, Wilhelm Dilthey, and Max Weber. Hegel's synthesis of idealitic thought posited that the ego was at the center of human existence and that it created a moral world. He went on to say that individual experiences exist in a parallel plane with the processes of nature. Hegel saw society as a social group where reason referred not to the individual, but rather to the collective thought of the social group. Hegel's "dialectics" may be best understood in the terms of thesis (where a reality is stated), antithesis (where the reality is challenged by other realities), and synthesis (where the two once conflicting views merge as one). For Hegel, like Durkheim, the individual cannot be known or understood outside her or his context and, as part of the world, the person cannot take an external perspective to that world. Therefore, objectivity or value-free knowledge is not possible; there is no way of knowing anything that is unaffected by one's social situation. Self-understanding is possible only through an examination of one's self in interaction between the self and the world. Hegel's influence is seen in the conflict ideology of Karl Marx as well as the existential thought of Kierkegaard, and the philosophical tenets of phenomenology (Lorraine 1991; Martindale 1981).

Wilhelm Dilthey's neo-idealism asserted that history's truth could only be known through cultural phenomena and therefore cannot be understandable in the same way as the natural sciences. To understand history one must analyze various social tendencies, deduce their commonalties, and explore their syntheses. Internal understanding for Dilthey comes when the thought processes that are derived from external forms become internal realities. Dilthey believed there were two ways of dealing with the world—nomothetically, as in the natural sciences, where there were knowable laws that governed phenomena, or ideographically (historically), where one described individual experiences. For Dilthey there was a sharp distinction between the cultural (what would become the social sciences) and natural sciences (what would become the physical sciences). The methodology for understanding and explaining natural science was the controlled experiment, while the methodology for understanding cultural science was the interpretation of observations of social phenomena. Empathic understanding and the idea that the ego is ever-changing and developing were Dilthey's contributions to the empowerment perspective (Gitterman 1991; Martindale 1981; Simon 1994; Solomon 1976; White 1989).

The social behaviorism of Max Weber tried to synthesize the views of Dilthey with the philosophy of Immanuel Kant by noting that the study of society required a scientific discipline, but that content, not forms, define society. Weber believed that the scientific method could be applied to the study of society and that there were certain laws about social interactions that could be known. Weber noted that to the degree behavior is rational it is knowable and understandable. He also realized that empathy and logic are both necessary for understanding and explaining behavior. Weber formulated the idea that power is rationally legitimate when based on legal sanction, charismatically legitimate when due to individual qualities, and traditionally legitimate when based on custom (Martindale 1981). These concepts of ways power is legitimized played an integral role in the development of the empowerment perspective, as well as providing ideas for the phenomenological views of the latter part of the nineteenth century.

However, before a discussion of phenomenology, but contemporary with positivistic organicism, idealism, neo-idealism, social behaviorism, and phenomenology, a theoretical perspective known as "humanistic elementalism" merits attention. Two major thinkers associated with this movement are Arthur Schopenhauer and Søren Kierkegaard. Schopenhauer's philosophy, considered by most to be pessimistic, diverged from the Hegelian ideology of collectivity and deemed perspective as an individual matter where there was, as Kant had noted, a differentiation between the world of things and the world of individual experiences. Schopenhauer viewed human nature as intrinsically evil, where humans were driven by passion as opposed to reason, and felt that any hope for a better future was merely illusion (Martindale 1981).

Kierkegaard, diverging from the popular Hegelian philosophy of his time and as a result of his rigorous study of theology, posited that one could only relate to God. This interpersonal and subjective "I-Thou" relationship between man and God made communication to others virtually impossible, and it is the individual as opposed to the collective that is of utmost importance. Unlike Hegel, who claimed to have a rational understanding of life and history, Kierkegaard viewed life as fraught with ambiguity where the highest truth was subjective. He thought that people must create their own circumstances through choices made in the absence of universal standards that were believed to be objective. His views on the subjective nature of reality played a key role in the emerging philosophical views that would be known as phenomenology and postmodernism.

Phenomenology, the philosophical view of Edmund Husserl and followed by Friedrich Nietzsche and Alfred Schutz, evolved naturally from the subjectivity of earlier philosophers. Husserl believed that consciousness was directed at something, and that it contained unchanging structures called meanings. The role of the philosopher was to study the essence of objects created in the imagination, similar to the Platonic "forms." Meanings are determined subjectively and phenomenology holds that it cannot be assumed that anything actually exists outside the perception of "things."

Nietzsche, influenced by the earlier thought of Schopenhauer and classic Greek culture, is popularly known for the assertion, "God is dead," his way of noting that Christianity had lost its power in the lives of individuals. More central to the concept of empowerment was his belief that every individual is motivated by positive power that is accessible within each person and that such power is the basis for creativity. Nietzsche's concept of the will to power was, to him, the most basic human drive that provided the framework for the idea of the "decentered self," where the self is always in a state of flux and always striving to become something else (Lorraine 1990; Martindale 1981).

Schutz studied Husserl and is considered the architect of the reconstruction of phenomenological sociology that examines the problems of day-to-day existence. His efforts to synthesize the work of Weber and Husserl formed the basis of his philosophy, the belief that the world of the individual is not private, but rather intersubjective and common to those who experience it. The interpretation of that world is full of contradictions, is inaccurate, and yet it provides meaning for past events and determines how the future is conceptualized. People live in a "taken-for-granted" world full of socially constructed ideas that are ever-changing. Further, most knowledge is not derived from personal experience, but rather from outside. There is a need for individuals to be part of the "in group" and the only means available for doing so is found in language. And it is through language that individuals interpret and construct meaning from the world around them. In Schutz's opinion, social scientists must first examine the world in which people live and then, using inductive reasoning, move to the development of hypotheses that tend to describe that world (Martindale 1981).

What followed phenomenology, and was no doubt a reaction to it, was the move to a more structured view of the world that would evolve in the philosophies of Marx, de Saussure, and Lévi-Strauss. Schutz and his predecessors provide a logical base for the conflict ideology of Karl Marx, the linguistic structuralism of Ferdinand de Saussure, and the structural anthropology of Claude Lévi-Strauss. Karl Marx preceded both de Saussure and Lévi-Strauss and provides a bridge between these earlier philosophies and what would eventually become known as "structuralism." Known chiefly for his *Communist Manifesto* (1848), *Das Kapital* (1867, 1885, 1894), and long association with Friedrich Engels, Marx set forth an ideology, known as "scientific socialism," that viewed as natural the cultural evolution from capitalism to communism. If the structure of society is created by those within it, capitalist societies constitute an inherent disparity where those with power exploit those without it. In the utopian communistic world there exists only a society of workers where all give according to their ability and take according to their needs (Martindale 1981).

As it borrowed from phenomenology and Marxism, structuralism took on two basic formats—the linguistic and the anthropologic. De Saussure moved linguistics from being merely the study of the historical origins of words to the "meanings" of words in the present. His structuralism deals with the "synchronic" or existing in the here and now (the study of language as a current system) as opposed to the "diachronic" or the study of language changes over time (the study of language historically). De Saussure's methodology calls for the study of culture as a system of signs and, from these shared conventions, cultural conclusions from which humans derive understanding naturally emerge (Appignanesi and Garratt 1991; Martindale 1981).

Lévi-Strauss moved from de Saussure's thinking to the development of structural anthropology in the late 1950s. His cultural model allowed for a universal model of the mind. Levi-Strauss' structuralism held that there were commonalties of language structure, behavior, and myth across cultures. These common, shared structures provided a framework that underscored and created understanding of human life (Appignanesi and Garratt 1991; Martindale 1981).

The philosophical thought that arose in opposition to structuralism has become known as "poststructuralism" or "deconstructionism" where our bodies and experiences have meaning only through the codes and senses at our disposal (Lorraine 1990). Following the critical philosophy of Immanuel Kant, whose philosophical ideas predate the structuralists, poststructuralists tend to explore the world in terms of how the concept of reason informs the world of experience. Kant reasoned that while an individual is not capable of understanding the nature of the universe, the person is capable of understanding, in a rational form, her or his own experiences. He further believed that what are commonly viewed as material things were merely products of our senses, that space and time exist only in the mind, and that the welfare of each individual was of utmost importance. And in seeming contradiction to this view, Kant gave scholars the distinction between "synthetic" and "analytic" statements. Synthetic statements are those statements learned by empirical means that add new, factual knowledge about the world. Analytic statements are those that do not require empirical substantiation (Martindale 1981).

This theme of the subjective experience is closely associated with what has been labeled as the empowerment perspective. Roland Barthes proclaimed that readers interpret what was on the written page according to their unique circumstances and worldview and that the texts created by the reader may not have the same contextual meaning for the reader as it did for the author. Jacques Derrida went on to assert that the basis of structuralism (the universal structures of meaning) is at odds with the individual who will give different meanings to experiences based on personal knowledge. Deconstruction becomes the peeling away of the layers of meaning and is a strategy for discovering, through each individual's "text" or story, the underpinnings of meaning. Meaning becomes what is (identity) and what is not (difference), and there is never one universally accepted meaning. Derrida, whose work has a major focus on language also noted that the text of the author may have more than one meaning and that oral communication, too, was subject to idiosyncratic interpretation. His peeling away or deconstructing the texts of others demonstrated that language was an ever-changing entity with ever-changing meanings (Appignanesi and Garratt 1995).

The poststructuralists/deconstructivists provide a logical link to the postmodern thought of Martin Heidegger and Michel Foucault. There is no universally agreed-upon definition of the term "postmodern," nor is there any agreed-upon date when modernism gave way to postmodern thought. For architects, the postmodern era began with the destruction of St. Louis' Pruitt-Igoe housing development at 3:32 P.M. on July 15, 1972

(Appignanesi and Garratt 1995). Artists have used the term since the late 1870s, and philosophers have used the term since the early 1930s (Appignanesi and Garratt 1995; Foucault 1996; Sawicki 1991). For the purposes of this book, the postmodern era in lesbian and gay culture will be considered to have begun in the early morning of June 28, 1969, with the Stonewall riot in Greenwich Village where gay and lesbian patrons refused to submit to the will of the New York City police as the police raided yet another gay bar (Marcus 1992).

Heidegger's main quest was to explore the philosophical question of existence (what it is, to be) and the kind of "being" human beings have. Humans are part of a world where natural things have utility but, people need to be cautious and not become submerged in the world of objects and technology. Rather people must broaden their perspectives beyond "things" and contemplate the meaning of existence. He did not isolate the self from the real world and noted that language was of the utmost importance because it is how humans create significance. His philosophy made no distinction between the inner and the outer experiences as individuals are what they think, what they say, and the actions they take. Heidegger's philosophy had a significant impact on the work of Foucault, a gay man whose work challenged traditional thinking about gay rights, prisons, welfare, and other social thought (Appignanesi and Garratt 1995; Foucault 1996; Lorraine 1990; Sawicki 1991).

Foucault's philosophy was also influenced by Nietzsche, who noted, as the reader will recall, that individuals have a will to power and that the traditional values of Christianity had lost its power in the lives of individuals, and by Heidegger who believed individuals did not pay enough attention to the question of existence. Foucault's work tried to demonstrate that the structures and truths people take for granted about society and human nature change across time and are constantly in flux. To make his point, he studied historically the concept of power as it related to its patterns within society and its relationship to the self. He analyzed power and knowledge as underpinnings for truth and rationality. Foucault perceived the individual as being composed of events in dynamic relationships with the ever-changing notions of societal truth (Appignanesi and Garratt 1991; Foucault 1996; Lorraine 1990).

Foucault's work has had a significant impact on the accepted notions of power and knowledge. He reasoned that power and knowledge are interdependent. Power is coercive, productive, and enabling and is a resourceful and tactical narrative that provides the texture for living. For Foucault, individuals "live" power rather than "have" power. Knowledge represents those controlling systems of thought that become legitimized and institutionalized and which an individual must master in order to be powerful (Appignanesi and Garratt 1991; Foucault 1996; Lorraine 1990). It is from Foucault that those practitioners involved with the empowerment perspective and the related strengths perspective gain much of their current ideology.

In summary, the empowerment perspective as envisioned by Barbara Solomon (1976), Barbara Simon (1994), Judith Lee (1994), Alex Gitterman (1991), and Germain and Gitterman (1996) and practiced under the label of the "strengths perspective" by Dennis Saleebey (1992) and Michael White (1989) comes from a rich philosophical tradition. From the positivistic organicists empowerment takes the concept that the world can be interpreted through one's direct experience of it. From the idealists and the neo-idealists comes the concept of social relationships and the notion that individuals cannot be studied outside of the societal context in which they live and that the individual is an ever-changing and developing entity. The Hegalian dialect of thesis, antithesis, and synthesis plays a key role in the empowerment perspective through the use of personal narrative and situation. Humanistic elementarism provided the empowerment perspective with the idea that there is a differentiation between the world of things and the world of individual experience and that through subjective choices individuals create their own circumstances. Phenomenology provides the viewpoint that day to day existence is of importance, that each individual is motivated by internal power, that the world is filled with contradictions found in language, and that socially constructed ideas are not static, but fluid and ever-changing. Structuralism allows empowerment advocates a method for studying the meanings of language and society across time and poststructuralism or deconstruction encourages practitioners to assist clients in peeling away the layers of perceived meaning in an attempt to uncover the individual's personal text or story. In this way, postmodern practitioners put the constructs of power and knowledge into an operational format for use in the empowerment process.

It is important to remember that when tracing the genesis of any philosophical viewpoint the path is not linear across time, but rather filled with loops and spirals. This is certainly the case for the evolution of the empowerment perspective. Ideas about the empowerment perspective as defined by social workers such as Solomon (1976), Simon (1994), Gitterman (1991), Germain and Gitterman (1996), and Lee (1994); the strengths perspective as delineated by White (1989) and Saleebey (1992);

and constructivism as characterized by Fisher (1991) are still being defined and debated. What seems clear to all these authors is that power and knowledge are important to the individual; that those in disenfranchised positions want to achieve empowerment; that people, communities, and societies possess internal power that can be uncovered and applied to oppressive situations; and that social workers working in partnerships with clients can discover the unique narratives that will tap and release internalized power. How then has the empowerment perspective been applied to the lesbian and gay movement?

Empowerment and the Lesbian and Gay Community

Before attempting to link the empowerment perspective with gays and lesbians, it is important to conceptualize the lesbian and gay community. Because social work is specifically involved with various populations the most significant demographic data include race, sex, and household income level. While there are hundreds of other statistics, these seem the most significant in defining this extraordinarily complex group. As the gay and lesbian community or its members are not easily visible, any demographic profile must be inferred. So it will be with the following profile. Census data note there are 260 million persons in the United States (U.S. Bureau of the Census 1992). Of that total number it has been estimated that between 3 percent and 10 percent are lesbian or gay (Kinsey, Pomeroy, and Martin 1948; Kinsey et al. 1953; National Opinion Research Center 1989–1992; Rogers 1993). This would mean that there are a total of 7.8 million to 26 million persons who are gays or lesbians in the country. The census data further define the population by ethnicity, stating that there are 33.6 million African Americans, 25 million Hispanics, 7.1 million Pacific Islanders and Asians, and 217 million Caucasians in the United States (Karger and Stoesz 1998; U.S. Bureau of the Census 1995). Applying the generally agreed-to percentages of gays and lesbians in the country to these populations would mean that there could be from 1 million to 3.6 million African-American gays and lesbians, from 750,000 to 2.5 million Hispanic gays and lesbians, from 213,000 to 710,000 Pacific Islander/Asian lesbians and gays, and from 6.5 million to 21.7 million Caucasian lesbians and gays in the United States.

Breaking these figures down by sex, census data show the population includes 124.8 million men (48%) and 135.2 million women (52%) (U.S. Bureau of the Census 1995). This means that it is possible that there are from 3.7 million to 12.5 million gay men and from 4 million to 13.5 million gay lesbians in the country. Of the total possible number of gay men, 48.8 thousand to 1.6 million may be African American, 360 thousand to 1.2 million may be Hispanic, 102 thousand to 340 thousand may be Pacific Islander or Asian, and 3.1 million to 10.4 million may be white. And, of the total number of lesbians, 524.1 thousand to 1.8 million may be African American, 390 thousand to 1.3 million may be Hispanic, 111 thousand to 370 thousand may be Pacific Islanders or Asian, and 3.4 million to 11.3 million may be white.

The U.S. census data also explore characteristics by total annual household income. In 1996, there were a total of 100.1 million households in the United States of which 30.1 million were classified as "nonfamily households" (Annual Demographic Survey 1996). Of those total households 24.6 million had an annual income of less than $17,500 (poverty or near poverty). And of those almost 25 million households, 11.6 million were in family households while the remainder (13.4 million) were in nonfamily households. There were a total of 85.1 million white households where 58.9 million were in family units and 26.1 million were classified as nonfamily households. Of all the households, 18.8 million had incomes of less than $17,500 while there were 8 million family households and 10.9 million nonfamily households similarly situated. There were 12.1 million African-American households where 4.7 million had annual incomes of less than $17,500. Of these, 8.5 million were family households where 2.8 million were at or near poverty. There were 3.6 million nonfamily African-American households where 1.9 million had similar incomes. Although similar data are not available on Pacific Islanders and Asians, there are 8.2 million Hispanic households where 6.6 million are classified as families and 1.6 million are identified as nonfamilies. Of the total number of Hispanic households 3.3 million had annual incomes of less than $17,500 while 2.4 million of the families and 94 thousand of the nonfamilies had similar incomes.

The 1990 census did make some attempt to identify persons who were living together and were not married. Presumably those are found in the "nonfamily" category identified in the section dealing with household income. Some of those individuals were gays and lesbians but, because the census survey did not collect data on sexual orientation, it is still difficult, if not impossible, to determine the exact number of lesbian and gay households. However, if one assumes, and it may be an enormous assumption, that 3 to 10 percent of all the households house gays or lesbians then there may be between 3.3 million to 10 million lesbian and gay households in the United States. And of that number, between 738 thousand and 2.4 million households are living in or very close to poverty. As many as 8.5 million white households, 1.2 million African-American households, and almost 1 million Hispanic households could be gay or lesbian. And of these as many as 1.8 million white households, almost 500 thousand black households, and 330 thousand Hispanic households have an annual income of less than $17,500.

If a household is white it is more likely to live closer to poverty in a nonfamily unit than in a family unit. But, for the two minorities of color for which data were available, fewer persons live in nonfamily households than in family households. While 22 percent of white households lived with less than $17,500 annually, 38.8 percent of African-American households and 40 percent of Hispanic households did so. Of these it is not known how many are actually lesbian or gay households, but it seems safe to assume that if one is a gay man or lesbian of color then it is more likely that he or she may be impoverished than if one is white.

A close look at these figures seems to demonstrate that there could be large numbers of lesbians and gays who may be in need of social services due to any number of variables, including socioeconomic status or being a member of a traditionally disenfranchised minority. However, a substantial amount of the research data that has been collected on gays and lesbians addresses well-educated, white, middle- or upper-class professionals, which means that social work professionals will have to extrapolate from what is known generally about lesbians and gays to populations for which little data exist. The empowerment perspective represents an excellent mechanism for providing services to the gay and lesbian community because of its approach.

As noted, the empowerment perspective utilizes an approach where the relationship between the client and the practitioner is built on mutual respect and reciprocity and demonstrates honesty, openness, authenticity, human caring, and naturalness. Clinical intervention is based on strengthening adaptive skills, reducing psychic discomfort, increasing self-esteem, providing information, and teaching coping skills that empower the individual to move toward the accomplishment of desired objectives (Germain 1979). The empowerment approach demonstrates a concern for empowering gays or lesbians functioning in an environment that, because of institutional, individual, and internal homophobia is oppressive. It further is one that is committed to working with disenfranchised, oppressed, and stigmatized populations—lesbians and gays clearly meet these criteria. The empowerment perspective also is one that is not based on a single approach as it can be successfully applied with individuals, couples, families, groups, communities, and organizations. Because the gay and lesbian community is not homogeneous, but rather includes all these facets, there is an excellent goodness-of-fit between the empowerment approach and the needs of those individuals, communities, and organizational structures that comprise and impact gays and lesbians.

Empowerment and Social Work with Gay and Lesbian Persons

As stated, those individuals who comprise the lesbian and gay community are a diverse population with social service needs as varied as their heterosexual counterparts. And, although gay and lesbian persons have been a persecuted, legally unprotected, and disenfranchised minority group for over 2,000 years, not all lesbians or gays require or need social service intervention. For those who do, it is essential that social workers be prepared to provide appropriate services. The social work practitioner must realize the impact of homophobia and the lack of legal and societal supports for gay people. Because gay men and lesbian women interact in both the nongay and gay worlds, it is important to remember that it is within the larger culture that the laws, policies, and procedures necessary to societal functioning are created and implemented. Because gay persons do not enjoy the same legal rights and privileges enjoyed by their nongay counterparts, the following section describes some of the societal and legal dilemmas faced by lesbians and gays.

Homophobia

Homophobia is probably the most singular factor that guides the development and implementation of public policy and opinion about lesbians and gays. Social work practitioners must be aware of the role homophobia plays in the lives of all gays and lesbians. Homophobia has generally been defined as "negative attitudes toward homosexual persons and homosexuality" (Herek 1990:552). It has been described as a prejudice against lesbians and gays that is similar to racism, sexism, and anti-Semitism and has three component parts—institutional homophobia, individual homophobia, and internalized homophobia (Tully 1995). When working with lesbians and gays, these three levels of homophobia must be recognized and the role each plays in the client's environmental interactions understood.

Institutional homophobia is the heterosexual macroculture's deeply embedded, and often unconscious, prejudice against homosexuals and homosexuality. As noted in chapter 1, it is centuries old and currently is evident in this country's overt and covert marginalization of sexual minorities. This is perpetuated overtly by public policy initiatives that fail to provide equal rights for gays and lesbians, and church doctrines that continue to condemn homosexual acts (Tully 1995; Vaid 1995). Such policies tend to make gays and lesbians mostly invisible until significant numbers become visible and demand equality. When this occurs, the non-gay social structures generally respond by increasing oppression. This ensures continued marginalization, discrimination, and hatred of lesbians and gays. Covert institutional homophobia tends to manifest itself in such ways as a lack of appropriate institutional recognition for openly gay or lesbian employees who often are denied adequate professional or personal recognition or such benefits as insurance for domestic partners because of their sexual orientation (Tully 1995). Institutional homophobia is found in all levels of the current societal structure (economic, political, familial, educational, social welfare, and religious) and must be take into consideration when working with gays and lesbians.

Individual homophobia is usually conceptualized as individual manifestation of institutional homophobia, characterized by open hostility toward sexual minorities by individuals. Such homophobia is manifested on a continuum from overt acts such as hate crimes (murder, rape, or other physical assaults of sexual minorities) to threats, teasing, harassment, queer jokes, ridicule, or other verbal attacks. On a more covert level, individual homophobia can be demonstrated by the lack of acknowledgment of a sexual orientation other than nongay and the expectation of conformity to the sexual majority—or what some have called the heterosexual assumption (Tully 1995). Because individual homophobia is present throughout both the gay and nongay cultures, the social work practitioner must not overlook this type of homophobia when working with sexual minorities.

Finally, internalized homophobia is that homophobia that is part of the gay or lesbian person's view of him or herself. Such self-loathing and contempt for one's personal sexual orientation may be operationalized through the gay person's learned fear and hatred of her or his sexual orientation that can cause personal crisis for the lesbian or gay client. Spawned by a society that is institutionally homophobic, and nurtured by those in society who foster individual homophobia, it is understandable that there are those gay and lesbian persons who dislike their sexual orientation. Such internalized homophobia can be demonstrated by a lesbian's insistence to her work colleagues that she is not gay (even though she has lived with her lover for the past twenty years), a gay man's entrance into therapy to be "cured" of his homosexuality, or the suicide of an adolescent lesbian. Such internalized homophobia may be psychically damaging to the individual and must be dealt with if the client is to be psychologically healthy.

Legal Dilemmas

Homophobia is evident in legal issues confronting lesbians and gay men. Three major areas in the legal arena that impact gays differently than nongays include child custody and parental rights, domestic partnership protections, and employment. At the current time there are no federal legal protections for lesbians and gays. In 1997, eleven states had decriminalized homosexual sexual acts between consenting adults, a number of cities or municipalities had nondiscrimination statutes or policies that protect some rights of lesbian and gay persons, and scores of major corporations and educational institutions had adopted policies that ensure domestic partnership benefits to gay women and men (NGLTF 1997). While seemingly notable, in the majority of states and countless other jurisdictions. lesbians and gays do not enjoy equal protection under the law simply on the basis of their sexual orientation (Jacobs 1991; Slavin 1991; Wilson 1991). Because of the lack of equality under the law, lesbians and gays may face personal and professional legal dilemmas and crises unknown to their nongay counterparts.

The nature of the American family is changing. No longer is it the norm for one woman and one man to be married, produce 2.5 children, live in the suburbs, and remain together until death. In fact, in 1997 only 24.8 percent of families comprised a heterosexual, two-parent family, raising children (U.S. Census 1997). There are more single mothers and fathers raising children, more grandparents raising grandchildren, and more lesbians and gays raising children. There are more single people living alone (young and old), there are more adult children moving back in with a parent, there are more people in communal settings, and there are more lesbians and gays living together. In essence, the American family has developed a previously unknown diversity, and in this diversity sexual minorities are creating what is being called "families of choice" or "wider families" (Marciano and Sussman 1991). Families of choice are those familial structures created outside the traditional legal structures and bound together only by the parties involved. Such families enjoy no legal protections and none of the entitlement benefits accorded to legally married partners such as tax benefits, parental and custody rights, property and inheritance rights, testamentary benefits, health care benefits, insurance benefits, bereavement leave, social security or veterans benefits, spousal testimonial benefits, probate designations, next-of-kin status to make medical or burial arrangements or special treatment under the U.S. Constitution (Slavin 1990; Treuthart 1990; Wilson 1990; Zimmer 1990).

Lack of domestic partnership protections poses another quandary for gay couples. While no state has yet legalized gay marriage many states, fearing that Hawaii will legalize such unions, have passed legislation specifically prohibiting gay marriage (Louisiana Electorate of Gays and Lesbians 1997). Lawmakers, usually slow to reflect any new societal formation, seem to be gradually incorporating pieces of policy that recognize nontraditional families of lesbians and gays (Treuthart 1990; Zimmer 1990). Such domestic partnership legislation may or may not include unmarried nongay couples, but does include domestic partners of gay couples who have lived together for some specified amount of time (usually at least one year), who share financial responsibilities, and who register as domestic partners (Louisiana Electorate of Gays and Lesbians 1997). These domestic partnership protections are now offered by numerous localities, companies, and universities and include such things as health insurance benefits, employment benefits, family leave benefits, housing benefits, and bereavement benefits (Louisiana Electorate of Gays and Lesbians 1997; Tully 1995).

Another area where gay people face discrimination is in the area of employment. Again, because there are no legal protections for homosexuals, the fear and reality of losing one's job because of sexual orientation continues to exist (Faderman 1991; Louisiana Electorate of Gays and Lesbians 1997). Gays and lesbians tend to be less open about their sexual orientation in the workplace because of fear of being denied a promotion or salary increment, fear of harassment, or fear of being terminated if their sexual orientation was public knowledge (Herek 1991; Rivera 1991). As with domestic partnership policies, some few states, municipalities, companies, and educational institutions guarantee protections and nondiscrimination on the basis of sexual orientation (NGLTF 1997), but because there are no federal mandates to protect the rights of lesbians and gays, discrimination, prejudice, and homophobia still thrive in the workplace.

In sum, the impact of institutional, individual, and internalized homophobia and its prevalence in the fabric of American society plays a significant role in the life of each and every gay and lesbian, as well as their nongay counterparts, and must be considered when providing social work intervention with them. The empowerment perspective does allow for the client and practitioner to struggle with the concept of homophobia and to confront it at the individual, couple, small group, community, and institutional level.

The following section describes how the empowerment approach can be applied when providing social work intervention with individual gay persons, gay couples, or groups (micro-level); intervention with communities (mezzo-level) and intervention in institutional settings (macro-level).

Conceptual Framework

Conceptual frameworks simply help provide a structure for better understanding. Inherent in each are basic principles that are assumed to be true. The conceptual framework to be used as the structure for the remainder of this book assumes the following:

1. That all lesbian and gay persons function at some level within the nongay society;
2. That the gay and lesbian subculture is part of the larger nongay society;
3. That lesbians and gays interrelate at three levels within the nongay society: micro-, mezzo-, and macro-levels;
4. That gays and lesbians interrelate at three levels within the gay and lesbian subculture: micro-, mezzo-, and macro-levels; and,
5. That, because gays and lesbians must negotiate both the nongay culture and the lesbian and gay subculture, the points for intervention are more numerous for them than for their nongay counterparts.

Figure 3.2 depicts the lesbian or gay person in society—a society that is both gay and nongay and one that comprises a number of complex interrelationships. As the gay subculture is assumed to be part of the larger, nongay world, the three innermost circles represent the social and familial (micro-level), cultural and community (mezzo-level), and work (macro-level) levels of the gay subculture while the three outer circles represent the personal (micro-level), communal (mezzo-level), and institutional (macro-level) levels of the nongay society. The gay or lesbian person in society, as represented by the bar, is seen to be interacting with all levels. While the graphic depicts the lesbian or gay person interrelating to all levels of both the gay and nongay society equally, this is not reality. Pragmatically, lesbians and gays have differing levels of interactions with various micro-, mezzo-, and macro-levels of each world depending on any number of variables. Before providing examples, a discussion of what is

FIGURE 3.2
The Lesbian / Gay Person in Environment

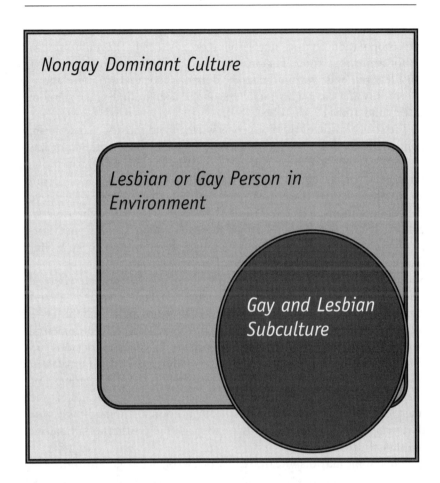

meant by nongay society, the gay subculture, and the three levels of inter-action (micro, mezzo, and macro) is provided.

The Dominant Nongay Society and the Subordinate Gay Culture

Although there is no precise way to accurately document the actual number of lesbian and gay persons in the United States, estimates vary from a high of almost 10 percent of the total population (26 million) (Kinsey,

Pomeroy, and Martin 1948; Kinsey et al. 1953) to a low of 3 percent of the population (8 million) (National Opinion Research Center 1989–1992; Rogers 1993). In either case, the numbers of lesbians and gays in this country are small when compared to the 90–97 percent of the total population that is not lesbian or gay (234–252 million). Data demonstrate that those persons who are members of minority groups must learn to exist within the larger dominant societal structure and this is certainly the case with members of the lesbian and gay community (Albro and Tully 1977; Tully 1989).

The social fabric of this country is woven from threads that were spun in the early English settlements and colonies: the Elizabethan Poor Laws of 1601 provide a pattern for the development and implementation of the current societal structure (Trattner 1994). The term "social structure" means the patterns discernible in social life, the regularities observed, the configurations detected (Blau 1975). In the context of the American culture, it is generally agreed that there are major societal institutions (economic, political, educational, familial, religious, and social welfare) that comprise the American societal structure (Vander Zanden 1979). Social institutions are defined as the principle structures where the essential tasks of life are "organized, directed, and executed" (Vander Zanden 1975:621). Within these social institutions an identifiable system of interconnected relationships exists and social structure becomes part of a differentiated yet interrelated collectivity in which all persons function (Blau 1975). The traditional dominant culture of this country is, and has been historically, defined by predominately white, male, nongay persons. By definition, lesbian and gay persons are a minority and, as such, must learn to exist in an often hostile, institutionally homophobic world that many have learned to negotiate through the creation of a homosexual subculture.

While some may dispute the reality of a lesbian and gay subculture that in many ways mirrors the dominant culture (Nicolosi 1991; Socarides 1962), others defend its existence (Faderman 1991; Gusfield 1978; Harry and Devall 1978; Murray 1979; Tully 1983, 1989; Vaid 1996). Ample data exist that demonstrate the reality of a lesbian and gay subculture. An identifiable gay and lesbian subculture coexists within the dominant heterosexual culture. The gay or lesbian person functions in both the gay and lesbian subculture and the nongay culture at the micro-, mezzo-, and macro-levels.

In using the terms "micro," "mezzo," and "macro" it might be helpful to recall that these terms have evolved from the older social work concepts of casework/group work, community organization, and administration. While the term casework does not merit an entry in the latest *Encyclopedia of Social Work* (1995), it is generally understood as an activity performed by a professional social worker who is adequately trained in psychiatric, psychological, and social concepts to provide professional intervention with individuals (Hollis and Woods 1990). Group work enjoyed a historically separate development in social work, but it too requires that a professional be trained in social science, psychiatry, and psychology in order to intervene effectively with groups (Schopler and Galinsky 1995). Both casework and group work have been categorized as "micro-level" intervention. So, for the purposes of this book, micro-level interactions will be defined as those professional social work interventions with individuals, families, or small groups. Community organization, while still current in the NASW encyclopedia (1995) has, like group work, been part of social work since the profession's start, and concerns itself with advocacy, service, mobilization, and organization within communities that promotes social change at the community level (Kahn 1995). While some use the term "macro" practice for community interventions (Meenaghan, Washington, and Ryan 1982), for the purposes of this book, the term "mezzo-level" intervention will be applied to those professional tasks and duties associated with community. Finally, social work administration has long been associated with the management of social welfare agencies and interactions with those agencies. The term "macro-level" intervention will be used in a slightly broader context to describe activities related to those social institutions with which individuals must interact in the course of living. Given these operational definitions, it is assumed that the gay or lesbian person interacts at all three levels in both the gay and nongay worlds.

How then do lesbians and gays pragmatically interrelate with the nongay and gay worlds? The proposed model assumes a systems theory/ecological perspective of social work (Compton and Galaway 1994; Pincus and Minahan 1973) that has evolved from the writings of Helen Harris Perlman (1957), Harriet Bartlett (1970), Gordon Hamilton (1951), and others (Hartman and Laird 1983; Germain 1979; Germain and Gitterman 1980: Middleman 1985). Briefly, this approach views all individuals as interacting in unique situations (person-in-situation) within a series of definable social systems. And, as opposed to the view that systems are static or mechanistic, the model assumes that all parts of the system are perpetually in a state of dynamic flux where there are constant transactions occurring between the individual and various systems and, in order to adequately manage, individuals must constantly adapt to new situations and new information. Such adaptation is a transactional process where the individual shapes, and in turn is shaped by, the environment (Woods and Hollis 1990). Hamilton noted that "the individual and society are interdependent" (1951:22) and that in social work, most problems are interpersonal.

For the gay male or lesbian who, by definition, continues to be part of an oppressed and disenfranchised minority and who has yet to win equality under the law, interacting with an often hostile and homophobic nongay culture may create interpersonal problems requiring intervention. Of course for the gay or lesbian person, interpersonal problems also may occur in the gay subculture as they do for nongays in the dominant culture. When the individual faces problems arising from life transitions, problems or needs in coping with the environment, or problems and needs associated with interpersonal crises (Compton and Galaway 1994) social work intervention may be appropriate. Such intervention focuses on the interface between the individual and environment and, according to Compton and Galaway (1994) seeks to help individuals and groups resolve or minimize problems; identify potential areas that may cause disequilibrium in an individual or group's social environmental system; and strengthen the potential within individuals, groups, and communities.

The previous review of social work's philosophy of person-in-society, homophobia, legal issues, and the many social roles played by persons who are gay or lesbian provides a backdrop for the application of the empowerment perspective in working with lesbian women and gay men. The conceptual framework for the empowerment model in social work is adapted from Lee (1994) and is characterized in table 3.1. It simply identifies four major constructs that underpin the profession of social work (purpose, value base, knowledge and theory, and methods) in terms of the empowerment perspective.

Using the conceptual framework in table 3.1 as a base, figure 3.3 depicts a model for using the empowerment approach with lesbian women and gay men. As mentioned, the gay person's environment by definition, includes both interactions in the gay and nongay worlds. And, in both of those worlds, there are opportunities for social work intervention that uses the empowerment approach.

This model also draws from the ecological perspective of Germain (1979), the life-centered model presented by Germain and Gitterman (1980), and family-centered practice described by Hartman and Laird (1983). The ecological perspective assumes that humans are in constant interaction with both their physical and social environments and that human needs and problems arise from those interactions. Humans strive

TABLE 3.1

The Empowerment Approach to Social Work Practice*

SOCIAL WORK PURPOSE

Concern for person in environment;

Commitment to empower those who experience oppression and poverty to enhance adaptive capacities; and,

Commitment to work collaboratively with others to change oppressive environments and structures.

SOCIAL WORK VALUE BASE

Commitment to working with disenfranchised, oppressed, stigmatized populations;

Responsibility to strengthening individual adaptive potentials; and,

Concern with the promotion of social and economic justice through individual and collective means;

KNOWLEDGE AND THEORETICAL BASES

Knowledge of theories and conceptual frameworks related to the person in environment, ecological perspective;

Understanding of empowerment principles in relationship to a variety of theories of human behavior, including personality development, ego functioning, cognitive and behavioral learning theories, feminist frameworks, postmodern thought; and,

Ability to pragmatically apply theory to practice at the individual, family, group, community, and organizational levels.

SOCIAL WORK METHODS

Ability to apply empowerment principles in micro-, mezzo-, or macro-settings;

Commitment to a respect for client's rights and responsibilities;

Utilization of the existing environment;

Fostering of motivation based on strength;

Concern for a collaborative, egalitarian effort between client and social worker; and,

Commitment to the process whereby client's find their own voice through personal narratives.

*Adapted from J. A. B. Lee (1994).

FIGURE 3.3

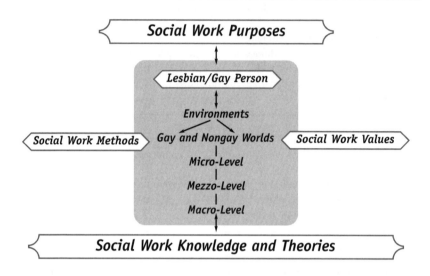

toward mastery and competency in an effort to impact their environments (Germain 1979; Germain and Gitterman 1980). The physical environment consists of the natural and built world while the social environment consists of a network of social relationships—both are vital to the development and sustenance of human potential (Germain 1979).

People adapt to the environment either by changing the environment to meet their needs or by changing themselves to meet the needs of the environment. The ecological perspective assumes people to be active, purposive, and goal-seeking where decisions are made using past memories with anticipation of future rewards. However, all persons are not able to take actions that will allow them to achieve their goals as some humans deprive others of the opportunity to do so by making it difficult or impossible to take action (Germain 1979). Gays and lesbians have been deprived of their ability to gain power and autonomy in their environments simply because of their sexual orientation.

Hartman and Laird (1983) present a family-centered view of social work practice where the unit of analysis is the family. In their early work, they note that all persons are deeply immersed in unique family systems, but fail to grapple with the issues of lesbian or gay family structures. They also point out that all families are embedded in the larger culture, but overlook the reality that gay men and lesbians in family units are also embedded in families of origin, families of choice, the gay culture, and the nongay culture. Their greatest contribution in their early work comes from the professional roles they advocate and from Laird's development of "eco-mapping" and their use of genograms. These ideas have exceptional utility when combined with the empowerment perspective.

Hartman and Laird (1983) turned the old social work truism, "Start where the client is," to "Start where the worker is." The empowerment perspective actually combines these two beginnings by starting where both the client and the worker are and moving with a mutuality that Hartman and Laird (1983) saw as each person bringing to the developing relationship a sense of individual personal meaning as derived from personal beliefs and values. From this emerges a mutual recognition from both the client and the worker of the potential for personal awareness and the capacity for growth in each. Like the family-centered approach, the empowerment perspective allows for flexibility to follow the client's story wherever it may wander with freedom of time and of space (Hartman and Laird 1983).

Both the life- and the family-centered models and the empowerment approach to social work intervention generally identify three major phases of social work treatment—the beginning, middle, and end. The initial phase of the relationship is characterized by the client and social worker getting to know one another. This process will undoubtedly be influenced by whether or not the client was seeking services voluntarily, or was required to have services because of agency policy. For example, if an older gay man seeks services because of his inability to deal with the continuing deaths of his social network because of AIDS, the initial contact may be easier than if a lesbian inmate is required to be seen because of ongoing suicide attempts. Irrespective of the voluntary or involuntary nature of the initial contact, the empowerment perspective, using techniques from the ecological perspective, can be a dynamic tool.

Relationships between clients and social workers need to be built on mutuality and reciprocity and should manifest what Germain (1979) identifies as honesty, openness, authenticity, human caring, and naturalness. Actions toward the individual should promote self-esteem, teach coping skills, reduce psychic discomfort, provide information and strengthen adaptive patterns (Germain 1979). In doing so the social worker assumes a variety of roles including those of enabler, facilitator, and teacher (Germain and Gitterman 1980). Actions between the client, the worker, and the environment should provide an opportunity for decision making, for mastery of the situation, for action, and for reshaping environmental situations to ensure a better goodness-of-fit between the client and the environment (Germain 1979). Just as no problem is one-dimensional, no solution should be one-dimensional (Hartman and Laird 1983).

The initial phase of interaction is where the client and the worker enter each other's worlds in a very literal sense. This can occur in a client's home, a social worker's office, a jail cell, a community center, or an organizational conference room. Wherever the first interaction occurs, both the client and the worker have done some preliminary work—generally referred to as cognitive and affective preparation. In this before-meeting phase, both the client and worker gather what is objectively and subjectively known about the other and anticipate what the meeting will include. Once the initial contact has been established, both the client and the worker enter into a transactional relationship where each brings her or his own experiences to the relationship. Rather than the client/worker relationship being one of superior/subordinate (where the worker is seen as superior), the relationship is rather reciprocal and mutual (Germain and Gitterman 1980; Hartman and Laird 1983). This beginning phase of service is one of exploration and contracting where the client tells her or his story, there is a mutual assessment of the current dilemma(s), and a tentative assessment of possible solutions. All of these steps are based on shared definitions, purposes, and expectations between the client and worker (Germain and Gitterman 1980; Hartman and Laird 1983). If the client is not a voluntary one, the initial conversations held between the worker and client center first on the definition of the array of services available and finding some common ground between the client and social worker. Once established then it may be possible to have the client share his or her story and come to mutually agreed upon goals (Germain and Gitterman 1980).

Hartman and Laird (1983) provide an interesting and, by the late 1990s, well-used method of initially gathering information about clients, their families, and their social systems—the eco-map and genogram. Although not specifically designed for use with lesbians and gays, it seems that by using these simple paper and pencil techniques with gays and lesbians, important data about their families of origin, their families of choice, and interactions with both the gay and nongay cultures could be gathered. This information should allow both the client and worker to visually identify sources of support (or strain) and define mutually agreed on courses of action. A detailed description of how to construct eco-maps and genograms can be found in Hartman and Laird's (1983) *Family-Cen-*

tered Social Work Practice, but a brief illustration of these techniques should demonstrate their usefulness when working with gays or lesbians.

The eco-map model proposed in Hartman and Laird's (1983) work assumed heterosexuality and also failed to account for cultural differences. The model therefore placed the unit of analysis (for Hartman and Laird it was the family unit) in only one sociocultural context. For gays and lesbians, as well as for ethnic minorities or minorities of color, a more accurate map would have to include social interactions within more than one cultural context. If an individual is an Asian lesbian, she would have to be depicted as functioning within the larger, white, nongay world; the nongay Asian world, the larger gay and lesbian world, and the relatively small Asian lesbian and gay world. If, as the empowerment perspective assumes, human needs and problems flow from continuous interactions between the individual and the environment, and both the environment and the individual are changed by changes in one system or the other, the Asian lesbian faces quite a challenge. Figure 3.4 attempts to diagram this example.

As seen in figure 3.4, it is quite possible that Mei, a 23-year-old stenographer working on her MSW part-time at night, has stressful relationships not only with the dominant white, nongay culture, but also with the predominantly white gay and lesbian subculture. Couple that with her own culture's anti-gay biases and it looks as though her primary source of support is found within the Asian gay and lesbian community—a very small community. School, work, and her recreational activities also provide support although her extended Asian family has difficulty in accepting her sexuality. She has adequate health care and yet this young woman may face incredible obstacles as the environments in which she functions have been polluted by what Germain and Gitterman (1980) describe as discrimination, poverty, and stigma—all of which have a tendency to have a negative impact on individuals. To complicate this eco-map, consider what the map would look like if Mei's partner was an African-American woman.

Similarly, while the use of the popular genogram has been used traditionally for diagramming intergenerational nongay family structures, using it to diagram lesbian and gay families of origin (which would use the traditional framework), families of choice, and relationship patterns would provide the client and worker valuable information about all three areas. Take for example a gay man who, although HIV+, is a long-term survivor and has responded positively to new pharmaceutical techniques but has lost virtually all of his former support system. Diagramming his

FIGURE 3.4
Lesbian / Gay Eco-Map

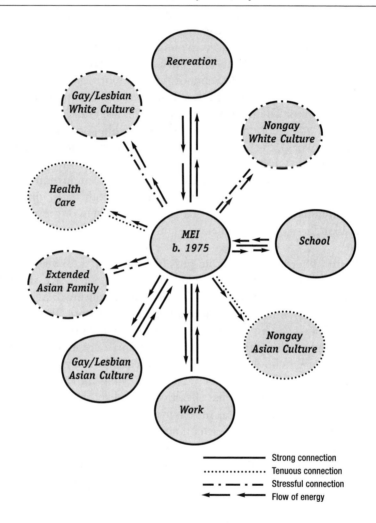

family of origin, family of choice, and relationships across time should provide excellent information from which professionally sound judgments can flow. Figures 3.5 and 3.6 attempt to provide such a view.

Figure 3.5 includes a diagram of the client's family of origin and his current family of choice, and of his past relationships. Figure 3.6 depicts his past significant relationships. In figure 3.5 Aaron's family of origin

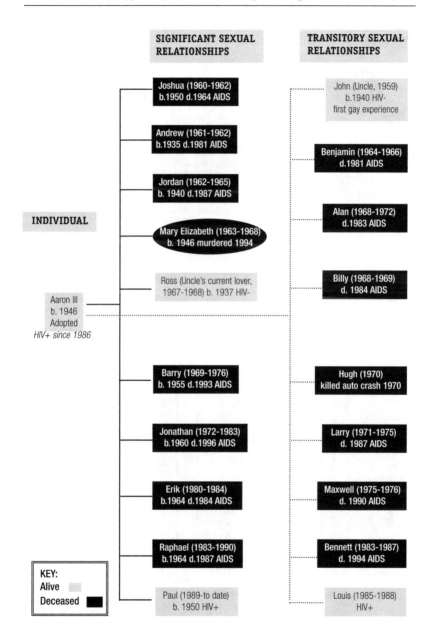

FIGURE 3.5
Gay / Lesbian Relationships Genogram

FIGURE 3.6
Family of Choice and Family of Origin Genograms

FAMILY OF ORIGIN

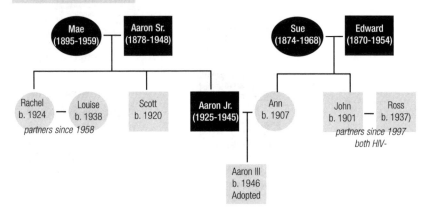

FAMILY OF CHOICE

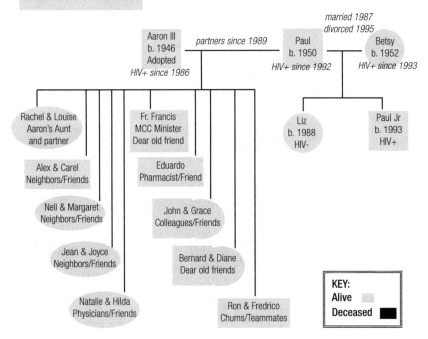

graphically displays that he was not the only family member to have been involved in a same-sex relationship; however the relationship between his uncle, John, and his current lover, Ross, was identified as strained (perhaps because, as figure 3.6 shows, Aaron has had sexual encounters with both his uncle and his uncle's current lover). The relationship with his aunt, Rachel, was described as positive and supportive, but his interactions with his uncle, Scott, are tentative. By diagramming these relationships it becomes clearer where sources of support and strain within the family of origin lie. Likewise, by diagramming Aaron's current family of choice, interesting patterns begin to emerge. For example, Aaron's current lover, Paul, is HIV+ as is his ex-wife, Bess, and his son, Paul Jr. Paul is cut off from his family of origin and his ex-wife as well. He does have a strong, positive relationship with both of his children. Aaron is relatively alone in terms of blood relatives, but has a long history of previous relationships as figure 3.6 depicts.

Aaron was born in 1946 and estimated that in his lifetime he had been involved in 10 significant relationships with men and one significant relationship with a woman. Figure 3.6 diagrams those relationships. The most significant pattern that is obvious from even a brief look at the relationship genogram is that most of Aaron's significant life partners, except his current partner, Paul, have died (as have most of his transitory lovers) and that he is currently HIV+. The diagram also points out that when he was involved with the one woman in his life, he was also seriously involved with other men. This pattern of non-monogamy appears to be of long standing because a closer inspection of the genogram reveals his continuing habit of being involved with more than one person at a time. What implications this information has for his current situation can be the beginning focus of the client/worker relationship. In sum, both the use of an eco-map and genogram would seem to have an important role in the empowerment perspective and approach.

Similarly, the social work techniques used in the middle phase and termination phases of the process—namely the working through of continuously shifting needs and solutions while working toward and arriving at agreed upon goals through the ongoing dialogue between the client and the worker—include the social worker's professional use of self. That creative use of self is particularly evident in the empowerment perspective where the worker is at liberty to, as Germain and Gitterman note, risk revealing her or his humanity, weaknesses, spontaneity, and humor by being "dependably real" and not "rigidly consistent" (1980:21).

From the life model of social work as described by Germain and Gitterman (1980) and the family-centered approach detailed by Hartman and Laird (1983), the empowerment perspective has incorporated the ideology of the unique interactions between the person and the environment where the dual nature of social work—of helping persons and changing environments—has been slightly altered to help persons by empowering them to remove whatever environmental blocks they see as impeding their progress. In doing so, there is an evolutionary development where humans are in constant interaction with their environments. This leads to a constant change in the environment as well as a constant change to those in the environment. Such growth should be concerned for the positive development of both the person and the environment where individual potential can be met and where environmental obstacles that fail to support the development of such potential will be reduced (Germain 1979). Both the life-model and family-centered model provide a foundation for the empowerment perspective's use of the individual's strengths to move toward positive growth and influencing social systems to be more responsive to human need. The empowerment approach has utility irrespective of the unit of analysis and can be equally well used at the micro-, mezzo-, and macro-levels of social work practice. For those working with lesbians or gays, this approach has a particularly strong appeal.

Micro-Level Intervention

Gay and lesbian people are not readily identifiable by appearance and because of institutional, internal, and individual homophobia they may not disclose their sexual orientation. So, the first obstacle facing a social worker is that of determining sexual orientation and avoiding the "assumption of heterosexuality." It is generally assumed that all persons are nongay and this is reinforced by standardized face sheets and other case forms and documents that ignore the possibility of other sexual orientations. Interviewers, too, may assume all their clients to be nongay which furthers the "myth of heterosexuality." Creative, nonstandardized face sheets and skillful interviewing, along with a willingness to confront homophobia, will make it easier for the client and the practitioner to overcome the dilemma of sexual orientation. Also, gay friendly literature in the waiting room or lobby makes the office accepting for lesbian or gay clients.

Once the issue of sexual orientation has been dealt with, the next myth facing the practitioner is that of "the homosexual as mentally ill." Despite ample research to the contrary, and fueled by the recent conservative movement, this myth still persists and feeds homophobia. While it is true that some gay persons, like some nongay persons, are mentally ill, or alcoholic, or depressed, most are not. And, while it is also true that some lesbians and gays require social work intervention, many (as in the nongay population) do not. Hence, the practitioner can not assume a homosexual cause of the presenting problem. The first phase of this and many treatment models (e.g., Compton and Galaway 1994; Germain and Gitterman 1980; Hartman and Laird 1983; White 1989) is to start where the client and the worker are. Social workers who are themselves heterosexist, homophobic, or otherwise uncomfortable with sexual identity issues may have difficulty separating what the client views as her or his problem from the client's sexual identity. And, workers who are not familiar with the lesbian or gay lifestyles and all of their complexities may also have difficulty comprehending some issues, but with the application of an empowerment approach these dilemmas can be resolved.

The empowerment perspective recognizes the egalitarian nature of the relationship between the client and the practitioner where the practitioner demonstrates concern for the person in environment. With these guiding principles as a base, the social worker must create a safe, homosocial environment where such a relationship can develop and flourish. Gay people often do not seek social services because of a perception of institutional homophobia (Tully 1989). But, there are some ways to make gay clients feel more at ease. Table 3.2 lists ways the practitioner can create a homosocial atmosphere and safe space for gay persons.

Social workers need to understand the gay person's environmental perspective and encourage the client to narrate her or his own story about seeking social work services. Social work practitioners bring to this relationship an ability to apply a variety of theoretical approaches that are synergistic with the empowerment perspective to deal with the presenting problem. The usual generalist roles of broker, advocate, teacher, case manager, and educator all have utility and these will be explored further in following chapters. Interventive treatment using the empowerment approach with gay men and lesbians varies little from the use of the empowerment perspective with any group, but some of the key issues might. Lesbians and gays often seek intervention for assistance during their "coming-out" phase (the assumption and identification as a lesbian or gay person), but gay people may also seek counseling for issues related to internalized homophobia, relationship development, health, family of origin issues, monogamy, gender identity, chemical abuse, spouse abuse, parenting, pregnancy, relationship dissolution, aging, the death of a partner, household management, or any of a number of related situations. As

---

TABLE 3.2
Creating a Homosocial Space

THE OFFICE SPACE

Avoid standardized face sheets and documents that presume everyone is heterosexual;

Include some lesbian and gay friendly magazines or newspapers in the waiting area; and,

Train staff to be gay friendly and nonhomophobic.

THE INTAKE INTERVIEW

Avoid questions that assume heterosexuality;

Be aware of institutional, individual, and internal homophobia;

Do not succumb to the myths of homosexuality; and,

Start where the client is and allow the client to define the presenting problem.

THE PROFESSIONAL SOCIAL WORK PRACTITIONER

Evaluate personal homophobia and bias;

Be willing to learn from your client;

Accept gay persons as members of an oppressed minority-not as pathological entities;

Learn about the gay community in your area;

Avoid myths and stereotypes about sexual minorities;

Become an advocate for lesbian and gay persons;

Remember that homosexuals are not a homogeneous group;

Understand the double and triple minority status of some gay persons; and,

Become a resource person for the gay community.

---

with any client, the presenting problem needs to be clearly defined and it may very well have nothing to do with the client's sexual orientation. The empowerment approach encourages client-professional interaction in the definition of the presenting issue and becomes part of the client's story. Once defined by the client, the empowerment approach can be applied to solving the predicament.

Table 3.3 provides some basic information to consider when providing micro-level intervention.

TABLE 3.3
Empowerment and Intervention at the Micro-Level

In order to successfully provide intervention at the micro-level using the empowerment approach, the social worker must:

Accept that sexual orientation is determined by a multitude of factors including both genetics and environment;

Understand the coming out process and its impact on individuals and their families;

Not assume that all persons are heterosexual;

Become familiar with issues related to families of origin and families of choice;

Be aware of the heterogeneity of the lesbian and gay community and the individuals who comprise it;

Have knowledge of the basic differences between lesbians and gay men (e.g., in relationships, sexual activities, at-risk behaviors, etc.);

Allow individuals to dialogue about their stories at their own pace and with your support;

Discover the reasons for the person's seeking intervention- sexual orientation may or may not play a role in the presenting problem;

Be totally aware of the ramifications of reparative therapies and spiritual interventions designed to "cure" homosexuality;

Have a knowledge base and know how to find information and resources related to those groups that are culturally different from your own (e.g., racial and ethnic minorities, hearing impaired, blind, etc.);

Develop a willingness to talk honestly and openly about matters of sexual activity and sexual orientation;

Be comfortable with your own sexual orientation;

Understand the impact of institutional, individual, and internal homophobia on gay men and lesbians;

Respect client confidentiality;

Avoid gay and lesbian stereotyping and mythology; and,

Not engage in homophobia at any level.

Mezzo- and Macro-Level Intervention

Although currently not as popular as working with individuals, couples, families, and groups, some social workers intervene at the community or institutional level. As defined, mezzo- and macro-level practice in social work deals with intervention at the community, state, or national level and is directed at creating changes or improvements at the societal level. It may include such activities as community organization, political advocacy, lobbying efforts, organizational changes, or policy development that differentiates it from micro-level social work practice (Barker 1995).

Working with the gay community means that the social worker must first be able to define for her- or himself what is meant by the term "gay community." And, although not everyone would agree that there is such a thing as a gay community, enough empirical data exist to support the premise that a gay community does exist (Faderman 1991; Gusfield 1978; Harry and Devall 1978; Murray 1979; Tully 1983, 1989; Vaid 1996). The lesbian and gay community (or subculture) exists in both the formal and informal structures of society. Formal structures include stores, bars, travel agencies, churches, counseling services, antique stores, real estate companies, dental and medical complexes, music companies, newspapers, magazines, coffee shops, novelty shops, exercise clubs and spas, restaurants, and a host of other businesses that are openly run by or cater to a lesbian and/or gay clientele. On an informal level, gays and lesbians have social clubs, friendship networks, reading groups, social support groups, sororities and fraternities, sports teams, choruses, vacation cruises, neighborhood associations, nontraditional family structures, and other ways to facilitate social relationships.

It is possible that the social worker could be asked to intervene with or on behalf of her or his client within the gay community or to be cognizant of and know how to access that community's resources. In order to successfully manage that the social worker needs to consider the suggestions in table 3.4.

To facilitate learning about the lesbian and gay community, the social worker is encouraged to discover the community within her or his own area. This activity will be made easier if the social work practitioner happens to live in an urban area where there are known gay communities (San Francisco, New Orleans, New York, Atlanta, Boston, etc.), but even in the most rural areas of the United States there are lesbians and gays participating in the routines of daily life. For the novice, the telephone book may be a place to start—just look for items such as "gay hot-lines" or women's centers. But, an even easier method is to search the Web. There are now countless Internet sites related to the lesbian and gay community and include chat rooms for lesbians only or for gays, lesbians, and bisexuals; literally thousands of pages of data related to information

TABLE 3.4

Empowerment and Intervention at the Mezzo-Level

In order to successfully provide intervention at the mezzo-level using the empowerment perspective, the social worker must:

> Distinguish between the nongay and gay communities;
>
> Identify the formal and informal structures within the gay community;
>
> Recognize institutional homophobia, heterosexism, and oppression;
>
> Understand the legal dilemmas facing the lesbian and gay community;
>
> Become knowledgeable about and supportive of the gay and lesbian community;
>
> Know what resources are available in the lesbian and gay community;
>
> Encourage dialogue between the gay and lesbian community and the social worker;
>
> Define a specific action plan that uses the resources of the lesbian and gay community;
>
> Evaluate and implement the action plan in light of homophobia or heterosexism; and,
>
> Become a resource person for the lesbian and gay community.

about gays; and endless places to search using a variety of search engines. What was once a hidden community has become quite easily found.

One of the interesting by-products of the AIDS pandemic has been a resurgence of community group work designed and implemented by gay men and lesbians. When first identified as a disease in the early 1980s AIDS was mostly overlooked as a major health issue until hundreds and then thousands of young, previously healthy gay men started dying. As a reaction to that reality, men of the gay community rallied and formed self-help groups to cope with the ever-increasing health crisis. Because AIDS was first identified as Gay Related Immunodeficiency (GRID), the nongay community paid little attention to a disease that seemed to only impact gay men. Gay men had what Middleman (1985) called a living awareness of the self in its relationship to other gay men that allowed for the informal development of self-help groups that eventually led to the creation of more formal community-based groups that evolved into federally funded city agencies that deal with HIV/AIDS. But at the beginning of the

HIV/AIDS crisis, HIV+ gay men helped other HIV+ gay men die and then lesbians joined forces with gay men to provide supportive services.

There were many gay male social workers, a lot of whom were themselves HIV+, who initiated self-help or mutual aid groups, provided crisis intervention, and helped their friends die one after another. Social workers continue to act as initiators of self-help groups for those with HIV/AIDS, and social workers also facilitate such groups, consult with such groups, make referrals to such groups, and act as advisers to such groups. Such mezzo-level interventions impact not only the individuals in the group, but also the community at large because the focus of such groups not only is on those with HIV/AIDS, but also on community resources available for those with HIV/AIDS.

Somewhat related, yet distinct from mezzo-level practice, is that of macro-level intervention. Macro-level practice is usually conceptualized as intervention related to changing societal institutions to make them less rigid and more compatible with current or evolving human need. Such practice would include political advocacy; development, implementation, and evaluation of public policy; and administration aimed at social change (Barker 1995; Meenaghan, Washington, and Ryan 1982). The practitioner who wishes to become involved in macro-level practice with lesbians or gay men, must consider the caveats in table 3.5.

Key to macro-level intervention is to know what political and social issues are facing the lesbian and gay community at any point in time. As laws change and as the general population becomes more familiar with the gays and lesbians in their midst so, too, do gay-related issues and dilemmas change. For example, the legal and social issues faced by a 1950s lesbian who was employed as a university professor by Tulane University are quite different than those faced by a similarly situated woman today when there are some university-level policy protections and social supports for her lifestyle. The practitioner must keep current with the "hot" topics facing gays and lesbians. In the early 1990s President Clinton's, "Don't Ask, Don't Tell" policy related to military personnel was in the forefront; but in 1997 congressional attention focused more on ending employment discrimination against gays and lesbians and the issue of same-sex marriage. Other current issues include hate crimes legislation, whether or not content related to gay and lesbian issues should be in the secondary school curriculum, and the status of gay clergy in the church.

Once familiar with the topics, the social worker needs to become an expert so as to be able to lobby, testify, and be prepared to ward off the assault of homophobia. So, too, does the social work practitioner need to

TABLE 3.5
Empowerment and Intervention at the Macro-Level

To be successful at macro-level intervention, the social worker must:
    Understand the many legal issues associated with lesbians and gays;
    Confront institutional homophobia at the state and federal levels;
    Become an expert in the field of gay and lesbian issues;
    Join and support pro lesbian and gay organizations;
    Lobby congressional appointees;
    Prepare gay friendly testimony for congressional hearings;
    Build networks using telephone trees for support;
    Construct coalitions that support the gay and lesbian agenda;
    Create constituencies and make allies that are pro gay;
    Be dignified and polite in legislative defeat;
    Learn to negotiate for an agreeable outcome;
    Be gracious, even in the face of homophobia;

build constituent groups and allies that will become a coalition to fight for pro-gay legislation and defeat legislation that is homophobic. The social worker must be prepared to win a few battles and to lose some hard-fought campaigns. But, whether the legislation is passed or defeated, one must be gracious and appreciative of all those who supported the effort.

Societal changes supported by legislation win acceptance more slowly and gradually than prevailing social customs, and they evolve more through persistence and tenacity than revolutionary tactics. Macro-level social work practitioners working in the field of lesbian and gay issues need to be comfortable with ambiguity and yet remain steadfast in their determination to encourage and foster social and legislative changes that will reduce homophobia and create legal protections for gays and lesbians.

This chapter has provided a discussion of the evolution of the empowerment perspective from a philosophic heritage that dates back more than two hundred years and includes concepts from positivistic organicism, idealism, neo-idealism, social behaviorism, humanistic elementarism, phenomenology, structuralism, post-structuralism, and postmodernism.

An operational definition for empowerment was provided as were the assumptions inherent in the empowerment or strengths perspective. How the empowerment perspective can be applied to the lesbian and gay community was discussed and an attempt was made to describe the demographics of lesbians and gays currently residing in the United States. Homophobia, heterosexism, and legal dilemmas facing the gay community were detailed and the concept of the gay individual's functioning in both the larger, dominantly white, nongay society and the gay community was noted. A conceptual model for social work using the empowerment approach within the micro-, mezzo-, macro-levels of both the dominant society and the lesbian and gay world was put forth. How that conceptual model can be applied is the focus of the following three chapters. Chapter 4 explores empowerment and gay and lesbian youth, chapter 5 examines the perspective's applicability to lesbian and gay adults, and chapter 6 describes how the empowerment perspective has utility when working with older gay men and lesbians. Finally, chapter 7 explores past, present, and future trends related to professional social work and its relationship with the queer community.

4

Empowerment and Lesbian and Gay Youth

My sexual orientation has not been caused by you, nor is it designed to hurt you, nor should you or I do anything to try and change it. What is hurting you is the misinformation you have about homosexuality that you have been taught by society. I know it will take you a long time to understand this, just as it has taken me. I am willing to give you lots of time to learn about this. I'll answer serious questions, provide you with information, tell you about my recognition and acceptance of my sexual orientation, tell you about my life and my friends lives as lesbians or gay people, tell you about my own fears and expectations, and discuss with you how you might handle the news with your friends and our relatives.

Savin-Williams 1996:175.

Just as the total numbers of gay and lesbian persons is unknown, it is also unknown how many gay and lesbian youths exist. The 1990 census data indicate that there are approximately 27.5 million (11.2%) persons in the United States between the ages of 12 and 19 (U.S. Census 1992). If one assumes, as has been reported, that between 3 and 10 percent of the general population are gay, (Kinsey, Pomeroy, and Martin 1948; Kinsey et al. 1953; National Opinion Research Center 1989–1992; Rogers 1993), then of those people between 12 and 19, anywhere from 82,500 to 2,750,000 could be lesbian or gay. The subject of lesbian and gay youth is new and, as recently as 1980, social workers writing in the area of homosexuality were warned not to discuss gay adolescence as the topic was "too sensitive" (Woodman and Lenna 1980:88). Most research dealing with this minority population dates from the late 1970s and is still an emerging topic of scientific inquiry.

Yet, even with a lack of years of data, significant issues related to lesbian and gay youths have begun to emerge. This chapter explores specific developmental tasks associated with becoming gay or lesbian, including the formation of a lesbian or gay identity, the coming-out process, legal difficulties associated with a sexual orientation different from the norm, mental health issues, and the development of relationships. The second section focuses on concepts, methods, and practice skills designed to empower lesbian or gay youths, and the final section presents case studies designed to help the practitioner practice her or his clinical skills with this population.

Growing Up Gay: Developmental Issues and Coming Out

Adolescence is generally defined as, "the life cycle period between childhood and adulthood, beginning at puberty and ending with young adulthood" (Barker 1995:9). With changes in the adolescent individual's biological, psychological, cognitive, moral, social, and sexual development, the struggle to define self-identity as an autonomous, independent individual who is not dependent on others for the management of personal affairs is characterized by this phase of development (Barker 1995; de Anda 1995; Hetrick and Martin 1987). For the lesbian or gay adolescent, this time of life can be extremely troublesome. While biologically developing in a similar fashion to their nongay peers, as they begin to consciously define the sexual orientation as something other than the norm, gay youths face psychological, cognitive, moral, social, and sexual issues that put them at high risk for social service intervention.

Conventional Psychological Theories

There are a number of psychological theories associated with the phase of adolescence (e.g., psychosexual, social learning, psychosocial) with proponents of each (e.g., Freud, Erikson, Bandura). Most are conceptualized as developmental, where the individual must successfully move through one phase of development in order to move to the next phase (de Anda 1995). Most psychological theories remain heterosexually biased even with the American Psychiatric Association's 1973 decision to remove homosexuality from its diagnostic manual of mental disorders (Talan 1997). As recently as the summer of 1997, the American Psychological Association was still debating whether or not it was unethical to convert, through reparative therapy, lesbians or gays to the more conventional heterosexual way of life (Talan 1997; Weiss 1997). There is evidence that some social work practitioners are not immune to homophobia (Clark, Brown, and Hochstein 1990; DeCrescenzo and McGill 1978; Tate 1991; Wisniewski and Toomey 1987); and gay and lesbian youths, when they are acknowledged, face the possibility of therapeutic alienation based simply on using theories that do not fit the population at risk.

Cognitive Development

Cognitive development during adolescence is characterized by the individual's increasing ability to comprehend, evaluate, and process more and more complex data that allows for the formulation and testing of hypotheses and identity confusion (Barker 1995; de Anda 1995). Most lesbian and gay children are raised in nongay family structures where they learn that being "different" is not good and being homosexual is horrific. Because as an activity homosexuality is illegal, so, too, it must be as an identity (Boyer 1989; Morrow 1993). As the young gay begins to comprehend, evaluate, and process information and create and test hypotheses about sexual orientation, he or she is confronted with myths, stereotypes, misconceptions, and contradictory data about the realities of a gay or lesbian lifestyle (Herdt 1989). The school library often has little or no information on the issue and teachers and school counselors may be unwilling or forbidden from discussing the subject with confused teens. Nongay parents are generally not a source for accurate information, there are few gay role models depicted on television or in the movies, and traditional church teachings condemn same-sex feelings (Martin and Hetrick 1988; Morrow 1993; Savin-Williams 1989b; Telljohann and Price 1993; Uribe and Harbeck 1991).

While the search for honest data about a gay lifestyle is still difficult for adolescents, more and more information is becoming available. Mainstream bookstores have entire sections devoted to same-sex issues, several gay oriented magazines exist, and there are now thousands of websites on the Internet devoted to lesbian and gay materials. Some social service agencies have programs designed for young gay people, and gays and lesbians are being depicted in the media as leading ordinary lives (Brown 1997; Marin and Miller 1997). But, until realistic depictions of the pluses and minuses of same-sex relationships are as plentiful as the depictions of nongays, the immature, struggling, gay or lesbian adolescent will have a difficult time.

Moral Development

Morally, the individual internalizes and incorporates the learning, values, and beliefs from childhood that differentiate right from wrong and are consistent with social mores (Barker 1995; de Anda 1995). Historically (as chapter 1 detailed), homosexuality has been variously defined and accepted across time. In recent history, it seems same-sex relationships have borne the brunt of stigmatization. School curricula generally overlook the issues of adolescent sexuality or, if sexuality is discussed, it is done so only in a cursory fashion. Homosexuality may be part of the high school curriculum, but it is generally glossed over by nongay faculty who may feel uncomfortable with the topic; when included in the curriculum, it often reflects continuing institutional homophobia within the school system (Telljohann and Price 1993; Uribe and Harbeck 1991). Such institutional homophobia can damage students psychologically by leading to the internalization of homophobia, which may create self-loathing in the student, a condition that places gay and lesbian students at high risk (CWLA 1991; Hetrick and Martin 1989; Martin and Hetrick 1988; Uribe and Harbeck 1991).

Internalizing positive values and beliefs about a generally illegal activity that is condemned by the church and is the source of stigmatization can be difficult for the adult gay or lesbian person (Tully 1989), but such an activity may cause the gay adolescent to be at high risk for depression, feelings of isolation or loneliness, developmental delays, suicide, lowered scholastic achievement, running away from home, or erratic behavior patterns (CWLA 1991; Grossman 1997; Hetrick and Martin 1987; Martin and Hetrick 1988; Sweet 1996; Telljohann and Price 1993; Vergara 1983/84). These developmental challenges are unknown to nongay youth, while the development of an acceptance of morality that deviates from the norm is closely related to the social development of the lesbian or gay adolescent.

Social Development: Relationships

The adolescent's social development is related to the person's growing autonomy and search for identity and intimacy with others, where the primary task is the creation of an independent functioning person who is dependent only on herself or himself in the management of personal affairs (Barker 1995; de Anda 1995; Browning 1987; Hetrick and Martin 1987). Identity as a concept is generally described as a view of one's self in relation to specific social situations (e.g., student, mother, father, worker, etc.). People have a variety of identities and all are not equally important to the person. While they may change with time, it has been noted there are three levels of identity: the least elaborate "subordinate identity," which is included in the more dominant "primary identity," which, in turn, is subsumed by the most elaborate and complex "super-ordinate identity" (Massey and Ouellette 1996). Though sometimes confused with "self-image," the concept of identity is differentiated from the concept of self-image. Self-image has been described as being broader than identity, as it includes the mental images people have of themselves and has countless social categories and dimensions (Troiden 1989).

Adolescence is a time for expanded development of ego identity. For the lesbian or gay adolescent it is a time of a dual socialization process—socialization to the mainstream of nongay society and socialization to the gay subculture with different norms and mores than the larger nongay society (Gerstel, Feraios, and Herdt 1989; Hetrick and Martin 1987). Lesbian and gay youths are traditionally assumed to be heterosexual and as such may feel isolated during adolescence because the nongay society's expectations of them differs from their identity and self-image (Massey and Ouellette 1996).

As members of a stigmatized minority group, gay adolescents must develop self-identity, self-image, self-esteem, social skills, social roles, and learn how to create and maintain interpersonal relationships—all within a hostile environment (Hunter 1995). Social development of the young gay person may be hampered because of this hostile environment where there are few if any adult role models for the adolescent to pattern or young people with whom to safely share the secret of homosexuality (Uribe and Harbeck 1991). Membership in a stigmatized minority group may lead to potentially psychologically harmful reactions like internalized homophobia, identification with the nongay dominant society, or denial (Martin and Hetrick 1988; Uribe and Harbeck 1991). Young gay people face violence, antilocution, discrimination, and the real possibility of being scapegoated at school or disowned at home simply on the basis of their sexual orientation (CWLA 1991; Hetrick and Martin 1987; Telljohann and Price 1993). Every gay or lesbian teenager must posses an incredible amount of psychological stamina to metamorphose into an adequately functioning individual. For the lesbian or gay teen, the journey and its struggles are even more precarious requiring much courage and resilience.

There seem to be a variety of ways young gay and lesbian people cope with the realization that their sexual identity differs from the norm. Some simply deny their same-sex feelings or activities by rationalization while others hide it by actively taking on roles and behaviors associated with the nongay society and engage in heterosexual behaviors as a "cover." Some internalize homophobia and loathe their same sex feelings or activities (leading some to suicide), and some openly flaunt their developing lesbian or gay identities (CWLA 1991; Grossman 1997; Hetrick and Martin 1987; Uribe and Harbeck 1991).

Gay and lesbian adolescents are as heterogeneous as their adult counterparts, but as a group are frequently overlooked as a minority population, or, if included, incorrectly thought to be a homogeneous group. If overlooked as a population, lesbian and gay youths are assumed by peers to be nongay; if included as a population, they are stigmatized (Herdt 1989). No small wonder then that one of the first things a developing gay or lesbian adolescent questions is whether or not her or his same-sex feelings are real. As adolescence is a time of both sexual and emotional development, denial is an easy path for one not ready or able to acknowledge a same-sexual or emotional orientation (CWLA 1991).

But once gay or lesbian identity has been acknowledged it becomes only part of a person's self-image. Creating a gay identity that is compatible with the teen's personality is often hampered by the adolescent's feeling of needing to hide her or his gay persona because of fear. While data demonstrate that college-age students are becoming more tolerant of same-sex relationships and sexual activities, junior and senior high school students are the most negative single group in their hatred of same-sex relationships (CWLA 1991). Data further demonstrate gay and lesbian youths whose sexual orientation is known or suspected are at extremely high risk of verbal abuse, physical abuse, victimization, harassment, sexual abuse, or institutional rejection from others while struggling with self-loathing, substance abuse, pregnancy, sexually transmitted diseases, mental health problems, or suicide from internalized homophobia (CWLA 1991; Grossman 1997; Telljohann and Price 1993).

Hiding seems a safe haven and many young gay and lesbian people go to great lengths not to have their true feelings made known. Adolescent lesbians may date, get pregnant, and have babies. Young gay men may engage in heterosexual sex, be the captain of the football team, or outwardly condemn "fags," "fairies," "fruits," and "queers." But, living a lie and a dual existence can take its toll on the young psyche and lead to symptoms such as depression or self-loathing which can lead to other risk factors, as noted. In sum, the socialization process of adolescents into both the nongay and gay worlds is a difficult one, posing special problems for gay youths. Unfortunately, it is a process often overlooked by professional social workers.

Coming-Out Models

Coming to grips with the social aspect of adolescence is accompanied by the awakening of sexuality. This development, characterized by the internalization of gender identity and role behavior, coupled with biological changes, adds a sexual dimension to the developing adolescent (Barker 1995; de Anda 1995). Biologically, gay and lesbian adolescents develop similarly to their nongay counterparts. The dimension that differentiates the two cohorts is that of sexual object—gay youths are sexually aroused by and emotionally attached to members of their own sex. As simple as this is to say, it is the cause of extraordinary anxiety, guilt, anger, fear, and self-destructive behaviors (CWLA 1991; Grossman 1997; Herdt 1989; Hetrick and Martin 1987).

The term "coming out" has been defined as the disclosure of a gay or lesbian identity to an increasing number of persons or the psychological and cultural processes by which people internalize a lesbian or gay identity (Savin-Williams 1990; Tully 1983). Since the 1970s several authors have created models that seem to define this developmental process for lesbian and gay people (Cass 1979; Chapman and Brannock 1987; Coleman 1981/82; McDonald 1982; Minton and McDonald 1994; Morris 1997; Savin-Williams 1996; Schneider 1989; Troiden 1989). While each has its own approach, the models tend to have certain shared characteristics (see table 4.1).

The social construction of the concept of homosexuality changes, given the historical era in which it is defined. So, today's queers, lesbians, and gay men are yesterday's lesbian feminists and gays; those terms having originated from earlier terms such as urnings, inverts, and homosexuals (Rust 1993). Also, there is general consensus that coming-out models, while appearing to be developmental and therefore linear, are not. A 60-year-old woman with grandchildren, for example, could come out as a lesbian without having gone through the agony of self-doubt or the confusion of identity clarification. More likely though, the development of a gay identity progresses through a series of multidimensional cognitive, behavioral, emotional, and sexual stages identified in the various coming-out models.

Frequently, though not always, the process of self-identification as a

---

TABLE 4.1
Common Themes in Coming-Out Models

Coming-out models tend to have the following elements in common:

An assumption that while appearing linear, the developmental phases are not. Individuals move through phases at different paces, may skip stages, or start at different places. This process is not related to chronological age.

An assumption that the coming-out process is multidimensional and includes cognitive, behavioral, emotional, and sexual aspects.

At some point the person feels different from the nongay individual because of an awareness of strong emotional attachments or sexual feelings for members of her or his own sex. These feelings may be ignored, repressed, denied, questioned, accepted, or acted on.

Once having identified the awareness and accepted its reality, the person begins to define the concept of homosexuality in an attempt to make it an acceptable part of the personality. This may include confusion about identity, initial involvement with the gay community, a beginning alienation from the nongay community, same sex experimentation, opposite sex experimentation, ambivalence, denial, or acceptance.

Having adopted a positive internalized acceptance of homosexuality as a social construct, the individual tends to become more closely involved with the gay community through the development of intimate personal relationships, the internalization of a gay identity, the disclosure to others of membership in the gay community, and the psychologically healthy view of self in spite of institutional homophobia.

---

gay or lesbian person begins quite early in life (Rust 1993; Telljohann and Price 1993; Troiden 1989), where the first stage in the development of a lesbian or gay identity seems to be an internal sense of feeling different from heterosexual people because of strong emotional alliances with or sexual feelings for members of the same sex. Some data indicate that young girls who do not fit stereotypic female roles in childhood or boys who are sensitive and more comfortable playing the piano than football tend to become lesbian or gay, but data are inconclusive as to the causes of homosexuality (Bailey et al. 1991; LeVay 1996). Sexuality, being a fluid construct, enables the individual to react to these socially unacceptable feelings in a variety of ways—from denial or repression to questioning, confusion, or acceptance (Cass 1979; Chapman and Brannock 1987; Coleman 1981/82; McDonald 1982; Minton and McDonald 1994; Morris 1997; Savin-Williams 1996; Schneider 1989; Troiden 1989).

Once an individual internally acknowledges the difference as being that of homosexuality, the person often becomes confused or ambivalent about being identified as a member of a hated and stigmatized minority group. This ambivalence and identity confusion is frequently unresolved until the person has a realistic perspective on what it means to be a gay or lesbian person that may be gained through increasing personal contacts with the gay community, interactions with gay friendly sites on the Internet, or information from scholarly publications. During this stage the person may engage in experimental heterosexual or homosexual liaisons in an effort to more fully determine and accept a sexual orientation different than the norm and gradually accept homosexuality as normal for him or her (Cass 1979; Chapman and Brannock 1987; Coleman 1981/82; McDonald 1982; Minton and McDonald 1994; Morris 1997; Savin-Williams 1996; Schneider 1989; Troiden 1989). If the person accepts homosexuality as a positive part of the self, heterosexuality becomes a negative force and attempts to change that person from a homosexual to a heterosexual orientation are intrapsychically damaging (Talan 1997; Weiss 1997).

Identity and social integration as a lesbian or gay person occurs once the individual has internalized what has been called a gay identity, where the person views her- or himself through a "self-identity" in social and sexual settings, a "perceived identity," where the person knows that others know of his or her sexual orientation, and a "presented identity," where the person presents openly in a variety of settings (social, educational, professional) as a gay or lesbian person (Troiden 1989). This final stage is variously referred to as the acceptance of a lesbian or gay consciousness (Morris 1997), a synthesis of gay pride and acceptance (Cass 1979), an integration of the private and public self into one self image (Coleman 1981/82), the establishment of a positive gay identity (McDonald 1982), the universalistic stage or last stage of ego development where role and ego identity merge (Minton and McDonald 1994), self disclosure (Schneider 1989), identity integration (Savin-Williams 1996), or quite simply, a choice of lifestyle (Chapman and Brannock 1987).

Coming Out as a Gay Youth: Family, Friends, and the Law

While coming out can be a confusing and difficult task for anyone, for those who question their sexual orientation early in life it is frequently a particularly harrowing experience. Disclosure of one's sexual orientation during adolescence has been shown to decrease feelings of guilt, help synthesize identity and ego integration, increase psychological adjustment, self-esteem, and positive identity, and increase the sense of individual freedom from having to live a lie. But, not telling because of the fear of hurting parents or facing rejection, harassment, or abuse immediately presents a psychological dilemma for the adolescent gay person who often wants to share this important part of the self with family members and others (Cramer and Roach 1988; Savin-Williams 1996).

Most gay and lesbian children are born into and raised in nongay family settings where parents, siblings, and other relatives have little understanding of, and often extreme negative feelings about, homosexuality. In short, many families are homophobic and the thought that a child in the family might be gay is horrifying to some parents. Parents assume children to be heterosexual and often the developing lesbian or gay adolescent is at odds with herself or himself, the family, and society (Tremble, Schneider, and Appathurai 1989). Data demonstrate that gay youths who do tell parents of their sexual orientation run the risk of having parents deny their statements, psychologically or physically isolate them, verbally or physically abuse them, or totally reject them. However, the scant data that have been collected on what happens when children tell parents of their sexual orientation show that as much as a decade may pass between when the child becomes aware of his or her sexual orientation and when the child shares that information with parents (Mallon in press; Patterson 1992). Parental reactions to the knowledge that they have a gay son or lesbian daughter are, at best, unpredictable, yielding mixed results (Cramer and Roach 1988; Savin-Williams 1989a).

Parents usually discover their child's lesbian or gay sexual identity by either finding it out accidentally or by having their child tell them. For example, Ella, a high school junior, and her best friend, Ruth, who was a high school sophomore, had come to the realization that what they felt for one another was more than mere friendship. When Ruth's mom attended a week-long medical convention, Ella had permission from her parents to spend the week at Ruth's so that Ruth would not have to be alone. When Ruth's mom came home unexpectedly and found Ella and Ruth in bed together, the reality of their situation became known.

Benjamin, age 17, had long thought of himself as gay and wanted to share this information with both of his parents. In preparation for this he had waited four years, rehearsing what he would say and when. When what he thought was the right moment came he sat with his parents in the living room and shared with them his secret.

Children live with the fear of being discovered. Whether their gay or lesbian sexual orientation is discovered by parents, siblings, or others

accidentally or whether parents or other family members are told voluntarily, those being told have usually not had much, if any, time to prepare
for what they are about to learn. This can set the stage for unfortunate
repercussions. A common parental reaction is guilt. A mother's lament,
"Have I been too overprotective? Did I cause my child to be this way?" is
frequently voiced. So, too, a father's anger as he denounces his gay son as
being a faggot and chastises his lesbian daughter as being a dyke. But, as
has been emphasized, the etiology of sexual orientation is unknown and
overprotective mothers or detached fathers are not generally seen as the
cause of same-sex behaviors.

Coming out to parents may yield unpredictable results. Some data
show that the better the relationship with her or his parents, the more
likely the parents will be to accept the child's atypical sexual orientation;
and the younger the child is when making sexual orientation known, the
easier it seems for parental acceptance (Cramer and Roach 1988; Savin-
Williams 1989a, 1996). Yet anecdotal data continue to point out how
hard it is for parents to accept a lesbian or gay child and that it is risky for
children to make their sexual orientation known to parents. It has also
been observed that the adolescent-parental relation tends to deteriorate
immediately after disclosure but improves with time. Mothers seem to be
more accepting than fathers and fathers who are poorly educated, authoritarian, and religious tend to exhibit greater hostility to a gay son. Telling
siblings seems to be easier than telling parents, and siblings tend to be
more understanding. Perhaps most significantly, the act of coming out,
while it may increase self-esteem and help the adolescent be honest and
feel closer to parents, is an extremely risky and difficult task, and the tim-
ing of the disclosure is of utmost importance (Cramer and Roach 1988;
Savin-Williams 1989a, 1989b, 1996).

Gay boys and lesbian girls tend to have same-sex sexual arousal feelings around the ages of 12 to 13, but boys usually act on those feelings earlier than girls. Boys tend to have their first same-sex sexual encounters by
age 15, whereas girls delay that event until they are 19 or 20 (Herdt 1989;
Rust 1993; Telljohann and Price 1993; Troiden 1989). One possible explanation may be that boys tend to place more emphasis on the physical act
of sex, where there is little need of a meaningful loving relationship. Girls
seem to want to develop a meaningful loving relationship with someone
before entering into a sexual relationship, and this often takes more time.

Living in a generally homophobic family environment where the family is not a source of support, where family members are not able to teach
the gay adolescent what it is like to be a member of an oppressed minor-

ity, and where there are usually no appropriate adult role models for the gay teen presents often unnecessary hardships on the adolescent, who must seek support outside the family unit (Gerstal, Feraios, and Herdt 1989; Morrow 1993).

Sadly, the problems encountered in the family setting are mirrored by those outside the family as well. Few community supports exist for the gay adolescent; schools are often hostile and homophobic places where the stigmatized lesbian or gay teen may face jeers, physical abuse, ridicule, or isolation; and friends, like family members, often do not understand. Coming out to friends may be easier than disclosure to parents and siblings, but telling friends may not always yield positive results, and the gay adolescent faces the possibility of peer rejection or isolation. As a result of institutionalized and internalized homophobia, young gay teenagers may avoid interpersonal peer group experiences because of the fear of discovery and, thereby, miss critical experiences for normal adolescent psychosocial development causing them to be at higher risk for physical and psychological dysfunction (Boxer and Cohler 1989; Grossman 1997; Herdt 1989; Morrow 1993; Telljohann and Price 1993; Uribe and Harbeck).

Those few social support structures whose sole mission is to provide services to lesbian and gay people frequently overlook the reality of lesbian and gay youth or are bound by state statute not to serve anyone below the age of consent. If services are offered to gay teenagers, it is not unheard of that the teenagers must have written parental permission to receive such services. Social service agencies designed to provide services to the general population tend to overlook all lesbians and gay people as a group and routinely assume that all adolescents are heterosexual. Finally, there are a few agencies designed specifically for gay and lesbian teens, but as with school counselors, workers must constantly be aware of legal constraints, religious beliefs, and social mores and values that often hamper the client-practitioner relationship (CWLA 1991; Hetrick and Martin 1987; Martin and Hetrick 1988; Schneider 1989; Sweet 1996; Vergara 1983/84). In sum, coming out for the young lesbian or gay person is not unlike walking through a minefield that starts at home and extends into every facet of society.

The Risks of Out-of-Home Placements

The relatively good news is that most lesbian and gay children live at home and manage to get through adolescence relatively intact. However, for those who are in need of out-of-home placements (placements in foster homes, group homes, or group care facilities), there are significant risk factors. The social work community, and indeed the community at large, tends to disregard gay and lesbian youths as a nonentity because of the generalized belief that children are not able to distinguish their sexuality. This population's invisibility is particularly evident in the child welfare community (Mallon in press).

The child welfare system has a responsibility to protect children, provide family centered services, promote permanent placements, provide culturally competent services, and place children in the least restrictive environment possible (CWLA 1991; Mallon in press). However, lesbian and gay youths who are either self-identified as such or whose actions make others identify them as such are often shuffled from placement to placement, abused by others in foster care, sexually molested, or beaten (Mallon in press). If in a foster home setting, the gay or lesbian youth is at risk of being assaulted, not only by other foster children but also by foster parents who do not want such a child in their care. If placed in a group-care facility, lesbian and gay children and adolescents also may face abuse at the hands of other group home residents or staff. For example, Juan, a 14-year-old Mexican American arrived in New Orleans during the spring of 1998. After living on the street for most of the summer he was arrested for petty theft and placed in a group home. His parents' whereabouts are unknown and he has been living on his own since he was 9 years old. He has a slight build, large dark eyes with long eyelashes, several pierced body parts, and a shaved head. His mannerisms are quite effeminate and he quietly acknowledges his gay sexual orientation. The first night he was placed in the group setting he was severely beaten by one of the other group members while the staff member stood by and watched. When the middle-aged social worker asked about his cuts, Juan remained silent.

Children who have been compelled into silence at home and in custodial care because of hostile environments have little recourse. How many gay and lesbian children are on the streets is not known, but it seems clear that for those who are unable to survive either at home or in traditional foster care settings or group homes the streets may seem a welcomed relief. In a country where there are only two social service agencies that provide services specifically related to lesbian and gay youths and their families (Gay and Lesbian Adolescent Social Services or GLASS in Los Angeles and Green Chimneys Services in New York City) (Mallon in press), there is great need to develop and implement services aimed at this underserved minority group. As noted, few persons are willing to discuss lesbian and gay children within the context of the child welfare sector. But one bold author and clinician, Gerald P. Mallon, whose book, *Let's Get this Straight: Issues of Sexual Orientation in Child Welfare* (in press) addresses these issues.

Multiple Jeopardy: The Racial or Ethnic Minority Gay or Lesbian

If coming out is thought to be difficult for a member of the white majority population, imagine the anxiety faced by adolescent gay members of ethnic minorities in the United States. While African-American, East Asian, or Latino families may be well-equipped to teach the gay adolescent what it is like to be a member of an oppressed ethnic minority, these families, like their Anglo counterparts, are ill-equipped to provide role models or even realistic information on growing up gay. Not only does the adolescent face racism but, too, homophobia. And the homophobia may be more feared than the racism (Liu and Chan 196; Savin-Williams 1996; Telljohann and Price 1993).

Several issues are associated with coming out for racial and ethnic minorities. Because of various cultural taboos, admitting to the traditional nongay family that one is gay presents difficulties; finding one's place in the usually white gay community without facing racism is awkward; and reconciling one's racial or ethnic identity with sexual orientation is hard (Tremble, Schneider, and Appathurai 1989).

Various cultures view homosexuality in various ways but, generally, for many of the cultures living in the United States, homosexuality as a social construct is not accepted as something to be valued or even tolerated. For example, East Asians (Chinese, Japanese, and Koreans) share the influences of Buddha and Confucius, where the family is seen as the most basic unit of the social structure and familial roles and obedience are highly honored and homosexuality is not part of the philosophical thought. Gay couples are not recognized and the concept of homosexuality is not well understood (Liu and Chan 1996). But in the Latino community some that practice homosexual acts may not be labeled as deviant, for only those men who assume a passive (feminine) role in same-sex sexual acts are so labeled. And some groups of the African American community think homosexuality is not indigenous to their community and therefore may ignore the concept as not germane (Grossman 1997; Savin-Williams 1996). Coming out for ethnic or racial minorities may put the adolescent in jeopardy of dishonoring the family by bringing shame and disrespect to the family unit or being rejected by often closely knit multigenerational families or communities (Hunter 1995; Liu and Chan 1996; Savin-Williams 1996).

Coupled with the conflicts associated with integrating a gay identity with that of a racial or ethnic identity within the family, the individual must also cope with trying to assimilate into the gay community. Racial and ethnic communities are often too small to support gay and lesbian communities within them and, in many cases, the white gay community may be only slightly more accepting of racial differences than the society at large. Where does a young person who is part of a racial or ethnic minority who is also lesbian or gay fit in? The answer is, sadly, yet to be defined (Savin-Williams 1996; Tremble, Schneider, and Appathurai 1989).

Another issue confronting the racial or ethnic minority gay adolescent is that of trying to reconcile a gay identity with that of a racial or ethnic identity. Often, as in the white community, there is little compatibility. Lesbian and gay children grow up in heterosexual families where they are socialized with values and beliefs that are different from their self-identification. And, for ethnic or racial minority youth, the problem may be compounded by the impact of both racism and homophobia. The lack of appropriate role models, adequate and realistic information, and family support may lead to issues of inadequate self-esteem; isolation; living dual identities; trying to cope with incompatible cultural and social roles and expectations; and psychological adjustments in dealing with the dominant social structure, the racial or ethnic subculture, and the gay community (Hunter 1995; Liu and Chan 1996; Savin-Williams 1996; Telljohann and Price 1993).

Like all gay adolescents, members of ethnic or racial minorities are at risk for a number of possible psychosocial problems from the nongay culture, families and gay community. Tables 4.2 and 4.3 outline the realities of being a gay adolescent and the risk factors associated with such status. Along with the many crises associated with growing up gay come opportunities for growth, self acceptance, the development of appropriate coping and social skills, the creation and maintenance of intimate same-sex relations, and the chance for developing a healthy gay identity.

The Empowerment Approach

Growing up in a homophobic society where the physical and emotional expression of one's love is vilified and, in many localities, illegal, has been associated with any number of potentially psychologically damaging feelings and behaviors, from loneliness to suicide ideation. The practitioner

TABLE 4.2
Realities of Growing Up Gay

The following represent realities faced by most young people as they struggle to develop a lesbian or gay identity:

A lack of easily accessible, adequate, and unbiased materials from which to determine the realities of a gay lifestyle;

A deficiency in the number of appropriate adult role models in life, books, or the media;

Inadequate resources to effectively cope with racial and ethnic diversity coupled with sexual identity;

An overabundance of misinformation, myths, and stereotypes about gays;

A scarcity of adequate social support structures at the micro-, mezzo- , and macro-levels;

Incongruity between the nongay norm and internal gay feelings or actions; and

Feelings of stigmatization, isolation, and anomie; the development of defense mechanisms to deal with such feelings.

must understand the realities of growing up gay, specific risk factors associated with lesbian or gay adolescents, and how pragmatically to use the empowerment approach when providing services to young gay clients.

Teenagers traditionally learn to be sexually mature individuals at home, in school, church, or peer group settings, or through activities with community agencies such as Boy or Girl Scouts, where they are taught not only about the physiological aspects of sexuality, but also attitudes, values, and decision making about sexual activity (Shapiro 1980). Because these traditional ways are heterosexually biased, the lesbian or gay youth, as previously noted, is at high risk for needing social work intervention as she or he negotiates both the nongay and gay worlds. The following sections explore, from an empowerment perspective, how social workers can work effectively with young gay and lesbian clients at the micro-, mezzo-, and macro-levels of social work practice.

Micro-Level Intervention

While adult gays and lesbians are virtually invisible, they do constitute an acknowledged minority; lesbian and gay youth are thought not to exist

(CWLA 1991; Grossman 1997; Liu and Chan 1996; Savin-Williams 1996; Shapiro 1980; Uribe and Harbeck; Vergara 1983/84). With this continuing assumption of everyone's heterosexuality comes the social worker's first challenge—the acknowledgment that gay and lesbian children, adolescents, and young adults do, in fact, constitute an at-risk minority population within the United States. Clinicians must also avoid the trap of believing that not all children are able to distinguish their lesbian or gay identity at a fairly early age. Although few data exist as to when children begin to think they are not heterosexual, some studies show that even very young children are able to identify their sexual orientation (Herdt 1989; Rust 1993; Telljohann and Price 1993; Troiden 1989). Once these realities are established, the clinician is in a position to approach the considerable challenges associated with working with lesbian and gay youths. Mallon (in press) believes clinicians should practice from a "gay- and lesbian-affirming perspective" that is rooted in the ecological perspective and affirms a lesbian or gay identity across a lifetime. Such a perspective also demands that the practitioner not try to change someone's sexual orientation or do anything to denigrate the individual's sexual identity. A lesbian- and gay-affirming perspective also is inherent within the empowerment perspective.

Adolescents seek psychotherapeutic intervention in regard to their sexual orientation for several reasons. They may be part of a highly structured, rigid, and punitive family environment that is extremely religious and rabidly homophobic; they may have had negative childhood experiences related to being deviant; they may have had specific antihomosexual experiences; they may be suffering from psychopathology that is affecting their sexual identity; or they may have been sexually abused. Further, they may be suffering from cognitive, social or emotional isolation, violence, or substance abuse (Hanley-Hackenbruck 1989; Martin and Hetrick 1988; Savin-Williams 1996). Therapeutic intervention with this population presents its own set of challenges based on general societal proscriptions, legal sanctions, and religious values.

A significant difficulty many social workers encounter is that because of homophobia (institutional, individual, and internal), lesbian and gay youths fail to identify themselves as such. So, the reality is that frequently social workers working with lesbian and gay youths do so without specific knowledge of a person's sexual orientation. A poignant example is that of Salvatore, a 12-year-old handsome bully who was just coming to terms with his sexuality. During a self-support group at the local gay and lesbian community center, the friend he had brought to the group meet-

TABLE 4.3
Risk Factors Associated with Lesbian or Gay Youth

Gay and lesbian adolescents have been determined to be at a high risk for the following:

FROM THE NONGAY SOCIETY

Verbal abuse;
Sexual abuse or exploitation;
Physical abuse;
Scapegoating;
Victimization;
Employment discrimination;
Oppression;
Stigmatization;
Cultural isolation.

FROM THE GAY COMMUNITY

Lack of appropriate role models;
Insufficient resources and services;
Ignorance of the population;
Fear of interpersonal relationships between adults and adolescents;
Legal restraints restricting interactions;
Racism.

FROM THE FAMILY

Verbal abuse;
Physical abuse;
Family disruption or crisis;
Rejection;
Emotional distancing;
Lack of compassion;
Guilt;
Isolation.

POSSIBLE CONSEQUENCES TO THE GAY OR LESBIAN ADOLESCENT

School dropout or lowered grades;
Depression;

TABLE 4.3 (continued)
Risk Factors Associated with Lesbian or Gay Youth

POSSIBLE CONSEQUENCES TO THE GAY OR LESBIAN ADOLESCENT

Isolation;

Fear;

Developmental delays;

Severe psychopathology;

Substance abuse;

Poor self image, lowered self-esteem;

Homelessness;

Increased chance of HIV, STDs, or pregnancy;

Suicide;

Prostitution.

ing, Carl, an effeminate-looking 15-year-old, was verbally harassed by other group members. Feeling responsible for getting his friend into an awful situation, Salvatore ran from the room as Carl wept. The issues of homophobia and the resulting consequences of it can be devastating at the personal, interpersonal, and institutional level.

In dealing with such situations, certain barriers to the provision of services must first be addressed. Such barriers include the clinician's lack of understanding of the needs of the population, a dearth of appropriate literature on the topic, general misunderstandings about lesbian and gay youth, few appropriate role models, lack of service integration, and few, if any supports for the families of gay and lesbian children and adolescents (CWLA 1991; Morrow 1993). Additionally, lesbian and gay youths may be hard to identify because their sexual orientation is often ignored, denied, considered irrelevant to the provision of social services, or assumed to be heterosexual. Agency personnel are generally inadequately trained to deal with homosexuality and the topic creates fear in both workers and clients. As a result, gay and lesbian youths may not use available social services such as health care, religious organizations, youth programs, welfare agencies, or other service providers (CWLA 1991; Martin and Hetrick 1988; Morrow 1993). In sum, in order to effectively empower gay and lesbian youths to help identify and solve their problems, these barriers need to be overcome or at least dealt with.

Overcoming these obstacles includes the creation of a homosocial and safe environment for the gay or lesbian adolescent to begin to find, accept, affirm, and integrate a positive self-image. To accomplish this, the clinician must realize that sexual orientation is nonvolitional, that it cannot be engineered through psychiatric intervention, that young people may need therapeutic intervention to discover a personal sexual orientation that will provide them the most fulfillment. Additionally, when working with ethnic minorities or minorities of color, the therapist needs an understanding of how long the family has been in the United States, what are the prevailing ethnic values and customs related to its culture, how strongly these mores are followed, what language is spoken in the home, what is the religious philosophy of the family, and what are the family's views and beliefs about gender roles, sexuality, and homosexuality (Grossman 1997; Liu and Chan 1996; Savin-Williams 1996).

For example, Thuy, a Vietnamese immigrant arrived in the United States during the late 1970s with her parents. She was 4 years old when she arrived and the family settled on the west bank of the Mississippi River in New Orleans, where several other Vietnamese families lived. She considered herself an American, but was culturally bound to her ethnic roots. She was now 20 and being seen at the gay community center's outreach social service program because she was experiencing difficulty reconciling her lesbianism with her Vietnamese heritage and was having a hard time finding an accepting peer group. The social worker, an Anglo, certainly knew about the young adult gay and lesbian activities in the city, but knew little of Vietnamese culture. The worker had initially prepared to meet Thuy by reading about Vietnamese culture and eating at a Vietnamese restaurant. Thus prepared, the two met and entered each other's world. Once an assessment was made both agreed to some tentative goals. This meant that the worker could learn about Vietnamese culture and that Thuy could learn about the young lesbian and gay culture in New Orleans. Such an egalitarian approach emphasizes a mutuality and willingness on the part of the practitioner and the client to start where they both are and move forward from that point.

While overcoming cultural and ethnic barriers is one area of concern, so, too, are factors related to the reactions of family members when they are confronted with the possibility that one of their children could be something other than heterosexual: the general lack of support for a gay lifestyle; proscriptive religious teachings about homosexuality; a legal system that supports only heterosexuality; and the promise of confidentiality between client and therapist. It is small wonder then that it has been said the primary task of psychotherapy with young lesbians and gays is to work on the effects of internalized homophobia that lead to psychological dysfunction (Sweet 1996).

The same kinds of interventive roles and strategies used with nongay populations can be used effectively with gay and lesbian adolescents as each has its place in the empowerment approach. At the micro-level, the roles of social broker, enabler, teacher, mediator, and advocate used with the strategies of sustainment, direct influence, exploration-description-ventilation and reflective discussion of the person-in-situation work well when combined with the use of a nonjudgmental and nonhomophobic approach to therapy where the client's narrative becomes the focus of the intervention and where the clinician is supportive and knowledgeable about homosexuality (Compton and Galaway 1994; Kaplan and Saperstein 1985; Simon 1994; Solomon 1976, 1985; Woods and Hollis 1990). Of additional use when working with lesbian or gay adolescents is assertiveness skills training where such techniques as modeling, instruction, behavior rehearsal, or video feedback are used (McKinlay, Kelly, and Patterson 1977). These techniques reinforce the individual's ability to find effective solutions to personal dilemmas.

And, just as traditional social work roles are used in the empowerment approach, so to are the traditional steps in the process. Those include initial preparation for the meeting between the client and the worker. Not only does the worker prepare for this encounter, so, too, does the client. Following the initial preparation comes the actual initial meeting. For those working with younger gays and lesbians this meeting may take place at school, in a client's home or foster care setting, at a community center, in a hospital, on the street, or in a juvenile detention facility. This initial meeting is crucial. A worker who will have success with younger clients must understand and speak whatever is current in "kid-speak" simply because standard English will quite probably be inadequate. Assuming the language between the client and social worker is not a barrier, assessing client strengths and appraisal of the current situation is the next step. The dialogue between the client and worker requires a mutual respect for one another—gaining this respect from some untrusting adolescents can create its own dilemmas and needs to be assured before real progress can be made. However, in this world of managed care and a demand for quick, measurable success, professional modeling of appropriate behaviors and affirming the client's identity may be more crucial than her or his respect for the worker. Once goals and possible solutions to problems have been identified, it becomes time for the client to test the solutions. If the solutions work and the problem is solved, the time for evaluation has arrived. At this point other issues may have surfaced or the end of service has come. In working with children and young adults the termination process needs to be one that allows for future services if the need arises.

For example, Dusty, a 19-year-old gay Phish follower and sometimes cocaine user, trails the band and is well known to social workers across the United States. Because of his drug habit he is often in trouble with the law, but his wealthy family bails him out. After the band played at the New Orleans Jazz and Heritage Festival in 1997, he decided he liked the city. He arrives in January each year and departs when it gets hot (usually around June). His requests from social workers center on food and housing. Once these needs are met he fails to keep appointments and disappears into the bowels of the French Quarter reappearing the following year with the same needs.

The same social work roles and processes work with the empowerment approach at the micro-level, but what about the choice of therapist? Data indicate that while college age gay or lesbian persons prefer therapists or counselors who are themselves openly lesbian or gay (Sweet 1996), no such data are available for those therapists working with gays and lesbians who have not yet reached the legal age of consent. This reality presents an ethical dilemma for the therapist, who must decide whether or not the young gay person and her or his parents should be made aware of the therapist's sexual orientation.

Self-disclosure of a social worker to a child or adolescent is not without risk. In the late 1990s there was a political surge from the religious right to ensure what has become known as "family values." These values, simply stated, are supportive of the traditional family comprised of a heterosexually married couple with children. Gay and lesbian persons are viewed as in need of psychiatric and religious intervention to extinguish same-sex behaviors. This conservative mind-set opposes gay rights in any form and views homosexuality as threatening the fabric of the traditional American family. One view, held by radical right conservatives, is that gay and lesbian adults recruit children to a homosexual lifestyle. This is done in the schools and must be stopped. While gay and lesbian groups lobby for equal protection as stated in the 14th Amendment, right-wing conservatives introduce bills condemning such equality.

What this means for the lesbian or gay practitioner working with gay and lesbian children and adolescents is simply that it may be illegal to discuss sexuality with children, much less approve of a same-sex lifestyle.

Social workers need to know what the laws of their area allow and, while not doing harm to young, confused, scared, or curious children who are dealing with their own sexuality, be as affirming as is possible. By assuring youngsters that they are not the only ones who have felt an attraction to a member of their own sex, by providing them with honest reading materials, by being affirming, and by being supportive the worker can convey a sense of trust and lack of homophobia even without acknowledging personal sexual orientation. Just as most people assume others to be nongay, most young clients also assume social workers to be nongay. So, by affirming their identity and struggles, lesbian and gay youths will be better able to work through their dilemmas.

Revealing one's sexual orientation can be awkward for both the professional and the client. It has been said that coming out is a lifetime process because we are constantly put in the position of meeting new people. It rarely seems to get easier, probably because of continuing homophobia. However, young gays and lesbians have few role models and, when possible, it is important for the social worker to be as honest with the client as is possible. Thus, revealing to a client that you are a lesbian or gay social worker can help the relationship simply because you are in an excellent position to understand the struggles and rewards of a gay or lesbian lifestyle. There are some social workers who, while lesbian or gay, tell their clients that their personal lifestyle is not germane to the therapeutic process and do not share this information. This nondisclosure seems somehow antithetical to the empowerment perspective.

Finally, the issue of the confidential nature of the interactions between the gay or lesbian adolescent and the clinician deserves special mention. Parents often feel they have a right to confidential information obtained as a result of conversations between their child and a therapist. In general, if a child is in therapy, the need for confidentiality about her or his issues is vital even in the face of prying or insistent parents (Woodman and Lenna 1980). Further, premature disclosure of an adolescent's sexual orientation before she or he has an opportunity to fairly well consolidate that sexual identity and self-acceptance can be damaging not only to the individual, but to the family as well (Savin-Williams 1996).

A key construct of the empowerment approach is that of the use of narrative where the client, in concert with the therapist, defines issues, possible solutions, and strategies for problem-solving. For example, a young Asian adolescent all-state wrestler has been referred, by the wrestling coach, to a high school social worker because his grades have dropped and, while not overweight, he has recently lost twenty pounds.

The therapist, knowledgeable of issues associated with coming out, and employing a nonjudgmental and nonhomophobic approach, allows the student to tell his own story in his own way. The narrative becomes the cornerstone for the definition of the presenting problem (lowered grades and weight loss) which, once the student feels safe, leads to a better understanding between the student and the therapist as to possible causes for the problem.

In this example, the student had been having feelings of same-sex sexual attraction for the past year and was unable to accept that he could be gay, as he was also sexually attracted to girls his own age. His family, second-generation Koreans, expected him, as the eldest son, to marry once he completed college and constantly praised him for his academic achievements and the grandchildren he would produce. The multiple issues confronting this adolescent get prioritized according to the client's needs and, as the young man, through a supportive therapeutic encounter, is empowered not only to identify the underlying causes for the presenting problem, but also to help create possible solutions. This egalitarian approach, where the client brings certain strengths to the clinical setting and the therapist encourages the ongoing narrative, does, in the case of lesbian and gay youths, require attention to those items identified in table 4.4.

Mezzo-Level Interaction

The empowerment of lesbian and gay youths at the mezzo-level begins with the social worker's understanding of and involvement with the gay community and its resources available to lesbian and gay youths. Sadly, in most communities, activities in the gay community for its young members are grossly inadequate if they exist at all. While the reasons for the lack of adequate social services and other resources for younger gays and lesbians are often rooted in a homophobic legal system (Schneider 1989), the gay community itself has been slow to embrace the needs of its younger generation in an inclusive way (Laird and Green 1996; Savin-Williams 1996; Woodman and Lenna 1980). This continues to be a serious problem, yet one that can be challenged and changed by social work practitioners willing to become community organizers and advocates on behalf of lesbian and gay youths within both the gay and nongay communities.

Community activism could include such activities as organizing events with and for gay and lesbian youths; working within existing community organizations such as churches, recreational facilities, neighborhood associations, etc., to dispel myths and stereotypes about gay youth; pro-

TABLE 4.4
Providing Services to Lesbian and Gay Adolescents

For clinicians working with gay or lesbian young people, the following points should be considered:

AT THE MICRO-LEVEL

Accept the reality that lesbian and gay youth exist;

Understand risk factors associated with being a gay or lesbian adolescent;

Avoid stereotyping young gay clients;

Do not assume all young clients are heterosexual;

Be comfortable with personal sexuality and not homophobic;

Act as a role model;

Understand the complex issues and stages associated with coming out;

View the young lesbian or gay person as a member of an oppressed minority, not as a pathological entity;

Do not assume that the presenting problem is related to issues of sexual orientation;

Be supportive and allow the young person the opportunity to tell her/his story;

Understand the triple jeopardy status of young gays who are also members of oppressed ethnic or racial minorities;

Become culturally sensitive and aware of racial and ethnic cultures different from your own;

Be cautious, but aware of reparative therapy and other dangerous techniques designed to "cure" homosexuality;

Realize that sexual identity formation is a complex issue and that sexual activity alone does not necessarily equate with a homosexual identity;

View the internalization and externalization (covert and overt behaviors) of identity formation as a time of stress;

Respect client confidentiality.

AT THE MEZZO-LEVEL

Become aware of the gay community and its resources;

View the person within the context of both the nongay and gay communities;

Become a community advocate for gay and lesbian adolescents;

Train agency workers to effectively work with lesbian and gay youth;

Implement agency nondiscrimination policies;

Adopt inclusive agency policies at all levels;

Include the needs of gay and lesbian youth in advocacy efforts;

Embrace youth empowerment.

(continued)

TABLE 4.4 (continued)
Providing Services to Lesbian and Gay Adolescents

AT THE MACRO-LEVEL

Understand state, local, and federal laws related to sexual orientation;

Become a state and federal advocate for gay and lesbian youth;

Build coalitions dedicated to the needs of younger lesbians and gays;

Challenge discriminatory laws and policies related to sexual orientation;

Confront institutional homophobia aimed at gay and lesbian youth at the local, state, and national levels;

Become active in organizations dedicated to assisting lesbian and gay youth.

---

viding lesbian and gay sensitivity training to volunteer workers at a teen center; or acting as the information and referral expert for lesbian and gay teens in crisis through a gay friendly crisis telephone hot line. Given the risks associated with being a gay or lesbian adolescent and the paucity of mezzo-level services that are currently in place, those social workers who have an interest in this level of intervention can have a tremendous impact on defining and implementing services that will provide a corner-stone for future development.

New Orleans has a large number of adolescents and young adults living on the street. The exact number of homeless lesbian and gay youths in the city is unknown, but that they exist is not in doubt. Their primary habitat, and the habitat of most of the city's homeless population, is the French Quarter. The French Quarter is a 70-block area, close to the Mississippi River, that was the original settlement of New Orleans, and now houses lovely historic buildings, antique shops, restaurants, bars, t-shirt and souvenir stores, striptease joints, and bars. It is also the center of the city's tourism and home to New Orleans' only community center for lesbians and gays. The center, funded through donations, is on a major thoroughfare and provides what minimal social services are available for the city's lesbian and gay youths. Although the City of New Orleans does not discriminate on the basis of sexual orientation and provides a domestic partnership registry, it is still illegal in Louisiana to engage in same-sex sexual behaviors. The center, while providing support groups and an information and referral services to gay and lesbian youths requires that those under the age of consent have written parental permission before services can be provided. Such restrictions decrease the numbers of potential clients and restrict the services that could potentially be available.

There is no full-time social worker associated with the center, but rather volunteer MSWs who run group programs provide information and referrals and do crisis intervention. Much of their work is with lesbian and gay youths—many of whom are on the streets. Coupled with this active volunteer staff is the equally active group, Parents, Families, and Friends of Lesbians and Gays (PFLAG) and an active board of directors. Children in the state of Louisiana, as they are in other states, are generally unable to act as advocates for themselves. This is certainly true in the case of lesbian and gay youths. But, when surrounded by a supportive and gay-affirming (Mallon in press) group of advocates, those voices that have been forced into silence will be heard.

In addition to the issue of who is eligible for services is the issue of reparative therapy. One young man, Doug, a native of New Orleans, sought services from the center because his parents had discovered his sexual orientation and were in the process of having him become involved in an inpatient program to cure his homosexuality. At 16 he was unable to go against his family's wishes, so he ran away. Sadly, for this individual there were no easy answers because of state law. But, what his situation demonstrated to those advocacy groups associated with the center was to provide more data that will eventually help promote policy change.

One avenue available was the use of the center's self-help support group for youth. This group, a dynamic boisterous one that meets weekly, has been part of the center's activities for about three years, and is a textbook example of what a self-help group should be. Membership is limited to young lesbians and gays. Formed and controlled by members, the group provides assistance in a timely, informal manner, each member helps other members, and group activities are based on personal knowledge and expertise. The role of the social worker was to get the group started, act as a consultant, and make referrals to the group. One of the social workers referred Doug to the group (King and Mayers 1985).

Doug's arrival into the group acted as a catalyst because other group members, too, had been faced with similar reactions from their parents. Group members did not believe being queer to be a bad thing, but it had bad consequences. Such consequences included harassment, abuse, rape, and a general lack of understanding. From the group process emerged a goal to make the needs of gay kids known. Supported by the social worker, board of directors, and PFLAG the initiative to provide a voice to their needs began.

This example of community organization merely skims the surface of needs related to lesbian and gay youths; however it does demonstrate how various opportunities lead to various solutions. And, while the solution to an individual problem (like being forced into reparative therapy) may not be immediately attainable, getting realistic information about the needs of gay and lesbian kids may eventually lead to better services for lesbian and gay youths.

Macro-Level Interaction

While services for lesbian and gay youths have been fairly well defined and implemented at the micro-level, but not too well defined or implemented at the mezzo-level, even fewer social workers are exploring the needs of gay and lesbian youths at the macro-level. And, although it has been acknowledged that institutional homophobia is a reality and that social workers are just as homophobic as the general population (Clark, Brown, and Hochstein 1990; DeCrescenzo and McGill 1978; Tate 1991; Wisniewski and Toomey 1978), there is little or no evidence that much of anything related to these issues is being investigated, challenged, or corrected. This reality presents endless opportunities for social work practitioners who have an interest in macro-level intervention.

Changing systems to accommodate the needs of those within the system has been one theme of social work since its inception and can trace its antecedent roots to the settlement house movement. Instead of changing people to accept their surroundings, the ideological philosophy of "changing systems" fits well within the empowerment perspective as it encourages those in need to challenge and redesign the existing social structures to meet the needs of a given population. For the practitioner who wishes to confront the prevailing system that has defined and implemented its policies related to lesbian and gay adolescents, the first step is to examine state, local, and federal laws related to that particular population. Armed with this knowledge, the macro-level practitioner is in a better position to refute existing policies and laws and, in turn, become an advocate for this overlooked population.

Coalition building is an extremely important activity for those who advocate on behalf of lesbian and gay adolescents and, as lobbyists soon learn, coalitions of groups are influential when challenging existing discriminatory laws and public policies related to sexual orientation. Coalitions, too, play an important role in confronting institutional homophobia wherever it is found.

The concept of leadership is of the utmost importance, for without individual leadership, coalitions will not be formed, letters to lawmakers will not be written, policies will go unchallenged, and issues related to gay and lesbian youths will suffer. Viewed from a person-in-environment, empowerment perspective, social workers are well suited to assume a leadership role at the macro-level and could be of extreme importance as services for gay and lesbian adolescents become more defined, staffs gain expertise and training in how to deal with this population, discriminatory laws and public policies are challenged, proscriptive religious dogmas are disputed, and social customs and traditions about younger gay men and lesbians evolve.

When considering lesbian and gay youths, there is probably no greater need for intervention at the macro-level than within the school system. The school system of the United States is a complex series of interlocking federal and state laws coupled with local school board ordinances, policies, and procedures. Implemented by individual principals and teachers the schoolroom provides an important forum for the development of this country's children. It is a powerful arena. It is so powerful that political forces on both sides of the liberal-to-conservative continuum are focusing attention to the issue of the teaching of sexuality, and specifically, the issue of teaching content related to same-sex sexuality (CCW 1998c; GLSEN 1998).

The first organization whose objectives include the ending of homophobia in the public school system (kindergarten through twelfth grade) is the Gay, Lesbian, and Straight Education Network (GLSEN). Begun in 1990, the grassroots organization of teachers, parents, students, and other concerned citizens conducts in-class/school training, acts as advocates, and is involved in community organizing. Its major aim is to eliminate antigay discrimination. To accomplish this goal GLSEN creates curricular modules, distributes educationally related resources, and is waging war on antigay laws, policies, and procedures. Teamed with other pro-gay youth organizations such as PFLAG, GLSEN and all those concerned with the rights of gay and lesbian children, adolescents, and young adults face fierce opposition from the religious right.

The religious right, coupled with some few psychiatrists and members of the political extreme right wing, contends homosexuality is a curable disease that warrants appropriate psychiatric and spiritual intercession. Even though the American Psychiatric Association removed homosexuality from its list of mental disorders in 1973, some clinicians still cling to the outdated and dangerous belief that reparative therapy can cure same-sex sexual behaviors (Bieber 1965; Nicolosi 1991; Socarides 1978). Children who exhibit what parents, teachers, or peers identify as inappropriate gender behaviors are vulnerable to being labeled as lesbian or gay. Parents, in an effort to cure their child, often take extreme measures.

Further, the religious right charges that through the classroom, lesbian and gay teachers recruit children to a homosexual lifestyle (CCW 1997). This belief furthers their attempts to thwart efforts on the part of pro-gay groups to ensure that realistic information about sexual development and sexual orientation is made available to all parents, teachers, and students through the school setting. Antigay groups are fighting to ensure that the pro-gay agenda remains outside the school setting. No doubt this, and other macro-level activities aimed at protecting the rights of a still virtually invisible minority, will be the focus of those interested in the well-being of a group whose voice must be made heard through others.

The Empowerment Model Applied

The preceding sections have provided an overview of empowerment and its general application at the micro-, mezzo-, and macro-levels of social work intervention with adolescents and young adults. Using an adolescent example, the following section demonstrates more specifically how the model can be applied. For this chapter, the model will be applied at the micro-level of intervention. Chapter 5 will include a mezzo-level example, and chapter 6 will use a macro-level example of the empowerment model. Referring to figure 3.3, and tables 3.1 and 3.3 may be helpful.

As an example, assume you are a social worker in an urban public high school. A 16-year-old male has been referred to you because of failing grades.

He presents himself as a quiet, ordinary-looking white teenager who is dressed totally in black. He is polite, had been an honor student until the past semester, has never been in trouble, and seems withdrawn and depressed. He is of average height and weight and characterizes himself as "not fitting in" with most of his student colleagues. Along with his books, he has a copy of a gay-oriented magazine, *The Advocate*. As his story emerges it becomes evident that he is struggling with his sexual identity. His parents are devoutly religious and extremely homophobic. He has gone on-line to find what he could, spent time in the library, had sexual relations with girls, and tried to talk to his best friend about his sexuality. His conversation with his best friend was not held in confidence and rumors about him being a "faggot" spread quickly throughout the school. For months, he has been taunted, marginalized, and made into a scapegoat. He is no longer able to study, he is flunking all of his courses, and he believes his life to have little meaning. He is not sleeping well, has little appetite, cares nothing about his hygiene or personal appearance, and is generally viewed as withdrawn. He stated he has considered suicide and sees that as a viable option.

In applying empowerment principles in this instance, you would allow the client's narrative to evolve in a nonthreatening way but with the realization that there is a real potential for possible suicide. Thus, the client must not be empowered to follow through with his thoughts of harming himself (or others), but rather empowered to identify more acceptable behaviors using resources identified by himself and you. This goal must be accomplished with a respect for the client's rights and an emphasis on his responsibilities in his existing psychosocial environment. Strengths can be assessed through the development of a genogram and eco-map that includes both biologic and friendship networks. A working knowledge of the coming-out process and its associated struggles may help to diffuse the volatile situation, and the development of an egalitarian relationship between you and the client may provide necessary support during this time of crisis. Understanding difficulties faced by most lesbian and gay teenagers as they struggle with issues of sexual identity in a homophobic social structure will also ensure better understanding between you and the client. In this case, the homophobia has been internalized and must be assessed in terms of what meaning it has for him. Likewise, how individual homophobia (homophobia directed at him by his friends) and institutional homophobia (homophobia as seen in the policies and practices of the school setting) have impacted his life must be evaluated through ongoing dialogue. In sum, a nonjudgmental approach where the client is allowed to give voice to his particular situation and is able to begin to differentiate a variety of approaches using all available resources, should enable him to successfully master the immediate crisis and ensure a positive resolution to what could have become a tragedy.

With these, and other empowerment principles in mind, the following provide opportunities for applying these concepts to case studies.

Case Studies

The following case vignettes, one each at each level of intervention (micro-, mezzo-, and macro-levels) are designed to stimulate thought and provide a basis for discussion. Items to keep in mind include a definition of the presenting problem; issues that underlie the presenting problem; the role of the client and the therapist; the supportive and nonsupportive environments of the client; the interactions between the gay and nongay communities as applicable to the case; the role of institutional, individual, and internal homophobia; and the application of the empowerment perspective.

Coming Out to the Family
Gregor is a 20-year-old whose parents were divorced when he was 8 years old. Since both parents share custody of Gregor and his younger sister Elena, age 17, they spend an equal amount of time in the household of each parent. With only a high school diploma, Gregor's dad, Sampson, was in a middle management position in a manufacturing company where he had worked his way up from the assembly line to his current administrative position. A burly fellow, Sampson enjoyed his evenings at the local bar and telling raucous, but loving, stories about his son and providing glowing accounts of his daughter's activities. He atoned for his overindulgences at the bar by never missing Sunday mass at St. Mary's Catholic Church he and his father before him had attended. He insisted that his children, too, be "good Catholics" and missing mass was not an option.

The children's mother, Helen, got a job as a waitress following her divorce and had worked her way up to the role of head hostess and cashier. Also a devout Catholic, she, too, believed in the power of the church and never missed mass. When the children were with her on Sundays, they went to her church, St. Luke's. In an attempt to better herself, Helen started taking night classes at the local college where she developed an interest in psychology. She will be graduated in another semester and is thinking about working on a master's degree either in psychology, counseling, or social work. Gregor attends the same college during the day. Helen is extremely proud of both her children, but especially of her firstborn, the strapping, talented, good-looking college quarterback, Gregor.

In order to save money, both children still live with their parents. Elena is completing her senior year in high school. Gregor, who has always been a well-developed lad, was the captain of the high school football team and dated the head cheerleader, Lara, throughout high school. Everyone assumed Gregor and Lara would eventually marry. However, Gregor, after years of denying his sexual feelings for other men, had come to realize that he was, in fact, homosexual. He had recently become sexually involved with an older college student, Armand, who was Ethiopian. Armand had been president of the college ACT UP organization, and was well known on campus as being gay. Gregor had told his sister last year about his sexual orientation because he was tired of living a lie. She was moderately supportive, but cautioned him against telling their father. Gregor and Armand were scheduled to have dinner with Helen next. Gregor wanted very much to tell his family who he was and Armand agreed it was a wise thing to do. Gregor has been coming to you for counseling about coming out. What steps need to be taken?

The School Prom

Kate, a 17-year-old high school senior, had been a sexually active lesbian since she was 15. Her family was aware of her sexual orientation, and while they were concerned about her lesbianism because of the stigma attached to homosexuality, they were generally accepting of her and her current girlfriend, Cecelia. Cecelia and Kate had been best friends since they had been toddlers. Cecelia, a year older than Kate, was enrolled in her freshman year at college. The two managed to see each other about twice a month and on holidays. Kate had been accepted to the same college Cecelia attended, and plans were being made for the two of them to live together in the gay dorm the following year. The relationship was flourishing and Kate was looking forward to being graduated within the next month. With few exceptions, Kate's high school colleagues and her teacher's were accepting of her sexual orientation and she, as Cecelia had been when she attended the school, a popular adolescent who frequently made the honor roll and would be in the top five percent of her class.

The senior prom was an event that Kate had looked forward to and wanted to take Cecelia as her date. They had contemplated going to Cecelia's senior prom the year before, but had been convinced by Ms. McGirr, the school counselor, that "school policies forbade such couples" and that "they should just forget it." After discussing the situation with their parents, Kate and Cecelia decided to forego attending Cecelia's senior prom with the idea that they would spend Kate's senior year challenging the system and attempting to get the school policies changed. You are the social worker assigned to Kate's high school. Kate and Cecelia have asked for your help. What, if anything, can be done?

Foster Care Placement

Juan, a 15-year-old teenager of Puerto Rican descent, was thrown out of his family when he was 13 because his father, Georges, confirmed his suspicion that his only son was gay. Prior to that time Georges had suspected his son of being a "faggot," and had verbally abused Juan since the boy had been small, calling him such things as "sissy boy," "fruit loop," and "queer" and in public often referring to the child as a girl. Juan's mother, Hilda, a gentle woman who loved her son even if he "was sick," prayed daily for his recovery, but could not allow him to remain in the household once her husband had thrown the boy out.

Juan was brought to the attention of the Department of Child Protective Services (CPS) shortly after he left home and was found under a bridge suffering from pneumonia and malnutrition. He had been living on his own for almost six months and had earned money through prostitution. Concerned about Juan's health, one of his tricks notified CPS where to find him. His HIV test was negative. Juan was 14 when he was placed in his first foster home. The foster home placement was headed by Mr. and Mrs. Bernard Valdez, a Cuban couple who had fled Cuba in the 1970s. They had in their care one other teenage boy, Chuck, and an 11-year-old girl, Rita. Chuck and Juan shared a bedroom. Chuck was 17 years old. The Valdez couple and their two other foster children had clear views about homosexuality—it was a sin, it was an illness, it was not normal, it was not to be condoned. When Chuck found out at school that Juan was gay, Chuck announced it to his foster parents, after he had beaten up Juan in the school parking lot. The Valdezes tried to convince Juan that he was just going through a phase, and that with time, reparative therapy, and prayer, he would be cured. Juan stated he had dated girls and even screwed girls, but that he found young men more sexually interesting and exciting. Furthermore he did not want to undergo therapy as he thought his homosexuality normal. His foster parents called CPS.

Juan, prior to adolescence, had always been, even in the face of his father's abuse, an excellent student and an outgoing child. While he had always thought of himself as different, it was only after defining and beginning to integrate the reality of his homosexual identity that he started to have difficulty in school and became isolated and withdrawn. Juan's depression is getting worse and he may be suicidal. He was the object of ridicule at school and has few friends. He has no contact with his natural parents and his foster family is ignorant about his needs, but Juan does have an ally in the school counselor, a gay man, who is painfully aware of the situation. The school counselor, Mr. Singleton, suggested to Juan that Juan be placed in a gay foster family and knows two gay men who would provide an ideal foster placement for Juan. While state law does not specifically prohibit gay couples from either adopting children or acting as foster parents, the Department of Child Protective Service policy manual denies all gays the opportunity to either adopt a child or act as foster parents. You are the social worker who has been following Juan's case since he became involved with foster care. Specifically what needs to be done to challenge this policy and how can you help or hinder the process?

This chapter has focused on the empowerment perspective and lesbian and gay youths. The developmental issues associated with growing up gay and coming out were explored in the context of conventional psychological theories associated with gay youths and cognitive, moral, and social development issues associated with being a lesbian or gay adolescent. Common themes associated with coming-out models were described as were dilemmas faced by members of racial or ethnic minorities who are also gay or lesbian. Some of the realities of growing up gay were described, and the risk factors associated with an adolescent gay or lesbian lifestyle were identified. Providing services to gay and lesbian youths using an empowerment approach was explored, the empowerment model was applied using a micro-level situation, and three case studies were presented for discussion.

5

Empowering Gay and Lesbian Adults

. . . there are as many gay lifestyles as there are gays, and any number of lesbian and gay communities, differentiated by age, class, ethnicity, common life goals, sexual interests, and gender. It should be recognized therefore that some problem areas may be of more concern to one group than to another and that as a result, the knowledge and skills mastered must always be considered in light of the specific client and the problem for which help is being sought. Woodman 1985:13.

As has been noted, there is no way to know exactly how many lesbian and gay adults actually exist, but assuming there are 260 million persons in the United States and 27.5 million are under the age of 19, there are 233 million adults in this country (U.S. Census, 1992). And, if one believes, as has been reported, that between 3 and 10 percent of the general population are lesbian or gay (Kinsey, Pomeroy, and Martin 1948; Kinsey et al. 1953; NORC 1989–1992; Rogers 1993), then there could be between 7 and 23 million adult gay and lesbian persons currently living in the United States. As with social work with adolescents, the idea of providing social services to lesbian and gay adults is a recent phenomenon having been a subject of social work interventive interest only since the late 1970s and 1980s (DeCrescenzo 1983/84; Gochros 1983/84; Hidalgo, Peterson, and Woodman, 1985; Messing, Schoenberg, and Stephens 1983/84; Moses and Hawkins 1982; Woodman and Lenna 1980), although therapeutic intervention with gays and lesbians has been of interest to the psychiatric community since the 1940s (Bieber 1965; Bieber et al. 1962; Duberman 1991; Gonsiorek 1982; Hatterer 1970; Hooker 1965). The interest in providing social work services to lesbians and gays emerged from the growing interest in national organizations like the National Association of Social Workers who, in 1977 adopted a policy statement describing gays and lesbians as a historically disenfranchised, at-risk minority (NASW 1977). It was not until 1992, after a long internal struggle, that the Council on Social Work Education (CSWE) mandated that content on lesbians and gays be included in the curriculum of all baccalaureate and master's level social work programs (CSWE 1992; Tully 1994). Social work knowledge and skills with this minority population is still an emerging area and, because gays and lesbians are such a heterogeneous group, the development of adequate knowledge in this area is years away. Even so, data do exist to begin to explore how the concepts of the empowerment approach can be utilized with lesbians and gays. The first part of this chapter will examine issues associated with gays and lesbians as they move through adult stages of development—such as issues dealing with families (biological and created), maintaining relationships, and coming out as an adult. The second part relates to concepts, methods, and practice skills designed to empower lesbian and gay adults, and the final section presents case studies designed to help the practitioner practice his or her clinical skills with this population.

Developmental Challenges

Developmental challenges, though keenly felt in adolescence, do not end when the adolescent becomes a physically mature, psychologically well-adjusted adult but continue throughout the life span. Although not unique to gays and lesbians, some of the challenges confronting them as adults have different impacts simply as a result of sexual orientation. This section explores the impact on the person as she or he moves from legally sanctioned families of origin into not legally sanctioned or socially recognized families of choice, how the individual forms and maintains relationships in a homophobic society, and issues associated with coming out as an adult.

In the Beginning: Families of Origin

Most lesbian and gay adults continue to be raised in traditionally nongay households where their sexual orientation may or may not be known to either their parents, siblings, or to themselves (Rust 1993; Telljohann and Price 1993; Troiden 1989; Tully 1983). Assuming the individual has personally acknowledged her or his sexual orientation to family members, that acknowledgment may be met with a range of emotions from overt physical hostility to mild confusion or sadness (Cramer and Roach 1988; Savin-Williams 1989), but rarely are family members overjoyed and totally accepting of the idea that their child or sibling is gay (CWLA 1991; Cramer and Roach 1988; Herdt 1989; Hetrick and Martin 1987; Savin-Williams 1989b). How the family of origin reacts to the lesbian or gay family member can have lasting effects on how that individual will react to and cope with future challenges of life.

For example, a gay man who grew up in a hostile environment with no positive social supports or role models may have difficulty in later life forming lasting relationships and may distance himself from his family of origin. But, a lesbian whose family was confused but supportive about her sexual orientation may find that her family of origin remains a strong support system for her across her lifetime. The literature generally does not differentiate between lesbian women and gay men with regard to issues associated with families of origin so the following has application to both.

If the individual has acknowledged his or her nonconforming sexual orientation to himself or herself and other gays or lesbians, but not to family members, other conflicts and challenges present themselves. Since family of origin members tend to assume that their loved one is heterosexual, this can lead to feelings of isolation and confusion because of the lack of congruence between family and societal expectations and self-image (Massey and Ouellette 1996). Leading a double life where the person is perceived as nongay within the family of origin and gay in other settings is confusing to the individual, presents many difficult social dilemmas, can cause psychiatric distress, and may be viewed as psychologically unhealthy: for example, the lesbian daughter who has never acknowledged her sexual orientation to her parents and finds it necessary to remove all her lesbian literature, books, and pictures from her apartment when her parents visit; or the gay attorney who finds that he must leave his partner at home rather than bring him to the weekly family Sunday dinners hosted by his family of origin.

Perhaps the most curious is the adult who has yet to acknowledge her or his sexual orientation to anyone—including herself or himself. While this individual may have some feelings of being different or feeling uncomfortable with the nongay role, the reality of being a gay or lesbian person is not yet in focus. The challenges for this individual may be seen in terms of dealing with a "developmental lag" where the chronological age differs from the developmental phase of life and where the individual has tasks to complete that others have completed at an earlier chronological age (Grace 1992). This concept will be examined later when we explore coming out as an activity not related to chronology.

In sum, families of origin play a significant role in the kind of families of choice the individual creates, the kind of relationship she or he develops and maintains. And while men and women deal with these issues in a similar fashion, that is not the case with other developmental issues associated with adulthood. As we will see, families of choice can take as many forms as families of origin, men and women approach these somewhat differently, and the social work practitioner must be comfortable with all of these permutations to empower adult lesbians and gays.

Families of Choice: Coupling and Maintaining Relationships

As adults we all select "families of choice" or those persons we select as friends, lovers, mates, and those with whom we will have children. For gays and lesbians the creation of families of choice is not accepted by the church, the law, or the social order. In short, creating fictive families that endure across time is a risky enterprise in a society where openly acknowledging your sexual deviancy can cause you to be evicted from your apartment, lose your job, earn you a dishonorable discharge from the armed services, lose custody of your children, be the victim of hate crimes, be the object of ridicule, be treated for homosexuality as a psychiatric illness, or be arrested (Jacobs 1991; Lloyd and Tully 1996; Nicolosi 1991; Slavin 1991; Vaid 1995; Wilson 1991). The fact that lesbian and gay relationships do develop, blossom, grow, and thrive for decades in spite of the toxic social structure in which they exist is a testament to the human spirit (Appleby and Anastas, 1998; Bieber 1965; Duberman 1991; Gonsiorek 1982; Grace 1992; Gunter 1992; Hatterer 1970; Hooker 1965; Isay 1989; Laird and Green, 1996; Moses and Hawkins 1982; Peterson and Stewart 1985; Tully 1983; Woodman and Lenna 1980). But, despite differences in approach and style, lesbians and gays do form loving relationships.

A current popular press book, *Men Are from Mars, Women Are from Venus* (Gray 1992), concludes that men and women are indeed different as they value different things, approach relationships differently, and have different basic needs. Likewise, studies that have been done using lesbian samples (Albro and Tully 1979; Armon 1960; Chafetz et al. 1976; Freedman 1967; Hassell and Smith 1975; Lott-Whitehead and Tully 1993; Tully 1983) seem to demonstrate that lesbians approach relationships and relationship-building and maintenance differently than men (Duberman

1991; Hooker 1965; Isay 1989; Kates 1998; Moses and Hawkins 1982; Woodman and Lenna 1980). Because women and men seem to enter into and maintain relationships somewhat differently (Decker 1983/84; Duberman 1991; Grace 1992; Gray 1992; Gunter 1992; Hooker 1965; Isay 1989; Kates 1998; McCandlish 1981/82; Moses and Hawkins 1982; Silverstein 1991; Terry 1992; Wilbur 1965; Woodman and Lenna 1980), this section will examine the development of families of choice from both a male and female perspective.

Lesbian Women Are from Venus

Gray's (1992) views that women tend to gain a sense of themselves through the quality of their relationships with others, that women tend to value communication and relationships more than tangible goods and assets, and that women need care, reassurance, respect, understanding, and validation is not refuted by research with lesbians (Decker 1983/84; Freedman 1967; Hassell and Smith 1975; Lott-Whitehead and Tully 1993; Mendola 1980; Saghir and Robins 1969; Tully 1983). Decker (1983/84) asserts that, for lesbians, love must exist before sexual intimacy occurs and that relationship skills are seen as an important aspect to falling in love. Further, it has been reported that lesbians have little practice with the concepts of autonomy and self-definition and therefore tend to fuse with their partners more than gay men or nongay women (Causby et al. 1995; Decker 1983/84; McCandlish 1981/82).

Lesbians create their families of choice based on individualized psychosocial needs, and these families are as unique as the individuals who form them. Lesbians may choose lesbians as partners, they may choose heterosexual men as partners, they may choose gay men as partners, or they may choose no one (Appleby and Anastas 1998; Laird and Green 1996; Tully 1995b). Lesbians tend to from relationships that are serially sexually monogamous, but there are instances of couples living together in nonmonogamous relationships where sexual fidelity is viewed as not important. Lesbian couples in committed relationships tend to last as long as or longer than nongay marriages and, as with nongays, face similar developmental issues across the life span (Albro and Tully 1979; Laird and Green 1996; Kehoe 1988; Tully 1983).

Many lesbians opt to live as couples in family units that, in many ways, are similar to nongay families (Appleby and Anastas 1998; Berzon 1988; Clunis and Green 1988; Laird and Green 1996; Lott-Whitehead and Tully 1993). Similar traditions enjoyed by both lesbian families and nongay families include such rituals as "marriage" ceremonies, baby showers, birthday celebrations, and funerals (Appleby and Anastas 1998; Butler 1990; Cherry and Mitulski 1990; Laird and Green 1996; Porter-Chase 1987). These family units may be conceptualized as a counterpart to traditional nongay family units, and in such families lesbians may or may not choose to have children.

It has been noted that the 1990s has been a decade in which a "lesbian baby boom" occurred (Appleby and Anastas 1998; Laird and Green 1996; Levy 1992; Lott-Whitehead and Tully 1993). Simply, more and more lesbians, whether or not they are part of a couple, are electing to adopt children or bear their own children. Adoption may be difficult for openly lesbian women because many states continue to consider lesbianism illegal and have passed laws prohibiting them from adopting children (NGLTF 1998c). Further, if allowed to adopt, in many states only one partner is allowed to bear legal responsibility for the child. Thus, the noncustodial parent has no legal rights. Some states do allow for second-parent adoption where both partners share joint responsibility for the child, but not all states agree on this issue (McClellan 1998).

Women who elect to give birth themselves become pregnant in a variety of ways. Some become pregnant through heterosexual intercourse, while others use sperm banks, or use sperm from friends or family of origin members. Insemination occurs either in the privacy of their homes or in a physician's office. It is not uncommon for lesbians to use fertility drugs to enhance their chances of becoming pregnant through artificial insemination, so there is an increased chance of having twins or even triplets (Lesbian Mothers Support Group 1998).

Whether children in lesbian families come from adoption, previous nongay marriages, heterosexual sexual intercourse, or artificial insemination, lesbian motherhood is a reality (Appleby and Anastas 1998; Gibbs 1989; Gottman 1989; Laird and Green 1996; Levy 1992; Lott-Whitehead and Tully 1993). While data on children raised by lesbians are still being gathered, data to date indicate that children raised by lesbian parents are no different than children raised by nongays other than they may be more tolerant of diversity (Gibbs 1989; Laird and Green 1996; Levy 1992; Lott-Whitehead and Tully 1993). Data also indicate that lesbians tend to take an active role in raising their children and do so in settings (such as schools, churches, social clubs) that may not have an appreciation or tolerance for lesbian families (Lott-Whitehead and Tully 1993).

Lesbian families of choice include more than couples in intimate relationships. As with nongay relationships, lesbians have friendship circles that may include former partners and other friends. These friendship networks often are viewed as extended families and include women and men of various ages who may or may not be gay and who play various roles and serve various functions in the lesbian's life. For example, a young lesbian mother whose preschool children require after-school care may call on a retired extended family member to fill that role. Or, because the lesbian network in any town is small, a former partner may be called on to help in a crisis.

In sum, lesbian families of choice are formed in various configurations from women living alone and couples with no children to couples with one or more children. Extended families of choice are also created by lesbians. Family configurations are based, as in nongay families, on individual psychosocial needs and such families of choice and the relationships within them play an important role in the individual's life across her entire lifespan.

Gay Men Are from Mars

Men are said to value power, achievement, and efficiency and, to gain a sense of self-worth, it is important for them to achieve results. Relationships and feelings are not as important as things (Gray 1992). Data related to gay men, who are after all socialized as men, tend to agree that relationships are secondary and that strength and winning are more important than emotional entanglements (Decker 1983/84; Moses and Hawkins 1982). While lesbians tend to equate love with sexual intimacy, this in not necessarily the case with gay men for whom sexual intimacy may not be confused with the emotion of love (Decker 1983/84). One consequence of this seems to be the lingering myths that gay men are not capable of forming long-lasting relationships, that relationships that are formed are unstable, and that they are all promiscuous (Appleby and Anastas 1998; Hooker 1965; Isay 1989; Moses and Hawkins 1982; Silverstein 1981).

Like nongay men, gay men may have difficulty maintaining stable relationships when they are younger and, also like nongays, may be more promiscuous than women as adolescents and young adults (Isay 1989; Moses and Hawkins 1982). But data also demonstrate that, while some gay men prefer a lifetime of anonymous sex without the intimacy of a long-term relationship, many gay men do form loving, stable relationships that can last a lifetime (Appleby and Anastas 1998; Isay 1989; Laird and Green 1996; Moses and Hawkins 1982; Silverstein 1981). Some research has been conducted that explores the nature of gay men's relationships and some present models of them (Isay 1989; Hooker 1965; McWhirter and Mattison 1981/82; Silverstein 1981). What these models tend to have in common is that, as with nongay men, various types of relationships exist based on individual psychosocial needs. And these types of relationships range from those men who have a lifetime of nothing but anonymous sex to those couples who have long-term monogamous relationships.

At one end of the relationship continuum is the male who participates in anonymous gay sex and may very well not identify himself as a gay person because the sexual act is simply that and nothing more. Another may strongly identify as being part of the gay community but prefers the excitement of the chase and having multiple sexual encounters. Others may prefer to have a series of partners with whom they may or may not have a monogamous relationship, and some may choose to have one lifelong partner (Appleby and Anastas 1998; Berger and Kelly 1995; Hooker 1965; Isay 1989; McWhirter and Mattison 1981/82; Shernoff 1995, 1998). Relationships tend not to follow any single pattern, but there does seem to be evidence that some gay men's relationships are not monogamous and that even with the decrease in sexual activity as a result of the AIDS pandemic, gay men may have more sexual partners in a lifetime than do nongay men or lesbians (Berger and Kelly 1995; Isay 1989; Moses and Hawkins 1982; Shernoff 1995). And, as with nongay relationships, gay men who are in coupled relationships face similar life tasks and crises as they move across time.

One such challenge is the formation of a family unit. As with lesbians, gay men, too, have rituals surrounding the formalization of their unions, the birth or adoption of their children, and other life passages. Like lesbian families, gay men who form family units do so within a social order that is generally not supportive of the relationship. In order to formalize their unions, gay men may hold commitment ceremonies where family of origin and family of choice members are invited, they may have a private ceremony of some sort where they exchange rings and vows, or they may do neither. They may live with each other or they may live in separate homes either in the same town or not. Gay couples may or may not be in monogamous relationships. Such couples may be totally open about their relationships, or they may hide the relationship, but most often they are neither completely open nor completely hidden as they choose to share their sexual orientation with those whom they can trust. Gay men may choose to parent children of their own with spouses or women friends, they may decide to adopt children, or they may opt to provide homes for foster children. All of these relational decisions are made based on the biopsychosocial needs and resources available to the men in the relationship.

Each relationship is seen as a separate entity with its own unique history, development, and life (McWhirter and Mattison 1981/82). Further, because gay men tend not to equate sexual experiences with love or commitment and tend to have a higher number of sexual partners across their life spans, the length of these relationships varies (Isay 1989; Shernoff 1995). Some research has been conducted on types of gay men's relationships and three categories of gay men have been noted. The first category is the "excitement seekers" who enjoy the thrill of the sexual chase and have lots of sexual encounters. Second are "home builders" who enjoy long-lasting relationships that may be monogamous, polygamous, or nonsexual. And third are the "nesting thrill seekers," who enjoy the comforts of a long-term relationship combined with the freedom to be a sexual predator (Silverstein 1981). Other research has identified that male couples go through various stages in their relationships. Couples may "blend" and "nest" during the first three years, then move to "maintaining" and "collaborating" in years three to ten. From the tenth year to the twentieth comes a "trusting" stage that is followed by a "repartnering" phase after twenty years together (McWhirter and Mattison 1981/82, 1984).

McWhirter and Mattison (1981/82) note that each stage is accompanied by certain activities and decisions that serve to maintain the relationship. In the first three years the couple blends (usually in year one) by falling in love, defining the nature and boundaries of the relationship, and enjoying high levels of sexual activity, exclusively with each other. This is generally followed by the nesting phase (years two and three), where the couple finds compatibility with one another and sets up housekeeping; during this phase ambivalence may replace the initial sexual exclusivity. Maintaining the relationship occurs in years three through five, where the partners begin to individuate from one another. More risk-taking and conflict appears in the relationship, and sexual exclusivity may vanish. This may be followed by a collaborative phase (years five to ten), where the partners collaborate with one another, establish independence from one another, and yet create a dependability on each other. The fifth phase is that of trust (years ten to twenty), where sincere trust between the partners emerges, monies may be merged, and the relationship taken for granted. Finally following twenty years together, repartnering occurs. This phase is characterized as including the realization of personal goals, an expectation of permanence in the relationship, and an awareness of the passage of time.

The creation and maintenance of family units of gay men is as complex as the individuals in the relationships and each situation is unique. Despite differences between lesbians and gay men and their approach toward creating and maintaining relationships, there are some similarities shared by both.

Common Relationship Dilemmas

As noted, men and women tend to have different values and approaches to the development and maintenance of relationships. But, there are also similarities. What they share is a common heritage of trying to form lasting relationships in the context of a homophobic society that creates obstacles to the development and stability of a healthy family unit. Such institutional homophobia can easily be identified in the following areas: the criminalization of same-sex sexual activities; the refusal by most businesses, communities, and states to acknowledge same-sex partners; the lack of support for same-sex marriage; the difficulty faced by gays and lesbians who want to have or adopt children; and the generalized lack of support in the nongay community for gay families.

By 1998, nine states had included sexual orientation in their nondiscrimination laws, eight states were considering the adoption of similar legislation, a number of municipalities had passed legislation protecting the rights of same-sex partners, and scores of universities and businesses had included nondiscrimination protections and domestic partnership benefits for gay families (Birch 1998; Mills 1997; NGLTF 1997). Yet, in most of the municipalities and businesses in the United States, basic human rights and judicial protections, routinely provided to nongays, are denied to lesbians and gays simply on the basis of their sexual orientation (Jacobs 1991; NGLTF 1997; Zimmer 1990). Lesbian or gay persons still lose their jobs simply because of their sexual orientation (Faderman 1991; Tully 1989). Many gays and lesbians are not open about their sexual orientation in the workplace because they fear discrimination, lack of promotional opportunities, or termination (Herek 1991; Rivera 1991). And, while some companies offer protections for gay employees, there are still no federal or state laws to ensure their rights. An example of discrimination is President Clinton's "Don't Ask, Don't Tell" (do not ask a member of the armed services his or her sexual orientation and the enlisted person will not tell) policy of the early 1990s. Although said to prevent discrimination, this policy has engendered gay and lesbian witch-hunts that have separated scores of enlisted persons from the armed services (Benecke 1998; Gelman 1993). The reality of this lack of protection has implications for gay families as they attempt to build and maintain long-term relationships and raise families.

As of 1998, no state has yet legalized same-sex marriage as most law-makers tend to view same-sex marriages as inappropriate (Slavin 1991; Treuthart 1990). Likewise, most traditional churches do not sanction same-sex unions although some churches and synagogues routinely per-form "commitment ceremonies" for same-sex couples (Butler 1990; NGLTF 1997; Porter-Chase 1987). And while many gay couples may choose to have a public ceremony to celebrate their relationship, the cer-emony has no basis in law and therefore may be viewed as illegitimate by many. As a result, gay families do not have the legal benefits of marriage such as inheritance and property rights, tax benefits, parenting and cus-tody rights, health care benefits, veterans pensions or social security ben-efits, or next-of-kin status (Slavin 1991; Wilson 1991; Zimmer 1990). These realities, too, have implications for gay and lesbian families.

While lesbians and gays have always parented children, many have done so in the context of heterosexual marriages. Thus, the concept of having a gay male couple produce or adopt and raise children is as new as that of having a lesbian couple raise children (Appleby and Anastas 1998; Gibbs 1989; Gottman 1989; Laird and Green 1996; Mallon 1998; Levy 1992; Lott-Whitehead and Tully 1993). Family law, the branch of law that most affects gay families, has been slow to react to and provide pro-tections for these newly emerging, nontraditional family structures (Lott-Whitehead and Tully 1993; McClellan 1998; Wilson 1991). Thus, while second-parent adoption is available for the noncustodial parent in a same-sex relationship, most states do not yet allow gays to adopt chil-dren, much less allow for a child to legally have two parents of the same sex (McClellan 1998). And while the laws are changing, the reality that homosexuality is still illegal and sinful continues to exist in the minds of many current lawmakers who fail to enact legal protections for lesbian women and gay men (Birch 1998; NGLTF 1997).

Just as creating families and dealing with life in a homophobic society may cause problems for couples, so too can health issues. Since the first cases of HIV/AIDS were reported primarily in the gay community in the early 1980s, it has become increasingly important to recognize that there are some health risks of which social workers need to be aware when working with lesbian and gay clients. While no disease is unique to the gay community, gay persons may be more likely to contract certain ailments more regularly because of their sexual orientation. For example, data tend to show that lesbians may be more prone to getting breast and ovarian cancer than their nongay counterparts and gay men may be more likely to get various sexually transmitted diseases (STDs) than heterosexual men and women (Shernoff 1995; Woodman 1995). Further, lesbians and gays are not immune from becoming disabled. Physically limiting impairments such as hearing loss, blindness, arthritis, spinal cord injury, heart disease, and others also impact the gay community.

Because gay couples tend not to be protected by traditional health insurance and laws and services that protect nongay family units, these health issues can be the source of crisis for the lesbian or gay family. For example, where can a lesbian turn when she is the victim of same-sex domestic violence? Battered women's shelters are generally not equipped to deal with such an event. Or, what protections does the lifelong partner of a gay man have when his lover is taken to the hospital in critical condition and hospital policies allow only family of origin members access to the patient?

In sum, these constraints that prevent lesbians and gays from being honest about their sexual orientation and prevent them from having equal protection under the law play an undeniable role in the development and maintenance of gay and lesbian relationships. These issues, as will be discussed later, can be the basis for gays to need and seek counseling. Another often ignored reality in the lesbian and gay community is that of hate crimes and domestic violence.

Hate Crimes and Domestic Violence

In addition to the relationship dilemmas, diseases, and disabilities that threaten the health and physical well-being of lesbian women and gay men, physical violence or hate crimes directed toward this group because of sexual orientation is fairly widespread. And, in addition to hate crimes, domestic violence is another form of assault that impacts the lesbian and gay community. Hate crimes and domestic violence are two distinct issues and will be discussed separately.

Hate Crimes

In the Hate Crimes Statistics Act of 1990 (Pub. L. No. 101–275, 104 Stat.140 Amending 28 U.C. 534), sexual orientation is included as a group for whom data should be collected, but this was accomplished only after much debate (Hartman 1996). In the Violent Crime and Control and Law Enforcement Act of 1994, the Congress defined a hate crime as, "a crime in which the defendant intentionally selects a victim, or in the case of a property crime, the property that is the object of the crime, because of the actual or perceived race, color, national origin, ethnicity, gender, disability, of sexual orientation of any person" (Hate Crimes: A Definition 1994:1). For the National Coalition of Anti-Violence Programs (NCAVP), an organization formalized in 1995, but which has been compiling annual reports on antigay violence since 1984, the definition of a hate crime has been modified somewhat by narrowing it to apply only to lesbian, gay, bisexual, trasgender, or HIV+ persons. The NCAVP definition of a hate crime states that it is "one in which there are sufficient objective facts to lead a responsible person to conclude that the offender's actions were motivated in whole or in part by the offender's bias about lesbian, gay, bisexual, transgender, or HIV-positive people" (1998c:2). The NCAVP cautions that in most localities verbal or sexual harassment is not considered a crime, so that statistics related to hate crimes do not include these forms of violence.

Hate crimes are certainly not restricted to the lesbian and gay community and its members. Such personal violence occurs against African Americans, Arab Americans, Asian-Pacific Americans, Caucasian Americans, Hispanic Americans, individuals with disabilities, Jewish Americans, Native Americans, and women. Further, hate crimes against property occur in these same groups (Faces of Hate Crimes 1998). Most hate crimes in the United States are directed against members of the African-American community, but violence against the lesbian and gay community increased 16 percent from 1994 to 1997 and shows no sign of ebbing (Faces of Hate Crimes 1998; NCAVP 1998h).

NCAVP (1998h) reported a general decline in hate crimes against most groups in 1997, but in the gay and lesbian community, hate crimes continued to rise. Most hate crimes against the lesbian and gay community occur in June, probably it is thought because June is the traditional month for Gay Pride activities and with increased media exposure comes increased violence. However, in 1997, the number of hate crimes reported to NCAVP in March ($n = 240$) and April ($n = 234$) were almost equal to those reported in June ($n = 254$). The reason for this may have been that during those months Ellen DeGeneres' television character came out causing quite a media sensation. Again, more exposure may have caused an antigay backlash.

The total numbers of persons reporting to have been victims of hate crimes is increasing. In 1995, 1,019 incidents were reported (Criminal Justice Information Services 1995); in 1996, 1,106 incidents were reported (Hate Crime Statistics 1996) (the NCAVP reported 2,399 that year); and in 1997, 2,445 incidents were reported (NCAVP 1998i). A word must be said about the use of such statistics. Hate crimes in the gay and lesbian community are grossly underreported for a variety of reasons. And, when looking at the statistics from 1995, 1996, and 1997 there are significant differences depending on what group collects the data. The lower figures were reported from the Criminal Justice Information Services Division of the FBI and include statistics obtained from law enforcement offices. The higher figures come from the NCAVP, who collects data only in 14 localities across the United States. The NCAVP's figures are no doubt more reliable, yet they agree their statistics are underrepresentative of the actual number of annual hate crimes.

In general there is a reluctance for lesbian, gay, bisexual, and transgender persons to report hate crimes because of a perception, apparently true, that the police fail to take such crimes seriously, or that in reporting such crimes the victim places herself or himself at risk of police brutality or having her or his sexual orientation become public. NCAVP reports that of the victims who reported hate crime incidents to it in 1997 ($n = 2,445$), only 24 percent ($n = 587$) also reported the incident to the local police. It is easy to see why the statistics on hate crimes in the lesbian and gay community are untrustworthy. What can be deduced, even from such poor statistics, is the reality that hate crimes against lesbian women, gay men, bisexual or transgender persons exist in great number and appear to be increasing when other hate crimes are diminishing.

Realizing the data on which conclusions are drawn come from but a small sample, what is generally known about the victims of hate crimes, the perpetrators of such violence, and the kind of hate crimes that are committed? The NCAVP (1998i) provide an overview. In the gay and lesbian community most (95%) of hate crimes were directed at individuals—not property. Most of the attacks (83%) were aimed at lesbian women, gay men, or bisexual women or men, but attacks were also made on nongay men and women simply because they "looked" gay or lesbian. Most were white (57%), although Latinos (25%) and African Americans (20%) were also targets and the majority ($n = 1,868$, 68%) were men. Most victims ($n = 1,013$, 42%) were between 30 and 44 years of age and were not HIV+. A composite of the average victim would be a white, gay, male adult who is not HIV+.

Because of the reluctance to report hate crimes, there is not much known about the perpetrators of these hate crimes. However, the NCAVP (1998e) also provides interesting data on offenders. In 1997, most offenders were white and 85 percent were men. They were usually less than 45 years of age (85%) and tended to be younger than their victims. Between 35 and 39 percent of these offenders were serial offenders and had committed from 1 to more than 10 reported incidents of violence in 1997. The four most common places for hate crimes to occur are, in rank order, the street or other public area, a private residence, the workplace, or in a gay/lesbian bar. The most common offender is a stranger to his or her victim, but landlords/tenants/neighbors, law enforcement officers, or employers also commit hate crimes against lesbian women and gay men. The NCAVP also reported that, in 1997, service providers were responsible for 311 hate crimes against lesbian, gay, bisexual, or transgender persons in 1996 and 1997. Those least likely to commit hate crimes are roommates, lovers/partners, pick-ups, or family members. A composite of a typical offender would be an adult male who had committed other hate crimes and was a stranger to his victim. The crime would be committed in a public area.

As with information related to hate crime victims and perpetrators, NCAVP (1998a, 1998d, 1998f) also provides much of what is known about the actual crimes committed against gay, lesbian, bisexual, and transgender persons. Such things as arson, bomb threats, unjustified arrests, and harassment increased in 1997, but so did murders. Assaults were actually down 1 percent, but across all categories assaults were down 14 percent. This seems to indicate that crimes in the lesbian and gay community are not being reduced at the same rate as other groups. Of those gay men and lesbian women injured in hate crimes, 71 percent required and received medical attention, but there were another 17 percent who should have received medical attention who did not get it. Of the 310 incidents with weapons, 51.5 percent ($n = 172$) were committed with bats, clubs, or blunt objects ($n = 39, 22.5\%$); knives or sharp objects ($n = 34, 20\%$); or guns ($n = 15, 9\%$). Another 25.5% ($n = 79$) were committed with rocks, bricks, or bottles. Because rocks, bricks, and bottles can be found almost anywhere and bats, guns, and knives need to be carried to a crime scene, it is hypothesized that many of these crimes against the lesbian and gay community were premeditated. Likewise, while guns tend to be the weapon of choice outside the gay and lesbian community, more brutal weapons like clubs, bats, or knives tend to be used in hate crimes against lesbian, gay, bisexual, or transgender persons (Appleby and Anastas 1998; NCAVP 1998a). These assaults, as well as murders in the gay and lesbian community, tend to be violent and brutal.

There were only 18 antigay related murders in 1997 that were reported to the NCAVP (1998d). Of those murdered only 3 (16.6%) were women, 1 (5.5%) was a male to female transgender person, 6 (33.3%) were African American, and 9 (54%) were between 30 and 64 years of age. Twenty-seven percent were between 30 and 44 years of age. Evidence exists that demonstrates 11 (61%) of the crimes occurred in a "pick-up" where the victim and perpetrator meet and agree to go somewhere for consensual sex. Of the perpetrators, little is known as only 4 arrests have been made. Of those arrested most were younger than their victims and were between 18 and 22 years of age.

In sum, data demonstrate that hate crimes against lesbian, gay, bisexual, and transgender persons not only exist, but are increasing as the lesbian and gay community gains more national attention through the media. Further, members of this community are disproportionately singled out for especially brutal attacks that often go unreported because of fear.

Domestic Violence

Although such hate crimes by strangers are rare in the lesbian community, both lesbians and gays can be the victims of domestic violence where partners harass, beat, or even murder their lovers (Renzetti 1992, 1995; Shernoff 1995). Domestic violence, although it is statistically counted as a hate crime, has been defined somewhat differently. In *The Social Work Dictionary* (Barker 1995), the term "domestic violence" is defined as abuse that occurs in the home and is committed by family members on spouses, children, older persons, or others living in the home. Barker further defines it at a more macro-level by saying domestic violence is a social problem where a family member's life, health, or property are harmed or endangered by the intentional behavior of another family member. The terms "family violence," "domestic violence," "spouse abuse," "spousal battery" are often used interchangeably, but all constitute variables within the same general construct of family violence. Family violence is usually viewed as any type of violence that occurs in any type of family (WISE 1998d).

In a paper on domestic violence in lesbian and gay relationships, Vickers (1996) defines domestic violence as a "systematic exercise of illegitimate power and coercive control by one partner on another" (2). She further defines lesbian domestic violence as patterns of behavior that involves violence or coercion where one partner seeks to control the behaviors, beliefs, actions, thoughts, or conduct of the other. This may include punishing the less-powerful partner for resisting the dominance of the more-powerful partner. Domestic violence in gay male relationships was defined as unwanted psychological or physical abuse or damage to property.

It is also important to differentiate between the concepts of domestic arguments and domestic violence. Domestic arguments are those conflicts that inevitably arise in any relationship between two people and may be in relation to job stress, children, finances, etc. As these conflicts get worked out arguments can erupt. Arguments are seen as the working out of conflict between equal partners where neither partner has more power or control than the other partner does. Domestic violence arises when there is an imbalance of power and control between the partners. One partner is afraid of the other or has been psychologically harmed or physically brutalized by the other (WISE (1998a). While domestic arguments can be, at times, helpful, domestic violence is never a positive way to approach conflict, and once violence has occurred in a relationship, it is likely to recur (Vickers 1996).

Lesbian and gay domestic violence is violence that is committed within the homes of members of the gay and lesbian community and is related to relationships and may be seen in a similar light as nongay spousal abuse. Most research on domestic violence has been centered on nongay populations, and most of the statistical information about this issue is on nongay populations.

While hate crimes are underreported, domestic violence in the lesbian and gay community was generally ignored as a reality until the 1980s when some few studies began to emerge that debunked the myth that abuse did not occur in lesbian or gay relationships and empirically demonstrated the existence of abuse in same-sex relationships (Berrill 1992; Renzetti 1992,1995). Many such incidents of domestic violence are not reported because of reasons similar to the reluctance of reporting hate crimes, namely that the police will not take the report as serious and that reporting the incident would create more trouble than not reporting it (Appleby and Anastas 1998; Shernoff 1998). Lesbians and gays are also reluctant to report domestic violence because they see it as a personal and private matter. But, and perhaps more importantly, they do not report these crimes because they fear coming out to the public, they do not want to betray an already marginalized community, they are uncomfortable

exposing their partner and themselves to a homophobic and not understanding legal system, and they fear there are no social services available
to them because of their sexual orientation (Vickers 1996).

There are no adequate statistics that portray the actual number of
domestic violence incidents in the gay and lesbian community. There may
be as many as 500,000 battered men in the United States, between 22 and
44 percent of all lesbians have been in relationships where violence
occurred, and perhaps as many as 15 to 20 percent of all gay or lesbian
couples are abusive (Appleby and Anastas 1998; Vickers 1996). The
NCAVP (1998f) data demonstrate that lovers were less likely to commit
violent offenses against their partners than strangers were, but in 1997
only 52 incidents of domestic violence were reported to them. Their data
further show that in 1996 only 27 such incidents were reported meaning
that there was a 93 percent increase in reported domestic violence
between 1996 and 1997.

Domestic abuse in gay and lesbian relationships can take the form of
verbal abuse, physical abuse, sexual abuse, destruction of personal property, psychological or emotional abuse, economic abuse, social abuse, or
spiritual abuse (Appleby and Anastas 1998; Trimble 1994; WISE 1998b,
1998e). It has also been noted, like in the nongay community (Zawitz
1994), that much of the abuse in gay and lesbian relationships occurs
within the context of drug or alcohol abuse (Shernoff 1998).

Because this is a hidden problem that occurs in the privacy of home
and those who experience it are reluctant to discuss it, neither the victim
nor the perpetrator is easily identifiable (WISE 1998d). There is no common profile for either although there is general agreement that domestic
violence stems from issues related to power and control within the relationship (Appleby and Anastas 1998). Some authors note that when
domestic violence occurs there is always an inequity of power between
the partners. Violence occurs when the more powerful partner coerces the
less dominant partner by either physical or psychological means where
the result is fear or harm to the less powerful partner (WISE 1998d). Data
from the nongay culture support the fact that most victims of domestic
violence (97%) are women and that Africa American, Hispanic, and Caucasian women are equally at risk (Zawitz 1994). Domestic violence is an
ongoing phenomenon, and lesbians and gays can be brutalized by a lover,
ex-lover, family member, spouse, ex-spouse, parent, or child (Appleby
and Anastas 1998).

How the issues of hate crimes and domestic violence need to be
addressed by the social worker will be detailed below. However, in addi-

tion to issues associated with violence, other dilemmas can confront the adult lesbian woman or gay man. Paramount among these dilemmas are issues related to coming out. There is no standard time for lesbian and gay persons to acknowledge their homosexual sexual orientation; hence, coming out can occur at any point in a life.

Coming Out as an Adult

As has been noted in previous chapters there tends to be a process related to coming out that follows various stages (see table 4.1). For a person who is psychically healthy, the individual first feels somehow different from the nongay world because of strong emotional attachments or sexual feelings for members of the same sex. Next, having accepted the feelings as a reality, the person begins to conceptualize the concept of homosexuality and make it an acceptable part of the personality. Finally, having accepted a positive internalized acceptance of homosexuality as a societal construct, the individual tends to become more closely involved with the gay community through the development of intimate personal relationships, the internalization of a gay identity, the disclosure to others of membership in the gay community, and a psychologically healthy view of the self.

While coming out for adolescents is an incredibly demanding life task, so it is also for the adult who may have always had same sex sexual affinities but denied them or repressed them until, as a middle-aged adult with grandchildren the feelings could no longer be denied. As data demonstrate, coming out can and does occur at any point along life's continuum and, as such, the adult who may have gotten through adolescence acting as a heterosexual is confronted with a new set of developmental tasks that must be achieved in order to facilitate continuity within the self (Berger and Kelly 1995; Shernoff 1995; Tully 1995; Woodman 1995). This "developmental lag" may cause the individual to act in ways more associated with an earlier chronological age such as engaging in behaviors that are not thought to be age appropriate. An example would be, the middle aged, newly identified lesbian who, after years of staying at home, suddenly decides to spend every evening in the local lesbian bar with her new-found friends. Or the thirty-year-old man who has just divorced his wife of the past ten years and purchased a motorcycle to be part of the gay motorcycle club.

Many gay men and lesbian women have been involved in nongay marriages that may have endured for years with the appearance of normalcy.

There is a natural confusion on the part of the emerging gay or lesbian with regard to expected societal roles (wife/husband, parent, grandparent, etc.) and newly defined psychic and sexual needs that are no longer met by the heterosexual relationship. Couple these needs with the legal issues associated with being gay, the lack of societal support, and the stigma attached to homosexuality, it is astounding that men and women do leave legally sanctioned marriages and families to enter into gay and lesbian family units. They do so realizing that they may lose custody of their children, their homes, their incomes, their families of origin, and their respect in the community. They do so at great personal risk and they face many challenges and opportunities in doing so. The challenges revolve around real and perceived loss, the opportunities revolve around an acceptance of the true self and an ability to integrate a previously incongruous part of the self into a whole identity. This is not done without struggles and, as will be noted, may be a cause for social work intervention.

As noted, there are countless challenges to be faced by gays and lesbians as they participate in society. So, too, are there countless challenges for social workers as they attempt to provide appropriate services for this population.

The Empowerment Approach with Gay and Lesbian Adults

Living in both the nongay and gay worlds is a reality for all gay and lesbian persons. This fact is one that presents challenges to lesbian or gay individuals in terms of the development and maintenance of their relationships, the creation of their family units, their employment opportunities, and their ability to use legal support systems. One way the practitioner can assist in simplifying the complexities of these issues is to use the empowerment approach. This approach has utility because it allows the person in the situation to define the issues and, with the support of the social worker, move forward to possible solutions.

Micro-Level Intervention

Adult lesbian and gay persons seek social services for a multitude of reasons that may or may not be related to issues associated with homophobia or sexual orientation. This section explores barriers to the effective provision of services, identifies common reasons gay and lesbian adults seek treatment, and provides pragmatic strategies for employing the empowerment approach with this disenfranchised minority group.

As with any population, services provided to adult gays and lesbians include those services provided to clients who voluntarily seek services, those to whom services are offered as a result of the situation in which the client finds herself or himself, or those services that clients are mandated to receive by virtue of their particular circumstance.

Barriers to Services

Before effective services can be provided the clinician must address barriers to service provision. In the case of providing services for lesbian and gay adults, barriers can include: the continuing generalized belief in the mythology and stereotyping of gays and lesbians, the lack of legal and religious sanctions for same-sex couples and families, the invisible nature of being gay or lesbian, and the lack of appropriate agency programs designed to provide services for gay families. There is a continuing pervasive mythology associated with being lesbian or gay to which even social workers fall prey (DeCrescenzo and McGill 1978). The myths and stereotypes are merely that and must be refuted with more informative data. Some of the more prevalent myths and stereotypes have been identified in table 5.1. This list is by far not inclusive, but does provide a basic understanding of how sinister homophobia can be and how widespread these beliefs have become.

In addition to prevailing myths and stereotypes, the practitioner must also confront the barrier of the lack of legal and religious sanctions for same-sex couples and the families of choice they create. The lack of legal and religious support for such unions not only creates stress and possible crises for practitioners trying to empower their gay and lesbian clients because of proscriptive agency policies grounded in homophobic legislation and religious beliefs, but also creates stress and possible crises for the lesbian or gay person in need of service. These omissions in the service network mean that appropriate and possibly necessary services to gays and lesbians and their families are simply not in place. But, before appropriate and adequate services can be provided to this population, gays and lesbians have to be made visible. Because it is not possible to distinguish gay persons from nongay ones by sight, the tendency might be to treat lesbian and gay families in the same way nongay families are treated. There are, as we have seen, subtle and not so subtle differences between the two. One way to begin to differentiate gay persons from nongay ones would be

TABLE 5.1
What Is True and What Is Not: Some Myths and Stereotypes vs. Reality

The following are myths and stereotypes that have long been attached to gays and lesbians. They have their roots in institutional homophobia and have no basis in fact. Practitioners must work toward eliminating these myths and stereotypes.

Gay men are pedophiles and child abusers;

Lesbians and gay men cannot maintain long-term, stable relationships;

All gay relationships are modeled on masculine/feminine (butch/femme) roles;

Gay and lesbians are psychologically damaged and sick;

Reparative therapy can cure homosexuality;

Sexual orientation is a choice;

Gay and lesbian persons hate members of the opposite sex;

Lesbians and gays are more sexually promiscuous than their nongay counterparts;

Homosexuals are easily identifiable because of the way they look/act/dress;

Gay men and lesbian women do not have children;

Children raised by lesbians or gay men become homosexual or are significantly disadvantaged;

Gays and lesbians have unstable relationships with their parents.

REALITY

While no truth is absolute, the following statements have their basis in research conducted with lesbians and gay men. Data do tend to refute the myths and stereotypes.

Most pedophiles and child abusers are heterosexual men;

Lesbians and gay male couples live in relationships that last from one date to a lifetime (just like nongay couples);

Gay and lesbian relationships traditionally are more egalitarian than nongay ones;

Homosexuality is not a psychological illness, although lesbians and gays can have mental illness (just like their nongay counterparts);

Reparative therapy, while perhaps altering homosexual behaviors for short amounts of time, cannot cure homosexuality;

Data demonstrate that sexual orientation is most likely determined genetically, so there is no choice involved;

Gay and lesbian persons have friends of both sexes;

Lesbian women have about the same number of sexual partners as nongay women; gay men tend to have more sexual partners across their life span than nongay men;

Gay men and women are indistinguishable from nongay persons;

More and more lesbians and gays are opting to have and raise children;

Children raised by lesbian or gay persons mostly grow up to be heterosexually well-adjusted adults with a high tolerance for diversity and show no ill effects from the experience of being raised in a nontraditional two-parent family;

Gays and lesbians generally have a history of stable relationships with both parents.

to use an intake form that does not assume heterosexuality. For example, rather than a form that lists only "single," "married," "widowed," or "divorced" as choices under marital status, the inclusion of other categories like "domestic partner," "companion," or "significant other" is more gay-friendly and will provide the social worker with more accurate information. In sum, prior to working with gay and lesbian clients, the practitioner must address these barriers and provide minimum agency supports that recognize the challenges faced by both clients and practitioners alike when working with this population.

Although social work practitioners are not immune from institutional homophobia (DeCrescenzo 1978; Shernoff 1995; Woodman 1995), internalizing a realistic view of lesbians and gays that is free of prevailing myths and stereotypes should be the first step for any clinician who wants to work with this population. Separating fact from fiction is a powerful tool and one that can empower both the practitioner and the client.

While the practitioner is unlikely to change more than four centuries of legal and religious discrimination, the social worker can create an office space that is homosocial and safe. This safe space can be created through the addition of gay magazines and newspapers to waiting rooms, the creation and use of gay-friendly intake forms that do not perpetuate the "heterosexual assumption," the training of receptionists and other agency personnel to allow couples to be viewed as couples, and the inclusion of sexual orientation as a protected category in the agency's nondiscrimination policy. Creating this homosocial space will also encourage gays and lesbians who could easily pass as nongays to share their sexual orientation irrespective of their presenting problem. Once the barriers that can be removed have been removed, the practitioner can move into the arena of exploring client dilemmas.

Common Presenting Problems

Lesbians and gays seek services for a variety of reasons. Such services may be voluntary, they may be suggested, or they may be mandated. While it is beyond the scope of this chapter to identify all the reasons that an individual might seek counseling, the focus will be on issues related primarily with sexual orientation that can create psychic stress significant enough to warrant intervention.

For those who seek services on a voluntary basis, data show that gay men often seek counseling for depression, anxiety, low self-esteem, an inability to form lasting relationships, coming-out issues (sexual identity confusion), relationship problems, internalized homophobia (self-loathing), sexual fidelity issues, AIDS anxiety, a bad marriage, discomfort in playing a sexually passive role, sexual dysfunction (e.g., premature ejaculation, impotency), mid-life crises, alcoholism, or suicidal ideation (Berger and Kelly 1995; Bieber et al. 1962; Gunter 1992; Hatterer 1970; Isay 1989; Moses and Hawkins 1982; Shernoff 1995). Lesbians most often seek counseling for relationship issues around fusion and independence, monogamy vs. nonmonogamy, finding a lover, courting behaviors, sexual problems, how to handle finances, sharing time between the office and home, issues associated with children, coming out, and terminating relationships (Anthony 1981/82; Bieber 1965; Causby et al. 1995; Gunter 1992; Terry 1992; Tully 1983; Woodman 1995). What is shared by both gays and lesbians who seek counseling is a tendency to seek help when confronted with coming-out issues, creating and maintaining relationships, or dilemmas around having and raising children. Given the homophobic nature of the social structure in which lesbians and gays function, it is hardly surprising that stress occurs at points when they confront the traditional nongay societal institutions.

Those social workers who work with clients where social services are offered as part of their interactions with particular social agencies—such as hospitals—also work with lesbians and gays. For example, Chloe, a 50-year-old lesbian was hospitalized for heart surgery. Her partner of fifteen years, Beryl, had Chloe's durable power of attorney for health care and was listed on the hospital records as "domestic partner." The hospital social worker assigned to the surgical unit's waiting room met with Beryl during the surgical procedure and met with Chloe and Beryl following the surgery. The couple was treated as a family unit and the social worker easily answered questions from both related to recovery time, scarring, and anxiety about renewal of sexual activity.

Dealing with voluntary clients and clients who are in position to accept or reject social services based on their needs is different from dealing with clients who, because of circumstances, are mandated to receive social services. Those who are required to receive social work intervention present interesting challenges for social workers because of the client's relative lack of power. For example, patients committed to institutions because of mental illness or those incarcerated because of legal convictions may be required to have counseling.

Not only may lesbians and gays may be found in institutional settings, some nongay persons in institutions may adopt lesbian or gay behaviors while institutionalized. Some normally heterosexual clients confined in sex-segregated institutions, such as prisons, may become involved in what has been called "situational homosexuality," where they engage in same-sex sexual relations within the institution, but once released resume heterosexual activities. Thus, the issues around sexuality become clouded. For example, Brad, a 27-year-old convicted murderer will spend the rest of his life in prison. He characterizes himself as heterosexual, but has been involved in consensual same-sex sexual behaviors with several inmates. Sandra, a 53-year-old lesbian, has been imprisoned since she was 28 for attempting to kill her lover. A somewhat maternal type, she has taken several newly incarcerated young, heterosexual women to her bed. When asked about their behavior both Brad and Sandra explained that the activities made them feel good and since no one was hurt and the sexual activities consensual they saw nothing wrong with it. Because institutional rules prohibit such sexual activities both Brad and Sandra were required to get counseling. Brad's institution allowed opposite-sex conjugal visits and the outcome of the intervention with Brad was that he was allowed such visits where he participated in heterosexual sex. The same-sex sexual activity was significantly reduced. But, because Sandra's institution offered no policy related to same-sex conjugal visits, intervention did nothing to stop her liaisons. In fact, her behavior caused her to be placed in solitary confinement on more than one occasion.

Common Stressors

Most of the stress of being a member of a minority group in any culture is generated from the dominant culture, and data suggest that for lesbians and gays questioning the efficacy of a homosexual lifestyle comes from outside before it is internalized (Berger and Kelly 1995; Lott-Whitehead and Tully 1993; Shernoff 1995; Woodman 1995). Table 5.2 identifies common stressors faced by adult gay and lesbian persons. Because of the reality of stress in the lives of gays and lesbians, the social work practitioner must develop the skills necessary to empower the minority group member not only to live in a hostile world, but to integrate the generally unacceptable social construct of homosexuality into a psychologically healthy being. Such would include an ability to separate external prejudices and homophobia from what a client has internalized (Decker 1983/84).

There are numerous stresses associated with the simple act of living across time that, for the lesbian or gay adult, may be more of a cause for concern than for her or his nongay counterpart. Some of those include rit-

TABLE 5.2
Common Stressors Faced by Adult Gays and Lesbians

The list following represents common areas that may produce stress for adult lesbians and gays:

STRESSORS FROM THE NONGAY SOCIETY

Prevailing myths and stereotypes;

Employment discrimination;

Legal proscriptions;

Hate crime violence;

Institutional homophobia;

Lack of adequate support systems.

STRESSORS FROM FAMILIES OF ORIGIN

Lack of understanding or acceptance about coming out;

Lack of familial support;

Individual homophobia;

Emotional distancing or rejection;

Violence or abuse.

STRESSORS FROM FAMILIES OF CHOICE

Creating, maintaining, and terminating relationships;

Monogamy vs. non-monogamy;

Children;

Second-parent adoptions;

Health;

Coming out;

Sexual orientation openness;

Finances;

Employment;

Internalized homophobia.

uals around the creation and dissolution of partnerships, the creation of families, and the death of a partner. While there are numerous rituals associated with the selection of a heterosexual mate—the pre-engagement, engagement, wedding shower, wedding, honeymoon, and creation of a nest—no such similar rituals exist in the gay and lesbian community. In fact, such rituals are banned either by law or by traditional values and mores. For example when Sam and Theresa met, fell in love, and decided to marry they had the support of both families, who were thrilled. Similarly when Henri and Costa met, fell in love, and decided to live together for the rest of their lives, those few in their families who knew were moderately supportive, those who did not know would have been horrified.

So it is, too, when lesbian and gay couples decide to have children. Elaborate rituals surround the birth of babies in the nongay world, but in the gay and lesbian community the discussion tends to center on how the child was conceived (if fresh sperm was used, whose was it and how did it get introduced; or, if frozen sperm was used, how was it obtained), or by what means was the child adopted (through traditional agencies or from a foreign country). An often overlooked reality is that children of lesbian and gay couples face discrimination because of their families of origin. To help them cope, organizations such as Children of Lesbian and Gay Parents Everywhere (COLAGE) can be found on the Internet (*http://www.colage.org*).

When Nanci and Brian decided to get a divorce it was a simple matter of filing the appropriate legal documents, waiting the specified amount of time, and working out an amicable divorce settlement that included shared custody of their two children. While not pleasant, both parties and their children were protected by law. When Andrea and Ellie decided to end their 8-year relationship that had produced three children, no legal protections were in place to provide an equitable settlement of their affairs, not to mention that because Ellie had borne two of the children and Andrea had borne one there were no safeguards in place to ensure the rights of the nonbiological parent.

When Frances lost her husband, Earl, family members gathered at the home, offered Frances support and condolences, mourned at the funeral visitation, attended the funeral, and promised to look after the widow. But when, after forty-five years, Abraham lost his partner, Hap, Hap's family of origin took control of the deceased's body, made the funeral arrangements, ignored Abraham at the wake and funeral, and made plans to sell the house Abraham and Hap had shared for thirty years.

These broadly defined life transitions are illustrative of the many ways gay and lesbian families are differentially treated. Not only are lesbians and gays treated differently with regard to stress associated with the passage of time and the transitions that occur simply because time passed, so, too, are they treated differently with regard to social services available to them. Issues associated with domestic violence and reparative therapy tend to illustrate this reality.

Dealing with Domestic Violence

As noted above, lesbians and gays are at risk of being the victim of a hate crime or the victim of domestic violence simply because of their perceived or actual sexual orientation. Because this reality of violence is present, many lesbians and gays never feel totally safe or secure (Mallon 1998). For social workers working with gays and lesbians, this ongoing insecurity should not be considered pathological—but rather an adaptive strategy for living in a homophobic, hostile environment (Germain and Gitterman 1996; Mallon 1998).

In order to better understand domestic violence, the following cycle of violence is presented. Authors have various conceptual frameworks for defining how violence occurs (Trimble 1994; WISE 1998a), but generally it is presented as a circular activity where the phases always return to a similar starting point. To these conceptualizations it seems necessary to add the idea that rather than being circular, the pattern of violence is a spiral, where each episode of violence moves up the spiral higher and higher until resolution occurs. Figure 5.1 demonstrates this point.

Starting at the bottom, the first phase that leads to violence is that of gaining power. This is where tensions between the gay couple begin to mount, where one is testing her or his dominance and power over the other in small ways. If left to fester, this development of an unequal power base in the relationship may lead to using and abusing power where the more powerful partner uses and abuses power to get her or his way and becomes angry when not in complete control of the less powerful partner. This phase can easily erupt into a violent exploitation of power that results in some type of violence against the weaker partner. Following this exploitation of power, the victim is often psychologically or physically hurt and vulnerable. The perpetrator often feels shame and guilt but blames the victim for causing the violence. This sense of powerlessness on the part of the perpetrator can include a sense of not being in control of her or his actions and yet feeling remorseful.

It is the subsequent remorse and perhaps guilt for the brutality that will

FIGURE 5.1
The Spiral of Violence

Violence has its own pattern that emerges and expands in a spiral fashion where the episodes are of increasing strength and likely to continue until some permanent resolution is determined.

lead the couple into an enabling phase where each is enabled by the other to forgive and forget. This "honeymoon" enabling phase is often one characterized by increased sexual activity, romantic dinners, gifts, and renewed promises that no more violence will occur. Sadly, this phase ebbs as the couple returns to a phase where the more dominant partner, empowered by the last sequence of violence, starts again to gain power by asserting his or her will. Where the circular models fail is in their assumption that after each sequence of violence the couple starts from the beginning. This model assumes that once violence has occurred it will escalate with each subsequent sequence until some resolution is obtained. Unfortunately, resolution tends to occur following the exploitation of power where a violent act has left one partner dead or has given the less powerful partner some way of ending the abusive relationship.

Many social service agencies that provide services to the lesbian and gay community have little understanding of violence within the gay community as it is an underreported crime, victims are often isolated and forced into silence, and it is generally believed that such violence does not occur between lesbian or gay couples (Shernoff 1998; Steinhorn 1998; Vickers 1996). And, while in the early 1990s there were 3,400 animal shelters in the United States, there were only 1,500 battered women's shelters and no shelters for battered men (Domestic Violence: The Facts 1994). As astounding as these statistics seem, most battered women's shelters, even in the late 1990s, do not welcome lesbians (Appleby and Anastas 1998; Vickers 1996).

This lack of support for battered lesbians raises an interesting quandary for social service providers working with same-sex couples and domestic violence. As with nongay domestic violence, the services provided must be aimed at both the victim and the perpetrator—often the service needs of these two groups widely differ. Victims of domestic violence may show signs of physical violence (bruises, burns, bite marks) or emotional damage (depression, suicidal ideation, alcoholism, drug use, anxiety, withdrawal, symptoms of post-traumatic stress disorder) that require intervention (Steinhorn 1998; WISE 1998c). Services for the victim need to include immediate crisis intervention where attention is given to physical and emotional safety needs and medical needs. This can be followed by positive reinforcement, necessary information and referrals, and empowering the victim to move toward resolving and removing the threat of violence (Appleby and Anastas 1998; WISE 1998c). These goals can be accomplished through the development of a supportive and empowering relationship between the client and social worker where the practical issues associated with the violence are met first (WISE 1998e).

Using the empowerment approach, the social worker has a unique opportunity to listen to the client's narrative and define with the client appropriate methods for dealing with issues. In doing so the social worker accepts the client as a whole being who has a unique story. Further, the social worker recognizes that she or he does not have all the answers or a hidden agenda, but rather a different perspective (Forrister

1992) that can be shared with the client in an egalitarian fashion in an effort to present as many views about the situation as are possible.

To facilitate this approach, the practitioner must have a thorough understanding of and ability to use interventive social work roles that will facilitate an open dialogue between the client and practitioner. Such dialogue could focus on such issues as the enormous number of psychosocial pressures faced by gays and lesbians or reframing lesbian and gay relationships as being worthwhile and valuable. In order to successfully accomplish such intervention, the practitioner must be well-informed about the gay community, gay history, and how homophobia has devalued and damaged countless millions of gay persons across time and place.

For example, the rape crisis center of Slidell, Louisiana, had no policies related to providing services to lesbians—their assumption was that only husbands or other male intimates abused their partners. Joy, a 31-year-old married mother with two children was confused about her sexual identity and had been having her first same-sex sexual relationship with Beth, a 35-year-old lesbian who, as a child, had been sexually assaulted and beaten by her stepfather. Beth wanted Joy to take the children and leave her husband so the four of them could be together. Joy was extremely concerned that her husband would not understand and that Beth might not be the right person for her. The situation had escalated from Beth's growing insistence on having Joy move in to having Beth verbally abuse Joy. The abuse included taunts that Joy must not be a "real lesbian" and if Joy did not leave her husband, Beth would out her to not only her husband, but her employers as well. Joy was still not convinced and continued to stay in what was becoming an increasingly abusive relationship with Beth because she felt there was no where to turn and she was emotionally and physically fearful of Beth. After five months of constant arguments, Beth issued an ultimatum—either Joy and the children move in with Beth or Beth was going to go to Joy's house and confront her husband with the truth. As Beth was moving toward her car Joy got between the automobile and Beth. Beth became enraged and began to beat Joy with her fists and rocks from the driveway. Bloodied and brutalized, Joy fled. Believing she could not go home because she feared what her husband would do to Beth, she parked the car and sat in it for hours. A police officer found her semiconscious and called an ambulance. She was treated at the local hospital where the social worker assumed she had been beaten by her husband and referred her to the battered women's shelter. She arrived at the shelter and became a further victim because of the "heterosexual assumption."

Ideally, Beth could have been empowered at the hospital to tell the truth about her abuser and more appropriate information and referrals could have been made. The focus could have been included the assessment of the meaning of the incident by the victim, an evaluation of the victim's resources and social supports, a ventilation by the victim to rid herself of the anger surrounding the incident, a move toward regaining her self-esteem, and a move toward allowing the victim to once again gain control and power over her own body (Appleby and Anastas 1998). Even more ideally, the battered women's shelter could have policies that protect not only the victim, but also the perpetrator. This brings up the second part of the puzzle—the service needs of the perpetrator.

It has been noted that issues of domestic violence revolve around issues of unequal power in relationships, and that there is a general denial of same-sex domestic violence. Because of the general invisibility of the problem, service providers have been slow to acknowledge its existence and therefore slow to develop interventions to address the problem. Just as lesbian victims tend to be seen as similar to their nongay counterparts, lesbians who batter tend to be viewed in a similar light with men who batter. In fact, lesbian batterers are not similarly situated with men who batter (Robson 1997). The differences have yet to be adequately defined, but many lesbians who abuse their partners have been victims of childhood abuse, victims of heterosexism, persons who have little actual perceived power, and victims of low self-esteem (Appleby and Anastas 1998).

Even less is known about gay male abusers, but all lesbian and gay batterers need to acknowledge and own the violence in terms of themselves and its meaning for them personally and for the gay community, learn to control the violence, explore personal needs and feelings related to violence, and explore the antecedent roots of violence within the context of their family of origin. Regrettably, many gay and lesbian perpetrators of violence simply disregard any kind of social services, disengage from the current relationship, and simply move on to new relationships where the violence continues (Appleby and Anastas 1998). With the current lack of appropriate services for either victims or perpetrators of domestic violence, this kind of violence will not be erased in the lesbian and gay community for some time.

Reparative Therapy

In addition to the ability to understand and apply interventive strategies that have a proven track record, the social worker also has to have a basic understanding of therapeutic interventions that, while still practiced by some, are not effective. One such method is that of reparative therapy. Evolving from the psychoanalytic school, reparative therapy has been a treatment approach designed to cure homosexuals from the "disease" of homosexuality. Historically, reparative therapy has been used almost exclusively with men. However, with the emphasis, in the 1990s, on the use of reparative therapy as a cure for homosexuality as lauded by the religious right, more and more lesbians are also being treated with this method. The methods used in this approach range from aversion therapy where the homosexual is given noxious stimuli (electric shock or other unpleasant stimuli) while viewing homosexually oriented stimuli (erotic photographs or other pleasing stimuli) to weekly individual therapeutic sessions or group therapy with other similarly situated persons.

While there has been a resurgence of this type of therapeutic intervention since the early 1990s, this approach has been denounced as, at best, ineffective and, at worst, damaging (Lloyd and Tully 1996). The American Psychiatric Association (1994) does not support the use of reparative therapy, stating that there are no scientific data to support the use of reparative therapy. Even those few practitioners who use this technique agree there is no lasting change from exclusively homosexual behavior to exclusively heterosexual behavior (Bieber 1965; Nicolosi 1991; Socarides 1978). While clinicians must be aware of all treatment options available, treatment modalities that approach homosexuality from a disease focus must be discarded in favor of more current methods.

In an effort to confront what the National Association of Social Workers deems as unethical, reparative therapy has been denounced by NASW. In a position statement dated 1992, the National Committee on Lesbian and Gay Issues of NASW stated that the use of reparative therapy violated the NASW Code of Ethics, as it condoned discrimination and encouraged homophobia. Further, the use of such therapies violates the 1987 NASW policy statement opposing discrimination directed toward gays and lesbians (NCLGI 1992).

Michael is a 17-year-old African-American who had come to terms with his nontraditional sexual orientation by the time he was 15. He lived with his parents and younger sister in an upper middle-class neighborhood in Brookline, Massachusetts. His father, a medical doctor with Harvard's medical school, was financially secure enough to send his only son to Andover Academy, an expensive private school. Michael's mother overheard him talking on his cellular phone to his boyfriend, Clark, and then discovered what she described as disgusting and loathsome love letters from Clark. His mother confronted Michael with her belief that he was a queer, which he did not deny, and then said some decisions would be made by his father. The decision made by Michael's father was that the boy would begin reparative therapy. After a lengthy Internet search about reparative therapy, Michael realized what lay ahead and sought support from the school's social worker.

Unknown to Michael, the social worker, Josef, was gay and knew about the Gay, Lesbian, and Straight Education Network (GLSTEN) and Parents, Families, and Friends of Lesbians and Gays (PFLAG). He also knew of the dangers of reparative therapy and, after two sessions with Michael where he determined his client's assessment of the current situation and identified possible strategies, scheduled a meeting with Michael's parents.

In sum, providing micro-level intervention to gays and lesbians requires the clinician to incorporate social work knowledge, skills, and values developed for work with any population and to then use knowledge, skills, and values germane to this particular disenfranchised minority group. This is true also when working with lesbians and gays at the community and institutional levels.

Mezzo-Level Intervention

As defined, mezzo-level intervention deals with social work activities centered at the community level. The gay and lesbian community has been conceptualized as a subculture existing within the larger, nongay society that is comprised of its own economic, religious, educational, social, and political arenas (Albro and Tully 1979; Harry and Devall 1978). Because the gay and lesbian community is a heterogeneous one, there have been few things that have united it to take action. One era of community continuity was the gay rights movement leading to and following the Stonewall Riots of the 1960s. This era, flowing from the civil rights and women's rights movements of the same time, witnessed lesbian and gay persons actively demonstrating for equal rights. This battle is still being waged but, because of different philosophical views promulgated by the two national organizations championing gay rights (NGLTF and HRC), the community is split as to how to best achieve civil rights. However, because the size of the lesbian and gay community seems large enough to accommodate various approaches as it works toward civil rights, this difference of opinion may be viewed as a strength.

The older of the two organizations, the National Gay and Lesbian Task

TABLE 5.3
Providing Services to Gay and Lesbian Adults

For clinicians working with lesbian or gay adults, the following points should be considered:

AT THE MICRO-LEVEL

Realize that most gay adults come from nongay families of origin;

Understand that coming out is not related to chronological age and can occur at any point in a person's life;

Be aware of all the complexities about coming out as an adult;

Do not assume that all persons are heterosexual;

Become familiar with issues around creating and maintaining families of choice;

Be willing to talk honestly about sexual matters;

Do not treat lesbian couples and gay male couples as homogeneous-women and men have been socialized differently and have different views;

Develop an understanding of emerging research related to gay and lesbian families;

Do not assume that the presenting problem has to do with sexual orientation;

Become culturally sensitive and aware of racial and ethnic cultures different from you own;

Be alert and cautious of reparative therapy and other dangerous psychological or spiritual techniques designed to "cure" homosexuality;

Be supportive and allow the individual to tell her/his story in her/his own way and time;

Do not view all lesbians and gays as the same-avoid stereotyping and do not be swayed by gay mythology;

Be comfortable with your own sexual orientation and not homophobic;

Appreciate psychosocial pressures faced by lesbians and gays.

AT THE MEZZO-LEVEL

Become aware of the gay community and its resources;

View the individual in the context of both the gay and nongay worlds

Learn about agency policies that impact lesbian and gay families;

Hold in-service agency training to ensure that workers are taught to work effectively with gay and lesbian family units;

Develop community services designed to include gay and lesbian familie;

Promote advocacy in the nongay community for the gay community;

Implement nondiscrimination policies that include lesbian and gays;

Challenge homophobia.

TABLE 5.3 (continued)
Providing Services to Gay and Lesbian Adults

AT THE MACRO-LEVEL

Develop an in-depth understanding about local, state, and federal laws that impact gay families;

Become an advocate for gay and lesbian causes;

Build coalitions to support lesbian and gay issues at the local, state, and federal levels;

Challenge discriminatory laws;

Confront institutional homophobia at all levels.

Force (NGLTF), emerged at a time when community organization was at a grassroots level and remains a champion of the oppressed, combating discrimination using techniques of civil disobedience, defiance, and other confrontational means. The NGLTF appeals to a younger, more liberal, less financially secure group. The Human Rights Campaign (HRC) is an organization dedicated to gaining human rights for lesbians and gays through the more established means of political lobbying, education, and information. The HRC appeals to more conservative, financially well off, older gays and lesbians. These two organizations seem to typify the schism within the gay and lesbian community of the 1990s and represent two means by which community organization has occurred in this community.

Another time of community coherence came in the 1980s with the emergence of the AIDS virus. Because the newly discovered virus hit the male homosexual community first and with such devastating outcomes (outcomes that are still being felt), gays and lesbians came together as a community to struggle with the effects of this horror. Centers dedicated to providing testing, counseling, and other social services emerged; laws about HIV/AIDS were passed, hospice services grew, and the community learned how to cope with the stigma of AIDS.

Social workers have had, and continue to play, a role in activities spawned by the radicalism of the 1960s and the devastation of the AIDS pandemic. Social workers are currently active with both the National Gay and Lesbian Task Force and the Human Rights Campaign. They are involved with such radical activities as storming the Georgia legislature with a group called Queer Nation and picketing the Centers for Disease

Control with ACT-UP. They are additionally involved with the Human Rights Campaign lobbying state legislators and forming political action groups. Social workers, too, have created and staffed countless AIDS centers and continue to play a vital role in the development of services for people with HIV/AIDS.

Barry was diagnosed as being HIV+ in the late 1980s. He considered himself a politically savvy young activist and joined NGLTF in order to empower himself and others like him to advocate on behalf of those with HIV/AIDS. As a grassroots organization member he spoke at local high schools and colleges, taught safe-sex seminars at the AIDS office, and handed out condoms on city streets to prostitutes and homeless persons. He was supported in these efforts by a social service network that not only empowered him to participate in these activities, but also provided a means for him to do so by helping him find a paid staff position with a local AIDS service organization. This example is one that was not possible during most of the 1980s when HIV/AIDS was considered a problem created by and confined to the gay male community. During the decade of the 1980s, the nongay community left the issue of HIV/AIDS in the hands of the gay and lesbian community.

In sum, the roles available for social work practitioners within the gay and lesbian community are generally defined by geographic locale (rural areas may have a high need, but few opportunities while urban areas offer more opportunities for intervention), community identification of problems (before the AIDS crisis needs were different), societal acceptance of a gay and lesbian community (southern and mid-western communities tend to be less accepting), community spirit (how actively involved are members of the gay community), and funding available for such community intervention. There is a great need for the gay and lesbian community to find a more common voice in its approach to the issues of the day, and yet to date we have not been able to meet that goal. Perhaps, as federal legislation is passed and institutions become more homosocial such unity can be achieved.

Macro-Level Intervention

Macro-level intervention is that intervention that involves social system changes that impact institutions and cultural mores. Admittedly fewer social workers are involved with macro-level interventions than interventions with individuals, families, groups, or even communities. Yet, this level of intervention can be exciting, challenging, and rewarding for those interested in policy development, implementation, and evaluation. One primary way social system changes come about is through the development and passage of public policy. Ideally, policy issues emerge from identified social problems that impact various populations and are enacted in order to solve some pressing social issue. Whether at the local, state, or federal level, policy development impacts significantly how social institutions are regulated and how members of society must relate to one another (Karger and Stoesz 1998). For example, without changes in social policy slavery might still be legal, women could not vote, and prohibition might still be in place. Within the sphere of macro-level intervention changes must be enacted to protect gay and lesbians by providing them basic human rights not currently protected under the law.

As noted in chapter 1, throughout history there have been a variety of legal sanctions and proscriptions against lesbians and gays. While some eras have been less harsh than others, gay persons have traditionally never enjoyed a time when they had equal rights with nongays and have generally been persecuted as being less worthwhile, mentally ill, and vile creatures unworthy of legal protections.

Since the 1960s there has been a gradual, but constant effort to ensure basic human rights and protections for lesbians and gays. Such has evolved through such protections as legally approved nondiscrimination policies, domestic partnership protections, durable powers of attorney, employment protections, repeal of sodomy laws, and second parent adoptions, as well as religiously sanctioned commitment ceremonies (Birch 1998; NGLTF 1997).

Even with such progress, as of 1998, only nine states include sexual orientation in their nondiscrimination laws while only seven others are considering such legislation (HRC 1998). Sadly, discrimination continues. A Baptist church in Texas came under fire for welcoming gay and lesbian persons as parishioners (Cropper 1998), gay and lesbian discharges from the armed services have increased 67 percent since the Clinton administration adopted the "Don't Ask, Don't Tell" policy (Benecke 1998), and more than 470 hate groups with more than 160 web sites on the worldwide web blanket America (SPLC 1998). In 1998, the radical right and Christian Coalition continue to promote discrimination on the basis of sexual orientation, Maine repealed its protections for gays and lesbians, and federal legislation ending employment discrimination on the basis of sexual orientation was narrowly defeated (Louisiana Electorate of Gays and Lesbians 1998; Louisiana Lesbian and Gay Political Action Caucus 1998; Salkind 1998).

These issues are but a few impacting not only gays and lesbians, but a variety of persons. And, these are some of the many issues needing macro-level intervention from social workers. As with services provided at the micro- and mezzo-levels, macro-level interventions use the same basic empowerment skills and knowledge—understanding the context of the issue at hand from the perspective and view of those impacted, acting in a collegial fashion to determine possible solutions, and then empowering self and others to create change. One example of how the gay and lesbian community has dealt with the AIDS crisis may serve as an example of the interplay between the micro- mezzo-, and macro-levels of intervention.

Dealing with AIDS

The early 1980s brought what was to become one of the issues around which gays and lesbians could reach common ground. As horrifying as the AIDS crisis has become since then, gay persons in the United States have worked together in coping with a disease that has ravaged generations of gay men, touched lesbians, and is now creeping into more and more populations, including minorities of color, drug abusers, and the elderly (Aronstein and Thompson 1998; Hooyman and Kiyak 1998; Gant 1998; Lloyd 1995; Shernoff 1998). By 1996, more than 500,000 persons have been estimated to have died from the disease, while almost one million people in the United States are HIV+ and 170,000 are living with AIDS (Gant 1998). While it is outside the scope of this book to discuss all the issues associated with social work with HIV+ persons, it is important for the social worker who employs an empowerment perspective to have a general understanding of some areas associated with providing interventive services to men and women who are HIV+. As with every social issue, AIDS can be addressed at the micro-, mezzo-, or macro-level. In an effort to examine some of the unique issues associated with this disease, we will briefly explore the impact of HIV/AIDS from all three perspectives.

At the micro-level, AIDS has created the need for a variety of services. When first identified in the early 1980s, this new disease was called GRID (Gay Related Immune Disease), and while that term was quickly replaced with the term AIDS (Acquired Immune Deficiency Syndrome), the lingering perception is that AIDS is a gay disease (Lloyd 1995; Shernoff 1998). Perhaps because when first diagnosed HIV/AIDS was primarily a concern for gay men, the gay community rallied to the support of its members. Self-help groups formed, individual gay men began learning about this

TABLE 5.4
Special Issues Associated with HIV/AIDS

The following represent special issues social workers must consider when working with persons impacted by HIV/AIDS.

AT THE MICRO-LEVEL

Learn the terminology associated with HIV/AIDS;

Know how the disease is transmitted and prevented;

Know the various manifestations of HIV/AIDS;

Assess client risk of exposure by asking about sexual behaviors;

Be aware of cultural situations that might indicate risk factors (e.g. male transmission to his wife);

Link clients and services;

Understand the ups and downs associated with the disease;

Be comfortable discussing sex and sexual behaviors;

Know "harm reduction" techniques and "safer sex" practices;

Counsel with clients before and after their HIV test;

Understand the ethical implications and confidentiality issues associated with HIV/AIDS;

Be able to assist terminally ill clients and their families;

Understand the differences between living with and dying from AIDS.

AT THE MEZZO-LEVEL

Know where anonymous or confidential HIV/AIDS testing is available;

Be aware of where appropriate services for HIV/AIDS persons can be found;

Learn about agency policies that impact HIV/AIDS clients and their families;

Hold in-service agency training to ensure that workers are taught to work effectively with HIV/AIDS persons;

Develop community services designed to include HIV/AIDS persons;

Promote advocacy in the nongay community for issues associated with HIV/AIDS;

Build bridges between client needs and agency services.

AT THE MACRO-LEVEL

Understand the legal and civil rights of persons with HIV/AIDS;

Develop an in-depth understanding about local, state, and federal laws that impact persons with HIV/AIDS;

Become an advocate for persons with HIV/AIDS;

Build coalitions to support HIV/AIDS issues at the local, state, and federal levels;

Challenge policies, practices, and laws that discriminate on the basis of medical status;

sexually transmitted disease, agency workers began to provide services to persons with AIDS, lesbians became involved in defining and providing services for gay friends, and hundreds and then thousands of gay men began to die (Gant 1995; Lloyd 1995).

Micro-level services have evolved from the volunteer staffed self-help groups of the 1980s to an entire network of federally funded services provided in the 1990s. Services include case management, discharge planning, acute care, bereavement care, hospice, advocacy, individual therapy, group therapy, and family therapy. These services are provided to babies, children, adolescents, adults, elders, parents, gay men, lesbians, ethnic minorities, nongay persons, urbanites, rural dwellers across every socioeconomic strata (Aronstein and Thompson 1998; Lloyd 1995; Shernoff 1998). Table 5.5 identifies some special areas social workers should consider when working with those dealing with HIV/AIDS.

Since its inception, the AIDS crisis has brought the gay and lesbian community together by providing a defined cause around which gay men and lesbians could rally. There remains a stigma attached to the diagnosis of HIV/AIDS and, despite advocacy activities and initiatives since the mid 1980s, community, organization, and governmental practices, policies, and laws fail to adequately address the ongoing devastation caused by this virus. A few areas that require intervention include the further development of adequate drugs, access to clinical trials, the regulation of drugs, insurance issues, the health care system's response to HIV/AIDS, nursing home regulations, federal and state legislation associated with HIV/AIDS, and ensuring adequate funding for services (Aronstein and Thompson 1998; Gant 1995; Lloyd 1995). Because as a social issue HIV/AIDS impacts virtually every segment of society, and because policies are still being developed, implemented, and assessed, social work practitioners working at the mezzo- and macro-levels continue to have had an opportunity to influence public policy in this arena (Lloyd 1995).

In sum, all social work practitioners will be confronted in some way by the HIV/AIDS pandemic. It becomes the professional's duty to be able to empower those affected to best confront the challenges that face those living with HIV/AIDS, those dying from AIDS, and their caregivers, families, and friends.

The Empowerment Model Applied

The preceding sections have explored a variety of concepts associated with adult lesbians and gays and the empowerment perspective. The following section demonstrates how the empowerment model can be applied at the mezzo-level when working with adult gays or lesbians. As in chapter 4, where a micro-level example was provided, it might be helpful to refer to figure 3.3, tables 3.1 and 3.4.

As an example, assume you are a social worker employed by the Long Prairie, Minnesota, welfare department as a community organizer. As a community, Long Prairie is a county seat but has fewer than 5,000 inhabitants. It is considered by some to be a heterogeneous, typically midwestern town that espouses traditionally conservative values and mores. The closest university, the University of North Dakota in Grand Forks, is approximately 190 miles northwest. Long Prairie and other surrounding towns like Bertha, Wadena, and Eagle Bend have been informed that a conference dealing with homosexuality is to be held at the university in the near future. Members of the communities are of differing opinions about whether or not such a conference should be held and tempers are beginning to boil. Several editorials have been printed in the local newspapers—some vow to picket the event, others vow to stop the protests at all costs. For the first time in history, the emergence of what seems to be a gay and lesbian community and its supporters becomes visible. Although you never thought you would need to know much, if anything, about the differences between the gay and lesbian community and the nongay community, you have been asked to ensure that the conference does not erupt into threatened violence.

A first step might be for you to specifically be able to differentiate between the nongay and gay communities. To facilitate this, you would need to be able to identify lesbian or gay persons willing to talk with you and then meet. One purpose of such a meeting would be to begin to identify formal and informal structures within the gay and lesbian community and to analyze where these structures were separate from, identical to, or overlapping with similar structures in the nongay community. By learning about the similarities and differences in the communities you are able to then begin to determine the role of institutional homophobia, heterosexism, and oppression in the lesbian and gay community.

Having established some understanding of the gay and lesbian community and its place in the nongay society, it is important to explore existing federal, state, and local statutes related to lesbian and gay persons in your area. This knowledge will also facilitate a better understanding of the role of homophobia in your area. Having gained a broader understanding of the gay and lesbian community and the laws related to lesbians and gays, it is vital to discover what resources are available in both the gay and nongay communities that will provide support for lesbian and gay issues. Accomplishing these things is best done in open and honest dialogue with those involved. By identifying issues, available resources, and strengths a specific action plan that uses supportive gay and nongay resources can be created and implemented.

Ideally, what would evolve from the above example would be an increased awareness of the needs and concerns of both the lesbian and gay community and the nongay community. The gay and lesbian community will, no doubt, discover support for their issues in places previously not thought of and the nongay community will have to begin to evaluate itself in light of previously ignored concepts like homophobia. The key to such understanding is that of dialogue between persons in specific social situations and the empowering of the community to ensure that the needs of all its members are identified and explored.

With these and other principles of empowerment in mind, the following case studies provide opportunities for applying these concepts.

Case Studies

The following case vignettes are designed to facilitate discussion and to stimulate various ideas for providing intervention. There is a vignette related to each area of practice (micro-, mezzo-, and macro-). Things to remember when exploring options to interventive services include: a specific definition of the presenting problem and issues that may underlie the problem, the role of the client and the clinician, the strengths and challenges presented by the presenting problem, possible solutions to the problem based on a realistic assessment by both the client and the clinician, interactions between the gay and nongay communities and how those impact the situation, the role of homophobia (institutional, individual, and internal), and how specifically the empowerment perspective can be applied.

The Visitor
Harry, a 66-year-old semiretired lawyer, had lived with David, a 48-year-old high school principal, for three years. Harry's previous relationship of twenty-seven years had ended following the death, due to complications from AIDS, of his partner, Roberto. Harry is HIV positive as is David. Both show mild effects of the virus, but are relatively well thanks to a continuing regimen

of drugs. David's previous relationship of fifteen years had terminated because Maximillian had decided he preferred to be single and had moved to Montana. Harry had no family, and David's family, who lived nearby, was aware and supportive of the relationship between them. David, a devout Catholic, attended mass every Sunday and participated in all the church rituals. Harry, a lapsed Baptist, had no objections to this. Harry and David seemed the ideal couple. Both were very much in love with the other and very involved in each other's lives both professionally and socially.

They were active in the nongay community where both were actors in little theater productions, enjoyed social activities with nongay friends, and assumed no one knew they were gay. The topic of their living situation never was discussed, each had his own telephone line, and personal communications were sent to separate addresses. Both were also extremely active in the gay community where both had been involved for more than twenty years. They attended and gave dinner parties for their gay and lesbian friends, went to a variety of social activities with gay colleagues and friends, and were well known within the gay community where they did not attempt to hide their relationship.

On the occasions where their gay and nongay friends happened to attend the same social event, no mention was ever made of sexual orientation. This generally seemed not to create any conflict between them as, professionally, both believed they had to hide their sexual orientation in order to maintain their professional identities and their employment. Because Harry's house had a swimming pool and was larger, when the two of them decided to live together it was jointly decided that David would rent his house and move into Harry's. This arrangement worked most of the time.

Annually, Harry invited a professional, nongay colleague, Beatrice, from out of town to teach a week-long seminar related to Harry's law firm. To save expenses and to prevent his colleague the discomfort of staying in a hotel for a week, Harry always invited Beatrice to stay at his home. Beatrice had met and stayed with Roberto and Harry for a couple of years before Roberto's death. The topic of sexual orientation never arose and the two men made every effort to have the home appear to be divided into separate living quarters. The time of Beatrice's annual visit arrived just after Harry and David had been living together for almost a year.

Because Harry did not want Beatrice to think that David lived with him, Harry demanded that David move out of the house for a week and go stay with gay friends. Harry said he would care for David's dog and cats, but that David must not spend the night in the house while Beatrice was in town and it must appear as though Harry and David were merely friends. Reluctantly,

David agreed to this arrangement and packed a suitcase. He spent the week with Mark and Luis who, while providing him a place to stay, thought the arrangement was insane and could not understand why David would put up with such nonsense. Unfortunately, David had not packed a week's worth of his medication and had to call Harry in an effort to get his pills. Harry was furious but agreed that David could come by the house when Beatrice was lecturing to pick up his medication. David did so. By the end of the week David had been home only briefly and had only seen Harry twice, both in social settings with Beatrice, where the conversation was extremely awkward. When Beatrice finally left and David moved back into his home, things were tense. Harry thought his actions were completely within reason, David felt confused, angry, and began to question the validity of the relationship.

Because both valued the relationship, they agreed to get an opinion from a third party. They have just arrived in your waiting room.

Seeking Shelter

Christine, a 35-year-old botanist, had lived with Carla, a 34-year-old lawyer, for twelve years. During their relationship both had gone through graduate school, had purchased a home in the historic section of the city, nurtured countless cats, and were always active in their neighborhood association. They were well known in the lesbian community and viewed by their friends as having a "perfect" relationship that seemed loving and free from stress. They had few financial difficulties as both were professionally employed in well-paying jobs. They enjoyed what most would call "the good life" where, at least on the surface, everything looked wonderful. There was, however, a dark side to this seemingly idyllic relationship.

For the first four years of the relationship things were fine. Both Carla and Christine worked on fixing up the house, getting comfortable with their relationship, and enjoying trips to the beach to bird watch. Once the two entered their respective graduate programs, things begin to deteriorate piece by piece. First, Carla wanted to have one of her law school professors join the couple for a trip to the beach. Next, Christine wanted to spend the weekend with her ex-lover. Realizing there were issues with monogamy, both decided to enter into a non-monogamous relationship with one another. This worked amicably for almost a year at which time Carla flew into a rage over one of Christine's latest love affairs. The result was the first physical fight between the two.

Totally distraught at her temper tantrum, a weeping Carla promised such a thing would never happen again and the two entered a new honeymoon phase in their relationship. This lasted for almost a year when Carla decided to place an ad in a local gay newspaper seeking someone with whom to have an affair. When Christine discovered a copy of the draft of the ad in the trash, she became infuriated, leading to another physical altercation where she threw a wineglass at Carla. The glass broke causing Carla to have to be rushed to the emergency room of the local hospital were 16 stitches were taken in her leg.

Realizing this kind of behavior was inappropriate, Christine vowed such an event would never happen again, and again the two entered a peaceful, honeymoon period. This pattern of behavior was to repeat itself often enough over the next several years to cause both Christine and Carla to lie about the bruises and broken bones they always seemed to have. By the start of the twelfth year together Christine had suffered both physical and psychological abuse to the point she could no longer keep her job. This infuriated Carla who, upon hearing that Christine no longer had a job, began to beat her, and threaten her with a knife. Christine finally broke down and left. She took with her only a few dollars and what clothes she had on. Although she had called a friend and had explained her situation, the friend was not in a position to be of assistance and suggested she go to the battered women's shelter.

Because she was terrified of returning home and felt she had no where to turn, Christine found her way to the battered women's shelter. When she arrived at the shelter and explained her situation, a social worker informed her that because she was a lesbian she would not be able to stay at the shelter. After being turned away from the shelter Christine went home and was found murdered the following day. Carla was arrested for the murder. As the social worker who was forced by agency policy to turn Christine away, you feel somewhat responsible and are anxious to implement agency policies that will protect all members of the community.

A Capitol Experience

Amy and Rose, a lesbian couple who have been together for several years, want to start a family. Because of several physical realities, they decide that Amy should become the biological parent. After a normal pregnancy Amy and Rose's babies (a healthy set of twins) were born. They are now 3 years old. Since their birth, Rose has been trying to legally adopt the children so as to have legal rights in matters that concern the twins. Amy fully supports this action and is also trying to ensure legal protections for the children should anything happen to her. While several states do provide for second-parent adoptions, the state in which the family currently resides fails to recognize the importance of such.

The issues Amy and Rose have encountered as they try and persuade their

state representatives include overt and covert homophobia—one state sena-
tor said in a committee hearing that "queer couples are an abomination
against God, and the legislature, as God's elected representatives on Earth,
should do everything possible to keep children out of the clutches of such vile
creatures." Other representatives have been less overt, but their homophobia
is evident; when Amy or Rose try and talk with them they retreat into closed
offices without comment.

Amy and Rose do have some support. Because the issue of second-parent
adoptions does not only impact lesbian and gay couples, the Child Welfare
League has agreed it to be in the best interest of the child to have, whenever
possible, two parents, no matter what sex. Their support, coupled with a
grassroots movement in favor of the legalizing of second-parent adoptions,
has led to having several house members introduce H.B. 987: Second Parent
Adoptions. The bill has been sent to committee for hearings.

As a member of Social Workers Concerned with Equity, you have been
called on to ensure passage of this bill.

This chapter has focused on the use of the empowerment perspective with
gay and lesbian adults. Developmental challenges for lesbians and gays,
families of origin, and families of choice were discussed. Differences
between lesbian women and gay men were addressed and common relationship dilemmas were identified. Issues assoiated with domestic violence, AIDS, and the special needs of HIV+ persons were detailed and
coming out as an adult was explored. Micro-, mezzo-, and macro-level
interventions with adult gays and lesbians were analyzed; the empowerment model was applied using a mezzo-level example; and case examples
in each area were presented for discussion.

6

Empowerment and Older Lesbians and Gays

*There is no longer any reason for the social work pro-
fession to ignore the needs of the older homosexual and
lesbian. As the elderly population increases in size, and
as greater numbers of gays and lesbians, young and old,
assert their sexual identity and their right to services, the
perspectives and needs of older homosexuals will come
to the fore. The social work profession can meet this
challenge only to the extent that it is knowledgeable
about this group.*   Berger 1982:241.

As mentioned throughout this book, gays and lesbians are not a visible
minority. Lesbian and gay youths have been identified as being at particular risk because of their invisible status, but perhaps even more at risk
are gays and lesbians who are no longer middle-aged, but old. This group,
whose numbers we will never know exactly, has been, until the 1970s, all
but ignored by society generally and the gay community specifically. Professional social work did not begin showing interest in the elderly population until the early 1970s, and another decade or more passed before
social work began to grapple with the needs and issues of this minority
(Berger 1980, 1982; Kelly 1977; Lee 1987; Tully 1983).

The estimated size of the older gay community has never been known,
but using census data that indicate a total population in the United States
of approximately 33.2 million who are 65 years of age or older (U.S. Census 1995), there may be as many as 996,000 (3% of the total number of
elderly) to 3.3 million (10% of the total number of elderly) older lesbians
and gays in this country. The numbers of older persons in this country are
growing each year. By the year 2050 the elderly population could be as
high as 80 million persons (U.S. Census 1995). This will mean an increase,

too, in the numbers of gay and lesbian elderly who, in 2050, could number from 2.4 million to 8 million persons.

No standard definition exists for the construct of "old age" and there are various definitions embedded within the term. Chronological age, the term most commonly used to operationalize the concept of age, refers to how many years an individual has actually lived. Psychological age refers to the person's psychic adaptive and coping mechanisms, and biological age refers to the rate at which the body is deteriorating in relation to a potential life span. For example, post mortem examinations on persons in their twenties have revealed hardening of the arteries, a condition more usually seen in older persons (Soldo 1980). Functional age is defined by how well one actually is able to function physiologically and mentally, and social aging refers to how one is fulfilling various social roles and expectations. If someone suffers a stroke at age 45, the person may have lived into middle age chronologically, but yet have a functional and social age of someone many years older. Similarly, one can be quite old chronologically, but have a psychological view of the world that is quite young. In sum, the concept of age and aging is multidimensional, being based on heredity, environment, and the individual's abilities to adapt. Gerontologists have yet to agree on a common definition of aging but frequently use chronological age as a standard. Because the passage of years has a more universally agreed upon definition and is perhaps the easiest to understand, chronological age is how aging is defined in this text. However, having said that, what constitutes old age?

Gerontology, the study of aging, is a relatively new science simply because until quite recently people did not generally live into old age. Even in the 1990s, the life expectancy of someone born in the United States was 72 for men and 79 for women (U.S. Census 1995). In comparison, persons who are today's elders—those born in the 1920s and 1930s who, when born, could expect to live to be in their sixties (U.S. Census 1995). Gerontologists have broken down the idea of age into four useful categories—the "youngest-old" (the fractious) or those between the ages of 50 and 64; the "young-old" (the frisky), those between 65 and 74; the "old-old" (the frail), those between the ages of 75 and 84; and the "oldest-old" (the fragile), those aged 85 and over. The last group, those 85 and older, are the fastest growing group of persons in this country, and 72 percent of them are women. Between 1960 and 1990, their numbers increased an astonishing 274 percent while the entire country's population increased only 45 percent (Hooyman and Kiyak 1996; U.S. Census

1995). These statistics foreshadow an increasing need for social work practitioners to become better acquainted with the needs and issues associated with older persons generally.

Specifically, this chapter will focus on the needs and issues associated with those possible one million to three million lesbian and gay elders that are currently living in this country, some of whom may need social work intervention. The first part explores what is already known about older lesbians and gays, including various issues associated with aging such as relationships, illness, death and dying, and legal dilemmas. The second section focuses on concepts, methods, and practice skills designed to empower older gays and lesbians, and the final section presents case studies designed to help the practitioner practice her or his skills with this client population.

Growing Older Gay and Lesbian: Gayging

Studying any aspects of aging is a fairly recent phenomenon having begun following World War II. So, perhaps not surprising, only since the 1970s have studies involving gays and lesbians been conducted with any regularity. The early studies of the gay community were centered almost exclusively on gay men because lesbian samples, while sought, were difficult to find (Berger 1980, 1982; Kelly 1977). Systematic study of the older lesbian began in the late 1970s. And, although studies using older lesbians and gays continue, this is an area of inquiry that still needs investigation. The following sections will explore what research has demonstrated about gays and lesbians and will then describe typical issues associated with growing older in a homophobic climate.

The Older Gay Man

Since the early 1970s there has been a growing number of studies that have explored the realities of aging as a gay man. Generally exploratory in nature, they examine the myths and realities of aging in our society, sexuality and aging, psychological and sociological adjustment to aging, relationships, community involvement, death and dying, and legal dilemmas.

As with other populations of lesbians and gays, older gays and lesbians face stigmatization and discrimination in a society that often fails to acknowledge or legitimize their existence. Often this discrimination is found in myths and stereotypes associated with the older gay man (see table 6.1). While the stereotype of the typical nongay older person is that of a politically conservative, religious, probably senile person incapable of sexual activity, the older gay man is stereotyped as one who ia a radical, sexual predator who preys on children or young males or has anonymous sexual encounters in public places. Further, the older gay man is seen as being old before his time, lonely, isolated, and unable to form or maintain lasting relationships. Finally, the older gay man is perceived as not being part of the gay community, preferring to remain hidden in the closet fearing exposure of his sexual orientation (Adelman 1980; Berger 1980, 1982, 1996; Francher and Henkin 1973; Kelly 1977; Kimmel 1977; Lucco 1987; Relkin 1990; Wahler and Gabbay 1997).

Because the older gay community is as diverse as its nongay counterpart, some of these generalities may apply to some members of the community of older gay men. However, data refute these stereotypes as nothing more than myths perpetuated by a society that is homophobic. When examining the intimate and sexual relationships of older gay men, the data do not support the myth of the older gay man as a sexual predator who seduces children, pays young hustlers for sexual favors, or opts for anonymous sex in public places. The portrait that does emerge about the sexual activities of older gay men is that these men are sexually active and sexually satisfied, although the number of sexual partners and encounters decreases with age (Adelman 1980; Berger 1980, 1982, 1996; Francher and Henkin 1973; Kelly 1974, 1977; Kimmel 1977, 1979; Lee 1987; Lucco 1987; Pope and Schulz 1990).

Data also indicate that many older men live with life partners in relationships that have been characterized by Berger (1982) as "committed." These relationships, often of long duration, are characterized by a commitment on the part of those involved to sustain the relationship. Such relationships may or may not be sexually monogamous. Other types of relationships in which older gay men find themselves include "independent," where the older man has a lifelong history of brief affairs and friendships, preferring to live alone and maintain a few close friends. Berger's third category, "ambisexual," would be termed "bisexual" in the 1990s. These men, many of whom have heterosexually married, maintain sexual encounters with both women and men. Some choose an entirely gay lifestyle once separated from their wives; others prefer to exist in both the gay and nongay worlds.

In exploring the question whether or not older gay men are lonely and isolated, research has contradictory findings. Some studies revealed that up to 33 percent of older gay men live alone (Berger 1982; Friend 1980;

Weinberg 1970) and loneliness has been identified as a problem for many older gay men (Kelly 1977). Other studies show that older gay men do not report loneliness to be a problem (Weinberg 1970) and that these men have significant friendships with three or more persons and regularly associate with persons who are their own age as well as those younger than themselves (Atchley 1977; Berger 1982; Friend 1980; Kelly 1977; Lucco 1987; Weinberg 1970).

When asked about their views on aging, older gay men did not perceive themselves as aging faster than their nongay counterparts (Minnigerode 1976), and may experience less anxiety about aging than other groups (Berger 1980, 1982, 1996). While some have negative attitudes (Berger 1980, 1982, 1996; Friend 1990; Kelly 1977), many have a positive view of aging (Jay and Young 1977; Lee 1987; Saghir and Robbins 1973). Aging gay men tend to experience similar anxiety to becoming older as all persons—fears of dependency, illness, loss of loved ones, institutionalization (Kelly 1977; Lucco 1987).

One stereotype that also seems to have little basis in fact is that of the older gay man hiding in the closet, fearful that someone will disclose his sexual orientation. Interestingly, older gay men (and lesbians) many of whom have already come out to families and friends, find being older allows them to be more open and honest about their sexual orientation generally. Having retired from their employment they face no recrimination from possibly homophobic employers. And while some older gay men choose not to reveal their sexual orientation, they do so less because of fear of disclosure but more as a matter of privacy—simply, their sexual orientation is not germane (Adelman 1980; Berger 1982, 1996; Francher and Henkin 1973; Kelly 1977; Minnigerode and Adelman 1978).

In sum, the exploration of the older gay man is still in its infancy. Since the 1970s fewer than 100 published articles (Wahler and Gabbay 1997 examined 58) exist on this population. Most explore general demographic characteristics of the population and have yet to gather data on differences between this group and nongay elders, housing needs, institutionalized gay men, rural and urban issues, the role of ethnicity, or a host of other research questions vital to the understanding of this disenfranchised population. Further, the data that has been collected on older gay men has been biased toward white, well educated, financially secure, healthy men using relatively small samples. What data do exist tend to support the idea that the older gay man is as heterogeneous and complex as his nongay counterpart and cannot be characterized by a set of stereotypic generalities.

Table 6.1
Older Lesbians and Gays: Myths and Realities

MYTHS AND STEREOTYPES

The following are myths and stereotypes associated with older lesbians and gay men. Their roots lie in institutional homophobia, have no basis in fact, and must be refuted by practitioners.

Generally, all older lesbians and gay men:

Are lonely and isolated;

Are unhappy and live alone;

Experience accelerated aging;

Are decidedly peculiar and senile;

Are unconnected with the gay community;

Are pathetic and tragic figures;

Older gay men:

See themselves "old" at 30;

Are increasingly effeminate ("old queens");

Are oversexed, but with an unsatisfactory sex life;

Prey on small children or younger men for sex;

Have anonymous sex in public places;

Are unable to form or maintain lasting relationships;

Are all hidden in the closet fearing disclosure.

Older lesbian women:

Are heartless and unemotional;

Have no families;

Attempt to seduce younger women for sexual gratification;

Are bitter;

Are chronically unhealthy;

Are physically ugly.

REALITIES

While no truth is absolute, the following are based on data and tend to refute the myths and stereotypes.

Generally, older lesbians and gay men:

Are not lonely, isolated or disconnected from the gay community;

May live alone, but do so generally because of the death of a partner;

Do not experience accelerated aging and may age better than nongays;

Are not particularly odd, peculiar, pathetic, or tragic.

TABLE 6.1 (continued)
Older Lesbians and Gays: Myths and Realities

REALITIES

Older gay men:

    Do not become overly effeminate as they age;

    Do not prey on children, lust after younger men for sex, or have anonymous sex in public places;

    Live in long-term relationships, short-term relationships, or alone;

    May or may not be open about their sexual orientation.

Older lesbians:

    Are not bitter, heartless, or unemotional;

    Are as healthy or healthier than nongay older women;

    Prefer women of their own age cohort for sexual activities;

    Are no worse looking physically than older nongay women;

    Have both families of origin and families of choice.

The Older Lesbian

If we know little about the older gay man, we know even less about the older lesbian. Research on this overlooked minority began in the late 1970s and continues, with little enthusiasm, today. Issues associated with aging are primarily related to women simply because women tend to live longer than men. Fifty-six percent of the population between the ages of 65–74 are female while 72 percent of the population over 75 is female (Hooyman and Kiyak 1996). Largely ignored by nongay society and gay society, subject to sexism, ageism, and homophobia, older lesbians may number between 558,000 and 18.6 million women—too large a population to be generally overlooked, but what do we know of this group?

The older woman is an invisible person in a youth-oriented society (Kehoe 1986a, 1986b; Laner 1979; Macdonald and Rich 1983; Moss 1970; Waite 1995) and lesbian women are even more invisible than their nongay sisters (Kehoe 1986a, 1986b; Laner 1979; Macdonald and Rich 1983; Tully 1983, 1989; Waite 1995). Older lesbians are at least at triple jeopardy facing discrimination in the areas of ageism, sexism, and homophobia; older lesbians of color must also endure racism and may face quadruple jeopardy. Ageism, sexism, homophobia, and racism exist not only in the nongay world, but also in the gay community, where the emphasis tends to be mostly on things male, young, and white. Older lesbians, who tend to be an extremely difficult population on which to gather data (Adelman 1980; Berger 1982, 1996; Kehoe 1986a; Kelly 1977; Laner 1979; Tully 1983; Waite 1995), continue to be overlooked in the literature.

What is currently known about older lesbians, as with samples of older gay men, is based on small samples and biased toward healthy, white, middle- to upper-class women who are well-educated professionals comfortable with their sexual orientation (Adelman 1980; Berger 1982; Kehoe 1986; Laner 1979; Minnigerode and Adelman 1978; Raphael and Robinson 1980, 1981; Tully 1983, 1989). These exploratory studies have collected data only since the late 1970s. The results are generally quite biased, having been based on responses from very few of the possible existing members of this minority group. With this in mind, the following presents an overview of those research findings.

Stereotypes of the older woman in general portray her as sexless, failing in health, alone due to being widowed or never married, heavily involved with church work, and physically unattractive but trying to look young (Laner 1979; Macdonald and Rich 1983; Moss 1970). The stereotypic older lesbian is viewed as heartless, bitter, unemotional, lonely, and isolated, living alone with no family or friends seducing younger women for sexual gratification (Berger 1982; Kehoe 1986a; Tully 1983). Because the older lesbian population is incredibly diverse, no doubt there are some older lesbians who meet one or more of the criteria in these stereotypes; however, existing research data demonstrate quite a different general view of the older lesbian.

Although not immune from sexism or ageism, the older lesbian woman is portrayed as one who, in spite of adversity and losses, has survived into old age doing relatively well. Many older lesbians have been married (or are currently heterosexually married) and have living children (Kehoe 1986a; Tully 1983). Their relationships with their husbands or ex-husbands may be from cordial and supportive to hostile or nonexistent (Kehoe 1986a). Relationships with children are similarly viewed, since many children, upon being told of their mother's lesbianism, have tremendous difficulties coming to terms with this fact. Most often, such difficulties become less pronounced when the child becomes an adult (Kehoe 1986a; Lott-Whitehead and Tully 1993).

In terms of relationships with women, many older lesbians define their acceptance of their sexual orientation as the singularly most important aspect of their lives (Adleman 1995). Across their lives most have been involved in sexually intimate relationships with other women that were serially monogamous; however, lesbian relationships also include partners living alone, heterosexually married women having lesbian affairs, living alone and having lesbian affairs, or not having a sexual relationship with anyone. Many of the women studied did live alone and were not sexually active. However, it is clear that had they been with a partner, they would have remained sexually active (Adleman 1995; Dunker 1987; Kehoe 1986a, 1988; Tully 1983). In general, older lesbians form and maintain long-term relationships that are sexually satisfying and exclusive with persons who are usually of their own age cohort (Kehoe 1986a; Tully 1983), but some may have a life partner who is significantly younger or older (Adleman 1995; Macdonald and Rich 1983). While older lesbians may have friends of various ages, they tend to enjoy and socialize primarily with those their own age (Kehoe 1986a; Tully 1983). Not prone to socializing in gay bars, they tend to enjoy small intimate gatherings with lesbian friends, but are also relatively active in the gay community as long as they are physically able (Adleman 1995; Kehoe 1986a; Tully 1983). Those living in rural areas are more apt to find themselves cut off from the gay community and other older lesbians as they become older (Tully 1983).

Psychologically, older lesbians may fare better than their nongay counterparts, who face accelerated aging and try to "pass" at being younger than their chronological age (Laner 1979; Macdonald and Rich 1983). Older lesbians do not experience accelerated aging and seem less concerned with their physical appearance than nongay older women (Laner 1979; Kehoe 1986a). In addition to not seeming to worry too much about physical appearances, older lesbians (like gay men) may face aging with more psychological reserves than nongay persons.

Older lesbians tend to have faced the "crisis of independence" (Berger 1996) earlier than their nongay counterparts. Realizing early in life that they would have to care for themselves financially and emotionally in a homophobic society, they have developed coping capacities to deal with the dilemma. This "mastery of crisis" or "mastery of stigma" (Berger 1980; Friend 1990) has been called "crisis competence" (Friend 1980) and refers to the older lesbian's (or gay man's) psychological ability to master the aging process with more ease than nongays simply because lesbians and gays have had to face challenges throughout their lives that nongays, by virtue of their sexual orientation, were spared. Thus, older lesbians, while still fearing declining health, financial crises, iso-

lation from friends and community, heterosexist policies, and institutionalization, face aging with a certain amount of optimism and life
satisfaction.

In sum, the small amount of information that does exist on the older
lesbian is woefully inadequate and merely explores demographic characteristics of the population. Data that explore the older lesbian in terms of
her similarities to nongay older women are virtually nonexistent, as are
data that explore coming out after retirement or how ethnicity or race
impact older lesbians. As with data on older gay men, data on older lesbians tend to demonstrate them to be an extraordinarily diverse population that cannot be characterized by stereotypic generalities.

Common Issues Associated with Gayging

While there is little actual data on the populations of either older lesbians
or gays there are some common issues associated with aging as a gay person. These include issues associated with relationships, health, and legal
matters. Although these issues themselves are not unique to older lesbians
and gays (Hooyman and Kiyak 1996; Schneider and Kropf 1992), older
gays and lesbians face unique challenges in these areas.

Relationships, History, and Coming Out

Older lesbians and gays, like their nongay counterparts, have relationships with a variety of other persons. Many older gay people have little or
no contact with their family of origin simply because of the lack of positive acceptance shown toward the lesbian or gay person by now-deceased
or living parents or siblings (Tully 1983). Further, if once married, often
spouses fail to demonstrate total acceptance for the older gay or lesbian
making the relationship between them strained (Lott-Whitehead and
Tully 1993). Relationships between older gay persons and their children
and grandchildren tend to range from being nonexistent to being loving
and supportive (Lott-Whitehead and Tully 1993; McClellan 1998). Older
lesbians particularly may find themselves in the position of having to care
for their own aging parent or parents. Women more frequently than men
provide caregiver services to aging relatives, and unmarried women tend
to become caregivers more frequently than married women (DeLombard
1995; McDonald and Rich 1983). Older lesbians also may provide caregiving services to gay men with AIDS or to an aging partner. These caregiving responsibilities can exacerbate stress on existing relationships and

are emotionally draining (DeLombard 1995). On the surface, this may seem a dim and hopeless situation for older lesbians or gay men. However, whereas families of origin tend to provide stress for older gays and lesbians, families of choice, friendship networks, and the gay community provide sources of social support and nurturance (Berger 1980, 1982, 1996; Kelly 1997; Tully 1983).

The older lesbians and gays of the late 1990s were born between the turn of the last century and roughly 1940. While there was a certain emancipation of women's roles and the documented existence of various gay communities (Bullough and Bullough 1977; Kennedy and Davis 1993) during the first half of the twentieth century, traditional social roles for men and women were still the norm. Women were expected to marry and stay at home and raise the children while their husbands worked to provide economic support. Marriage was viewed as a life-long commitment, bearing children out of wedlock was unacceptable, and divorce was scandalous. Unmarried sons and daughters often stayed in the family home and assumed responsibility for aging parents. Unmarried sons usually worked outside the home, daughters did so on occasion. Because of the emphasis on women's higher education during the later part of the nineteenth century, women who had the financial means were able to attend college and train for certain professions. However, professional employment for women during the early part of the 1900s was restricted to certain "women's professions" such as social work, teaching, and nursing. Those women now in their 80s and 90s would have had fewer professional opportunities than those now in their 60s and 70s. For lesbian women who chose not to heterosexually marry, the year of their birth played a significant role in the opportunities afforded them.

For example, Ella was born in 1899 and, upon her completion of her baccalaureate degree, she was accepted as the first female law student at a prestigious Virginia university. Having been awarded her law degree she quickly discovered no law firm would hire her simply because she was a women. She eventually found employment in the post office where she worked until she retired. Jessica, who was born in 1937, found more professional opportunities open to her. Following her graduation from undergraduate school she enrolled in a combined master's/doctoral program in chemistry and completed her Ph.D. in the early 1960s. With the emerging women's movement and emphasis on hiring women, her sex was viewed as a benefit. She accepted a management position with DuPont and stayed with the company until she retired.

In addition to those lesbian women who opted not to marry, there are untold numbers of now older lesbians who, because of prevailing social norms and proscriptions against homosexuality, married, had children, and lived rather conventional appearing lives. There are no known data that describe the total numbers of lesbians or gays who have married and have lived under the guise of heterosexuality and who have never made their same-sex practices common knowledge. The data that do exist on these older gays and lesbians indicate that many of the older lesbians and gays of the 1990s have been heterosexually married and have children. Some hid their sexual orientation during their marriages while others denied their same-sex orientation until after a spouse had died. Some divorced because of the acknowledgement of a lesbian or gay identity.

Older gays and lesbians have a tendency to prefer to socialize with persons within their own age cohort although they may have some younger friends. They seem to enjoy small social gatherings and tend to shy away from bars. When younger, these persons would have found that bars were in dangerous parts of the city where they were hard to find and prone to police raids. Because bars have not played a major role in the lives of some older persons in the past, they do not now play a major role. As for the gay community itself, during the time most of these people were growing up, the gay community was nonexistent or at least difficult to locate or to break into. Because of this, the elder gays of today had to discover friends and social outlets on their own. This activity generally became important to the developing gay person when she or he identified herself or himself as gay.

As with other groups of gays and lesbians, older persons tend to discover their sexual orientation at various points along their life span (Berger 1980, 1982, 1996; Kehoe 1986a, 1988; Tully 1983). Those who came out during their adolescence or early adulthood (in the 1930s, 1940s, 1950s, and 1960s) faced a very different social climate in relation to homosexuality than did those who embraced their gay status after the Stonewall Riots of 1969. Those who comprise the group called the "oldest-old" (the frail), 85 years old, were born in 1915 or before. Those in the "old-old" (the fragile) are now between the ages of 75 and 84. They were born between 1916 and 1925 and would have reached adolescence and early adulthood between 1929 and 1938. As they moved through the complex developmental phase of puberty and sexual awakening in the late 1920s and 1930s, both of these groups would have experienced the institutionalization of Freudian thought, the commonly held belief that homosexuality was a mental illness that required a cure, the "Red" baiting of the late 1920s, the Great Depression, and the New Deal. These historical events and commonly held beliefs about their sexual orientation would impact their views about openness, relationships, and self.

The "young-old" (the frisky) were born between 1926 and and 1935 and would today be between the ages of 65 and 74. And, the "youngest-old" (the fractious), now between the ages of 50 and 64, would have been born between 1936 and 1950. These two groups came of age between the 1940s and the late 1960s. The 1940s saw the rise of gay bars for men and lesbian bars for women, the emancipation of women due to World War II, the popularization of the first novels with gay and lesbian protagonists, the continuing view of homosexuality as an illness, and the beginning development of a gay community in urban areas.

The 1950s found gays and lesbians retreating further into their closets to escape the McCarthy era's witch hunt for "commies, pinkos, homos, and spies"; the emphasis on the "corporate man" and his family; the race to the suburbs to escape the crises of the inner city; and the return of women to their appropriate place in the home. Gays and lesbians were still viewed as engaging in aberrant behaviors and few felt comfortable being "different." The gay community remained virtually invisible to much of the gay world and to all of the nongay world. However, even in the homophobia of the 1950s, the Daughters of Bilitis (a lesbian organization) was founded in 1955 and the Mattachine Society (a comparable organization for gay men) began in 1951.

The 1960s burst the conservative bubble of the 1940s and 1950s with stunning legislation in the area of social justice and civil rights not seen since the 1930s. Previously disenfranchised minority groups suddenly had political and legal clout. The Civil Rights Movement of the 1960s empowered racial minorities to push toward legal inclusion. The Women's Liberation Movement and the Gay Liberation Movement emerged in that era and changed the way society would view women and gays. The gay community began to flourish during the 1960s, homosexuality was challenged as a socially constructed issue that did not constitute a mental illness, and gay persons began to demand equality.

The 1970s brought with it the declassification of homosexuality as a mental illness by the American Psychiatric Association, an increased public awareness of gays and lesbians and the gay community, a generalized fear of homosexuality spurred on by Anita Bryant and her "Save our Children" campaign, a growing gay community, the creation and sale of lesbian and women's music, and the creation of an increasing number of support groups and organizations for gays and lesbians. The National Gay and Lesbian Task Force emerged in 1973, the National Organization for Women endorsed gay rights, and the National Association of Social Workers created its first policy supporting lesbians and gays.

The 1980s saw an increase in the numbers of publicly identified lesbians and gays who were challenging local, state, and national policies, running for (and being elected to) public office, and the passage of some legal protections for same-sex couples and gay people. It also brought the start of the HIV/AIDS pandemic and the growing fear of homosexuals and homosexuality on the part of the religious right. The 1990s included the continuing challenges to existing laws, policies, and practices that discriminate on the basis of sexual orientation, the ongoing issues associated with HIV/AIDS, the military "Don't Ask, Don't Tell" policy, the repeal of gay rights protections, and an increase in the Christian Coalition's attempt to return homosexuality to the category of mental illness. Through it all older gays and lesbians continue to come to grips with a sexual orientation that is different from that of the majority.

To say that history, and the historical era in which they personally identified themselves as gay, plays a role in how the older lesbian or gay person views her or his situation may seem simplistic; however, it does have a significant impact on their current view of themselves. It is quite obvious that those over 85 years old who came out in the 1920s or 1930s will have a different perception and world-view of their situation than those who came out post-Stonewall. Because those who now comprise the fractious, frisky, frail, and fragile older gay population generally came to terms with their sexual identities prior to the advent of the Gay Liberation Movement of the 1960s and 1970s, they may still harbor internalized homophobia and an unwillingness to be particularly open about their sexual orientation (Berger 1982; Kehoe 1986a; Kelly 1977; Tully 1983). This may be one reason that older lesbians and gays are so difficult to identify. Certainly some older gays and lesbians are actively involved in the gay community, but the gay community, too, tends to isolate and not include its elders (Kehoe 1986a; Macdonald and Rich 1983). Perhaps this is why many older gays and lesbians tend to prefer small intimate social activities at home or with a few friends rather than spending time in bars.

In sum, older gay persons tend to get social support from persons like themselves and may be alienated from their families of origin, spouses, or children. They are difficult to find and identify and choose not to be terribly public about their sexual orientation. How they view themselves and their sexual orientation is related to the historical era in which they grew up and came out and they are an extremely heterogeneous group.

Health Quandaries

As with other older populations, older gays and lesbians may have issues related to health. But, because they are lesbians or gays, they may also have problems related to the health system that are distinct from the nongay population. Older gays and lesbians are not immune to the various conditions of aging that include changes in sensory and cognitive abilities, chronic and acute diseases, and mental disorders. Such include decreases in sensory perceptions and muscular strength, a declining physical resiliency, organ deterioration, increased illnesses, cognitive slowing, declining memory, and a decrease in psychomotor ability (Hooyman and Kiyak 1996; Kehoe 1988). Also, HIV/AIDS has not segregated itself to simply the younger population. By the time the first HIV/AIDS cases were reported in the late 1970s, most of those who are currently older gays and lesbians were well into middle age and were not the primary target of the virus. However, for whatever reason, HIV/AIDS is increasing in the older population generally and older gay men seem to be at risk (Hooyman and Kiyak 1996). There are also some data that tend to suggest that older lesbians and gays may be at greater risk for alcohol or drug abuse (Armon 1960; Bell and Weinberg 1978; Bieber 1965), but due to early death rates, alcoholics are less likely in the over 60 group (Hooyman and Kiyak 1996). Further, because older persons generally abuse over-the-counter medications (Hooyman and Kiyak 1996), it is impossible to know how many older gays or lesbians fall into these categories. Finally, some data also suggest that older lesbians and gays may be more prone to depression than the general population, but the data are inconclusive and contradictory as studies tend to demonstrate that older gays and lesbians, because of their ability to master crises, are less prone to depression (Berger 1980, 1996; Dunker 1987; Humphreys and Quam 1998; Kehoe 1988; Kelly 1977; Macdonald and Rich 1983; Pope and Schulz 1990; Relkin 1990; Tully 1983; Wahler and Gabbay 1997).

While gays and lesbians face the same health dilemmas as the rest of the population at large, how they are defined and treated by the medical and health care communities differs. Gerontological specialists in the medical community, while not as rare as they were in the 1970s and 1980s, still are not easily found. And medical personnel who have been sufficiently trained to deal with lesbian and gay elders are virtually nonexistent. Medical staff may tend to assume that patients are all hetero-sexuals and treat them accordingly. Couple that with an older gay person's unwillingness to share her or his sexual orientation and one has the ingredients for creating a less than ideal patient to health care provider relationship. Further, medical facility policies do not generally include provisions for persons who are not "blood" relatives; insurance companies do not recognize domestic partners; and there are few built-in social supports in the medical community for gays and lesbians. This lack of support, as we shall see, may cause the older lesbian or gay unnecessary stress in situations. In such cases, an informed social worker can ease the situation.

Legal Dilemmas

Public policy that discriminates against older lesbians and gays is found not only in the medical community but in the social order generally. As the creator and watchdog of the social order, perhaps the best example of continuing institutional homophobia is found in the legal system. As noted, since the 1980s several steps have been taken to ensure equal protection under the law for gays and lesbians. But, with the continuing tug-of-war between the far right conservatives on one side and the moderates and liberals on the other, pro-gay legislation may be passed in one legislative session only to be repealed in the next. The process is slow. What this has meant for lesbians and gays is that they have had to make do with existing legal protections and try to ensure that their interests are protected even in a homophobic climate. For older persons this has special meaning because it is during the declining years that gays and lesbians have need of special protections that are automatically in place for non-gays. These include issues related to durable powers of attorney, living wills, and wills.

Created while the person is well and capable of making rational decisions, legal documents that describe the individual's wishes before a health crisis occurs make dealing with less than supportive policies at least somewhat easier. One of the by-products of the HIV/AIDS crisis has been that the medical establishment has better learned to honor durable powers of attorney whereby a designated person can act on behalf of the incapacitated partner in all matters from health care to selling the car. Further, living wills made before the health crisis leaves one unable to care for herself or himself, specify the kinds of treatment and under what conditions treatment will be administered once the individual can no longer make those decisions. Finally, wills that specifically state what the individual wants done with his or her personal property at death make it easier for the surviving partner to circumnavigate the legal quagmire.

This is not to say that the protection of these legal documents will, in all cases, allow the partner of a dying man entry into the intensive care unit, or ensure that the final wishes of a deceased lesbian will not be contested by her estranged relatives. But, taking such measures before there is a crisis may help the surviving partner or caregiver.

In sum, the process of growing older, while being as challenging as it is for all persons, may be even more challenging for lesbians and gays. Functioning as an invisible minority both in the gay and nongay communities, facing issues associated with coming out and families of origin, and battling the medical and legal establishments for equality, all create stressors and that may require the empowerment of older gays or lesbians.

The Empowerment Approach with Older Gays and Lesbians

As with all populations of older persons, older lesbians and gays face problems that are associated with the aging process itself while also dealing with issues associated with their sexual orientation. This section explores various stressors associated with aging that may create a need for psychosocial intervention and then looks specifically at using the empowerment approach at the micro-, mezzo-, and macro-levels.

Common Stressors Associated with Gayging

Older gays and lesbians face possible stress from the nongay community, the gay community, families of origin, spouses, children, and families of choice. Stressors from the nongay society include a belief in stereotypic views about aging combined with myths about older gays and lesbians that can prevent an honest appraisal of them. Further, the nongay society has had a tendency not to recognize its elder population in general, thus making the older gay person virtually invisible. Although, as the baby boomer generation ages, older persons are becoming more visible in the popular media, older lesbians and gays are still not portrayed. Such invisibility may force older lesbians and gays to remain hidden. The nongay world generally provides inadequate support systems for older gays and lesbians, perhaps because of their lack of recognition. Furthermore, the public policies that are in place demonstrate a continuing institutional homophobia that fails to support same-sex relationships. These policies are particularly evident in the health care system where domestic partners are not recognized as family and in the legal system where a surviving partner can be disinherited if a will is contested by even a distant relative.

Sadly, the gay community, too, may be a source of stress for the older lesbian or gay person. The gay community is not immune to believing the prevailing myths and stereotypes about aging and, unfortunately, may not move beyond these to learn about what they will eventually become. Often, the active gay community is still one of youth which may fail to routinely include its older members. This lack of recognition, as in the nongay world, renders the older lesbian or gay invisible and means that adequate support systems for this minority may be generally overlooked.

Stress for the older gay man or lesbian woman may also arise from relationships with family of origin members, spouses, or children. If the older lesbian or gay never married and integrated her or his sexual orientation into her or his personality and lifestyle years ago, issues with the family of origin may have already been worked out and the pain of rejection or isolation dealt with years ago. The tendency is for older gays and lesbians to distance themselves from those in their families of origin who are not supportive, choosing to remain close only to those who provide some type of emotional support.

However, if an older gay or lesbian never disclosed his or her sexual orientation to family members, married, had children, and came out later in life, there may be problems. A typical problem for married or once-married older gays and lesbians is that of disclosing their sexual orientation to spouses and children. Often, perhaps due to individual homophobia or a lack of understanding of the awkward situation in which the older gay or lesbian finds himself or herself, family members may reject or emotionally distance themselves from the individual during the coming-out phase. Such lack of understanding is a clear source of stress coupled with the stress and anxiety of coming to terms with sexual orientation issues generally.

Other sources of stress for the aging lesbian or gay may include caregiving responsibilities for aging parents, disabled spouses, or sick children. Women find themselves in the position of being caregivers more frequently than men, and it may be safe to assume that older lesbians do provide more caregiving services than older gays. However, no data exist to support or refute this assumption. What data do exist suggest that older gays and lesbians may find themselves in the role of providing care-

TABLE 6.2
Common Stressors Faced By Older Lesbians and Gays

The list below represents common areas that may produce stress for older gay men and lesbian women.

STRESSORS FROM THE NONGAY SOCIETY

Prevailing myths and stereotypes about gays and aging;

Lack of recognition (invisibility);

Lack of adequate support systems;

Homophobic public policies (especially in the health care system);

Lack of adequate legal supports (especially in terms of wills);

Institutional homophobia.

STRESSORS FROM THE GAY COMMUNITY

Prevailing myths and stereotypes about aging;

Lack of recognition (invisibility);

Lack of adequate support systems;

Stressors from families of origin, spouses, and children;

Lack of familial support;

Emotional distancing or rejection;

Individual homophobia;

Lack of understanding about coming out;

Providing care to aging parents, disabled spouses, or sick children.

STRESSORS FROM FAMILIES OF CHOICE

Providing care for a partner;

Failing personal health;

Finances;

Death and dying;

Internalized homophobia;

Ensuring appropriate legal protections.

giving services to aging parents, disabled spouses, and sick children and doing so produces a significant amount of stress.

Finally, the older gay or lesbian may find stress from the family of choice he or she has created. While often viewed as a source of support, which it is, lesbian and gay fictive families may also cause stress. The most common sources of stress for older gay families centers on the failing health of one or the other of the partners, the processes of dying, the inevitability of death, and the failures of the health and legal systems to assist in making those final passages with honesty and integrity. Internalized homophobia, perhaps decades old, may cause anxiety and an inability to acknowledge sexual orientation which, in turn, may create barriers to ensuring that adequate legal protections are in place to protect either the partner or the individual. In sum, there are multitudes of areas that may cause stress to the older gay or lesbian person, and the clinician must be sensitive to each when applying the empowerment approach.

Micro-Level Intervention

As noted, older gays and lesbians are at risk of stress from a variety of sources. Stress and lack of necessary social supports may cause them to seek help. It should be noted that the research that has been conducted on this population, while biased toward white, middle-class, financially secure, professionals who were open about their sexual orientation and fairly healthy, generally indicates that this group is not prone to seeking psychotherapeutic intervention but tends to use friendship networks to help solve personal dilemmas (Berger 1980, 1982, 1996; Kelly 1977; Kehoe 1988; Kooden 1997; Tully 1983; Wahler and Gabbay 1997). Because no data have been collected on the kinds of older gay or lesbian persons likely to require social services, social workers must have a general understanding of the needs and issues of the older gay or lesbian simply because whether or not the individual identifies openly as gay, social workers will encounter some of these individuals in their practice.

One of the first dilemmas faced by any clinician who wants to work with older lesbians and gays is a philosophical one about whether or not services for the older gay group should be separate from, or integrated with, services for other senior citizens. The "separate but equal" mindset, like SAGE (Senior Action in a Gay Environment) in New York, believes that to ensure that appropriate services are being provided to older gays and lesbians, such services must be developed and implemented by the gay community. This model has been the prevalent one since the 1970s and remains an important source of social services for older gays and lesbians. The disadvantages of this model include the reality that to obtain services from this kind of agency one has to be open about one's sexual orientation. Data tend to demonstrate that not all older persons are willing to patronize such agencies because they are not open about their sexual orientation.

The other model requires that appropriate services for older gays be provided in the more traditional social service agencies, where openness of sexual orientation is not an issue. The disadvantages of this model include the reality that most employees will assume that all clients are heterosexual and treat them as such and that most agency staff are ill-equipped to provide services to older gays and lesbians. Further, agency policies that are not supportive of same-sex relationships may create barriers to effective services.

Many older persons choose to remain extremely private about their sexual practices and sexual orientation, believing it is no one else's business. While this may cause discomfort on the part of the clinician, unless the presenting problem is related to sexual orientation the privacy should be honored. The clinician can facilitate a more honest and open discussion if she or he is willing not to press, but rather is alert to clues provided by the client. Such may include references to a special friend, long-time roommate, partner, or companion, and an absence of discussion about a husband, wife, or children. If the client has been married, clues to a gay identity might also be references to a special person other than the spouse. The professional helper should listen, not pass judgment, and create an environment that will facilitate the older gay or lesbian's willingness to be open. The clinician should, however, be warned that, if the individual has not been honest with herself or himself about her or his sexual orientation and is deeply homophobic, labeling the individual as gay may create an enormous barrier to providing services. Internalized homophobia must be viewed in terms of its source and must be respected in terms of its relationship with the client.

Because many older lesbians and gays view their coming out as the singularly most important event in their lives, it is vital that the clinician be able to place in an appropriate historical context when that occurred. For example, the older gay man who came out in the 1930s as a young man will have had a different experience from the older gay man who came out in the 1960s after retiring and raising a family. Knowing the historical era of the older person allows the practitioner insight as to the older person's views about coming out and internal homophobia and will allow for an honest exchange between the client and clinician. Because the concept of homosexuality is a constantly evolving social construct, its definition changes from one era to another. The older person who came out during the 1930s when being gay was defined as a mental illness may believe that being gay is an abnormal mental deficiency. Likewise, the older person who came out in the 1960s when gay liberation was blossoming may tend to view same-sex sexual orientation as normal.

Social workers possibly may deal with older lesbians and gays who are in the process of coming out, who have recently come out, or still have scars from the coming-out process. The practitioner must understand the complexities about coming out and the stresses that may ensue from identifying as gay in later years. An example is that of Rose, a 60-year-old woman who, following the death of her husband of thirty-eight years, accepted what she had known most of her life—she was a lesbian. As a young child Rose had been a tomboy, but had married her high school sweetheart because in the early 1950s she was expected to do so. Although never quite sexually satisfied with her relationship with her husband, she had four children and what appeared to be a normal American family. After the children left home her husband died. She was totally alone and began having sexual fantasies about her best friend. This was so emotionally upsetting she became involved in counseling.

The issues raised in the initial session revolved around Rose's newly emerging identity, what that meant for her children, for herself, and her friends. The identity she had only been marginally aware of for most of her life was in conflict with what she had been taught and she felt confusion between feeling shame and guilt for her feelings and feeling relief and excitement over finally accepting who she had always been. Also, because the lesbian and gay community was an unknown place for her, she needed information about resources.

During a series of counseling sessions, the social worker and Rose identified issues, defined strategies for dealing with those issues, and evaluated the success of how those strategies were implemented. For example, Rose found it particularly difficult to identify herself using the term "lesbian." She preferred to self-identify herself as bisexual because of her long marriage and family. The social worker, realizing that labels are just that, allowed Rose to self-identify in a way that felt comfortable. As the coming-out process moved through its various phases and Rose became more comfortable with her same-sex sexual identity, the internal homophobia began to dissipate, and Rose began identifying herself as a lesbian. Not all social workers are as nonjudgmental and accepting as Rose's.

Just as social workers are homophobic (DeCrescenzo 1983/84; DeCrescenzo and McGill 1978; Tate 1991; Wisniewski and Toomey 1987), so, too, they may believe stereotypes and myths about aging itself and about older lesbians and gays. Clinicians working with any population of older persons must be informed of the realities of aging and overcome the temptation to ascribe to the prevalent myths and stereotypes. This is particularly true when working with older gays and lesbians. For while not much scientific data exist on this minority, what data are available strongly refute the myths.

Older lesbians and gays are as heterogeneous as the general population and are represented in every socioeconomic stratum and in every ethnic or racial community. Being an older gay person places the individual at risk for discrimination on the basis of age and sexual orientation, but for the older gay or lesbian who is also a member of an ethnic or racial minority, the threat of discrimination becomes threefold—they may be subject to discrimination on the basis of age, sexual orientation, and race. Add to this the reality that most older people are women and consider that an older lesbian who is also African-American faces the possibility of quadruple jeopardy in that added to ageism, homophobia, and racism, is sexism. Having an understanding of how these areas can possibly impact the older gay or lesbian is vital for a clinician wanting to empower those without clout.

Consider the older African-American gay man who, because of a stroke, has been confined to the hospital's intensive care unit. The hospital, long known for its racist practices, began treating African Americans in the 1970s and has few doctors or nurses who are minorities of color. Most of the hospital support staff are Hispanic or African American. The patient's Puerto Rican lover, a 70-year-old retired artist, is kept from visiting because he is not considered a family member. Because he believes the true nature of the relationship to be a private matter, he remains quiet. The hospital social worker, being sensitive to the perceived needs of the patient and his friend, arranges for visitation. There are times when empowering individuals requires institutional flexibility.

Barbara Macdonald (Macdonald and Rich 1983) noted that the best and only way to truly empower older gay people was to openly acknowledge their existence and treat them with respect. Both the nongay and gay communities do a poor job of first recognizing the existence of older gays and lesbians, much less respecting their wisdom. Perhaps she is right.

In sum, the empowerment perspective values the egalitarian nature of the relationship between the older client and the clinician, where the client is allowed to share her or his narrative in a safe space and where the presenting problem and subsequently identified issues are solved by the creative thinking of both the client and the clinician.

Mezzo-Level Intervention

Because both the nongay and gay communities tend to overlook older lesbians and gays, perhaps the most significant impact related to providing services for this group can be at the mezzo- and macro-levels. At the community level, practitioners must become aware of the social service networks available to older gays and lesbians. In large urban areas this may not be as difficult as it may be in smaller localities. Resources available include the venerable organization, SAGE, headquartered in New York City. But, not all communities have such resources. Most do not. Therefore the practitioner must see the older gay or lesbian person in the context of both the gay and nongay worlds and must provide services within the service network available. In doing so, the practitioner must be aware of agency policies that discriminate on the basis of sexual orientation and be alert to even the subtle nuances of heterosexism, ageism, and institutional homophobia found in many social service agencies.

For example, are staff members trained to acknowledge and accept the reality that all persons seeking services are not heterosexual? Do intake forms, or other agency documents reflect a nongay bias? Are workers aware of the realities of being an older lesbian or gay or do they believe stereotypes? What community supports are in place for older gays and lesbians? How are homophobia, ageism, and sexism within the agency addressed? Workers in community agencies have a responsibility to ensure that all older persons in need of service, including those who are gay or lesbian, are treated with respect and that issues associated with homophobia are confronted.

With the explosion of communication technology and the development of the Internet, there has been a surge in the development of web sites devoted to older lesbians and gays. Self-help groups for this population have been slow to develop, but the Internet provides useful and relatively safe activities for older gays and lesbians. For example, PRIDENET has a resource list for older gay, lesbian, bisexual, and transgender persons with links to several areas of interest (*http://www.pridenet.com/senorg.htm*). The Senior Cyborgs also have a useful homepage that has chat rooms, library resources, information about disabilities, legal links, home and garden tips, insurance information, meeting spots, pets, and topics related

TABLE 6.3
Providing Services to Older Gays and Lesbians

For clinicians working with fractious, frisky, fragile, and frail older lesbians and gay men, the following should be considered:

AT THE MICRO-LEVEL

Grapple with the philosophical dilemma of whether or not services for older gays and lesbians should be separate from or integrated with services for other older persons;

Be aware of the complexities of coming out as an older person;

Respect personal choice about sexual orientation openness;

Understand the role internal homophobia may play in the lives of older gays and lesbians;

Do not assume that all older persons are heterosexual;

Do not fall prey to stereotypes and myths of aging;

Be aware that older lesbian and gay persons face at least double jeopardy (ageism and homophobia) and perhaps triple jeopardy (ageism, homophobia, and racism) or even quadruple jeopardy (ageism, homophobia, racism, and sexism);

Have a working knowledge about the historical era in which the elder grew up and came of age;

Understand the stressors faced by older gays and lesbians;

Create a safe space for older lesbians and gays;

Be comfortable with your own sexuality and aging and not homophobic or ageist;

Recognize the older lesbian or gay as an important entity.

AT THE MEZZO-LEVEL

Become aware of the social service network available to older gays and lesbians;

View the older lesbian or gay person in the context of both the gay and nongay worlds;

Become familiar with agency policies that discriminate on the basis of sexual orientation;

Develop community services designed to meet the needs of older gays and lesbians;

Implement nondiscrimination policies that include older lesbians and gays;

Challenge homophobia.

AT THE MACRO-LEVEL

Have a working understanding of the Older Americans Act;

Be able to differentiate between all levels of service available-from the federal level to the area agencies on aging (AAAs);

Challenge laws and public policies that discriminate on the basis of sexual orientation;

Confront institutional homophobia at all levels.

to death and dying (*http://www.online96.com/seniors/gay.htm*). Some of the self-help groups that are emerging to assist older lesbians and gays include the Pride Senior Network, the Prime Timers, and the Gay and Lesbian Association of Retiring Persons (GLARP). The Pride Senior Network seeks to promote services that enhance the well-being, health, and quality of life for older lesbians, gays, bisexuals, and transgender persons (Pride Senior Network 1997). They seek to do so through education and community advocacy. The Prime Timers is more of a social organization that seeks to provide older gay men and those who admire older gay men, an opportunity to get together and enjoy recreational, social, and educational activities (Original Prime Timers Worldwide 1998). GLARP provides retirement information and services and raises money for the development of gay and lesbian retirement communities and resorts (GLARP 1998).

Such cyberspace community resources are used frequently by seniors who have access to them. Chat rooms are an easy place for seniors to meet other gays and lesbians, and there are untold numbers of resources available for seniors who can master the information superhighway. Clearly, those seniors with access to the Internet have resources not available to all seniors. Social workers have a mandate to work with those who may not have such resources. However, if the social worker has access to the Internet, a wealth of useful information about gay and lesbian seniors is easily accessed and can be shared with clients.

Obviously not every older gay or lesbian client will have an interest in or need for cyberspace technology. Some may be suffering from terminal illnesses, be mentally unable to grasp the technology, or simply not care. The computer generation after all was not their generation. For those older clients who require hospice or palliative care support efforts may need to be directed to their families. At both the micro-level and the mezzo-level, dealing with the families of older gays and lesbians can be a challenge. Many older lesbians and gays have children, siblings, ex-marital partners, ex-lovers, current lovers, assorted friends, and perhaps even living parents. This mixture of families of choice and families of origin can create interesting dynamics.

For example, Hector, age 67, and Ivan, age 71, had been lovers for more than twenty years. Ivan's invalid mother, now 93, had lived with the couple for half of that time. Hector and Ivan were part of a close-knit gay and lesbian community in Rutland, Vermont, where they had both grown up. Community members provided the couple respite care so they could occasionally get away from their caregiver responsibilities. Ivan was diagnosed with bone cancer, underwent chemotherapy, and was thought to be responding well when an aortic aneurysm was discovered. Ivan died on the operating table. Because Hector was not legally related to Ivan, members of Ivan's family of origin claimed the body, assumed responsibility for the funeral service, and tried to take over the house Hector and Ivan had shared for decades. Ivan's invalid mother was placed in a nursing home and Hector was despondent. Because of Ivan and Hector's involvement with the lesbian and gay community, members of the community and members of the couple's family of choice rallied in support of Hector. This support was spearheaded by a hospital social worker known to the couple who had provided services to both while Ivan had been hospitalized. And, because the couple had the foresight to create strongly worded wills, the family of origin retreated. This mobilization of the community was possible primarily because the social worker was aware of the existence of the community and knew how to ensure its action.

Creating social change is never easy and doing so may mean community organization designed to challenge prevailing social thought, agency policies, and law. To accomplish such community organization and action requires knowledge of the gay community in general, insight and interest in the world of older lesbians and gays in particular, and a willingness to challenge and confront increasing condemnation from the growing conservative right. Whether or not community services for older gays and lesbians are provided in segregated settings or in traditional social welfare agencies, social workers are in the position of being able to play a significantly increasing role in assuring that appropriate services for older gay people are institutionalized.

Macro-Level Intervention

As challenging as work in the community may be, it is at the macro-level where perhaps the most challenging work related to older lesbians and gays is to be found. All persons who work with older persons must have a working understanding of the Older Americans Act (OAA) and its amendments. This one piece of federal legislation articulated universal entitlements to those over 60 regardless of income or need and created a national network of comprehensive service delivery systems, including planning, coordination, and the actual delivery of services (Special Committee on Aging, U.S. Senate 1986). While sexual orientation is not mentioned in the OAA, it is vital for the practitioner to be able to differentiate between all the various federal (Administration on Aging), regional (ten regional offices), state (state offices or units on aging), area (area agencies on aging—AAAs), and local (local providers of services) branches. For, as noted, homophobia can lurk at each level.

For example, a state where homosexual sexual activity is illegal may be reluctant to institute policies in the state unit on aging that would be supportive of same-sex older couples. The area agencies on aging that report to the state unit (and from where the money flows) may also be queasy about the issue of services related to gays and lesbians. So, this institutional homophobia is transmitted from the state level to the area level. How then will the local providers of service, who are dependent on the AAAs for funding, tend to treat older gays and lesbians? Sadly, the institutional homophobia may be most evident at this level where older gays and lesbians can be made invisible by uninformed service providers.

Practitioners wishing to empower older lesbians and gays can begin to do so at the macro-level by challenging institutional homophobia at every level. This may be accomplished by working with national organizations such as the National Gay and Lesbian Task Force or Human Rights Campaign and by ensuring that gay organizations do not overlook the issues and needs of older gay community members. If struggling with huge bureaucratic federal systems is not practical, perhaps working within smaller (though perhaps just as intimidating) state systems holds more appeal. In working with state systems it is imperative to meet and get to know the legislators who, with help from various constituency groups, create and pass state legislation. Tracking legislation (at either the federal or state levels), writing and presenting testimony for or against various bills, and joining with other advocates will provide ample opportunities for the practitioner to have input into the legislative process and issues associated with older gays and lesbians. It will also allow the practitioner an opportunity to confront homophobia and ageism at the state level.

If state-level intervention is too complicated, another way of confronting homophobia and ageism is to become an expert at policies and procedures within the agency setting. An in-depth knowledge of the agency philosophy, mission, and policy manual will help the practitioner understand where homophobia, ageism, sexism, and racism are institutionalized. With this knowledge, the social worker is well equipped to confront and challenge ethically unacceptable policies, procedures, and practices.

For example, Carmen was a social worker employed by one of the West Virginia State Office on Aging's Area Agencies on Aging (AAA). She not only reviewed and implemented public policy related to West Virginia's senior citizens, she also saw clients. Carmen's older brother had been gay and died of AIDS in the mid 1980s and Carmen had been witness to the discrimination and difficulties he had faced during his illness.

Carmen was extremely sensitive to the needs of gays and lesbians and had been active with Parents, Families, and Friends of Lesbians and Gays (PFLAG) for years. However, she was ill-informed about older lesbians and gays but realized her agency's policies and practices assumed all clients to be heterosexual (the heterosexual assumption).

To effect agency change she met with staff, developed new intake forms that were gay-friendly, added lesbian and gay-oriented materials to the waiting room, and provided staff training related specifically to the needs of older gays and lesbians. As a result of Carmen's initial awareness of lesbians and gays and her willingness to consider the needs of older same-sex oriented individuals, the AAA in one West Virginia area was able to expand its policies and practices to include gays and lesbians. The initial changes made in this one AAA were eventually expanded to other AAAs in the state, demonstrating that the policy ideas of one person can be developed and implemented across a wide spectrum.

In sum, there are enormous challenges for those wishing to question and confront homophobia, ageism, sexism, and racism at the mezzo- and macro-levels. Because older persons in this country have been and continue to be stigmatized on the basis of age (not to mention sexual orientation, sex, or race), there are unique opportunities for those who wish to become involved to help those who are powerless and invisible to gain power through visibility.

The Empowerment Model Applied

The preceding sections have explored a variety of concepts associated with older lesbians and gays and the empowerment perspective. The following section demonstrates how the empowerment model can be applied at the macro-level when working with older gays and lesbians. As in chapter 4, where a micro-level example was provided, and chapter 5, where a mezzo-level example was provided, it might be helpful to refer to figure 3.3 and tables 3.1 and 3.5.

As an example, assume you are a social worker who has been hired by American Association of Retired Persons (AARP) as a legislative advocate working at the state level. One of your jobs is to build coalitions between AARP and other groups in order to pass legislation supported by AARP and to lend AARP's support to other groups when legislation is seen as mutually beneficial. In reading summaries of state house and senate bills that had been introduced the previous day you notice that a house bill dealing with legislation mandating durable medical powers of attorney had been referred to the House Committee on Health and Welfare. Because AARP had supported similar legislation in other states you were aware that medical powers of attorney allowed for decisions about health care to be made for an incapacitated individual by someone legally sanctioned to do so. Similar legislation had been positively supported by AARP in other instances and you began to identify sources of support and nonsupport regarding this particular bill. Your research lead you to the sponsors of the bill—a Republican from an extremely conservative section of the state, two liberal Democrats from the two largest metropolitan areas in the state, and the Speaker of the House, who was considered a political moderate.

Further investigation led you to discover that the bill had been written by members of the Human Rights Campaign (HRC) in an effort to ensure that terminally ill AIDS patients and other gay and lesbian couples could allow their partners the right to make medically necessary decisions for them when they were no longer capable of making those decisions for themselves. You also discovered that the American Medical Association (AMA) and the state association of nursing home administrators also supported the bill. The only opposition to the bill is from the religious right, which opposes it because of its genesis in the gay community and because it would allow lesbian and gay couples rights they currently do not enjoy.

AARP's position was that such legislation provided all older couples— gay or nongay—with appropriate options for health care in later life. The AMA supported the legislation because it relieved medical personnel from having to make decisions for patients, and the nursing home lobby agreed that such legislation allowing nursing home residents the option of selecting an individual to make such health care decisions was in a resident's best interest. HRC and the gay lobby believed the legislation would further the rights of gays and lesbians irrespective of age.

Your job is to ensure that all these disparate groups with different value orientations and different reasons for wishing the legislation to pass were in agreement with the intent and language of the proposed legislation and that appropriate testimony would be presented when the bill came before the House Committee on Health and Welfare for public debate and comment. You also have to ensure that those who oppose the bill do not mount an effective campaign to have the bill defeated before it reaches the floor of the house. To effectively succeed, the empowerment approach can be a helpful tool.

The basic principles of empowerment include collaboration, the use of existing structures, a concern with the promotion of social and economic justice, and a commitment to working with disenfranchised populations. The proposed legislation allows for the application of all these concepts. Additionally, it allows you an opportunity to see the relationship between legislation and the individual and the lack of power and legal rights afforded some members of the community—it is not uncommon for older gays or lesbians to have no say in the health and welfare of their partners because of their lack of legal status. The proposed legislation, like most legislation that impacts gays and lesbians, has implications beyond the lesbian and gay community. Medical powers of attorney impact numbers of the population, hence the popularity of the bill even though it had been developed by the gay community.

In order to effectively broker agreements with the various constituency groups that vocalized support for this bill, you would need an understanding of the legal issues associated with it from both a gay and nongay viewpoint and an ability to confront vestiges of institutional homophobia that might be found in some of the bill's more conservative supporters. Because passage of the bill requires the efforts of all the constituency groups, it is important to know the pro and con arguments related to the bill and to be able to advocate for its passage even if the radical right poses a significant threat. Helpful tools include use of telephone trees to have coalition members directly contact legislators and voice support, the preparation of legislative testimony for coalition members to use in committee hearings, and the continuing use of negotiation in the creation of coalitions.

In sum, knowledge of the intent and language of the proposed legislation, an ability to articulate the pros and the cons of any argument raised about the legislation, and the capacity to bring seemingly disparate groups together in support of common goals using the empowerment perspective should provide the advocate opportunities for success at the macro-level. Using the empowerment perspective allows for the dialogue of difference to be heard and incorporated into positive outcomes. No doubt you will discover, the unions made in political arenas are, as noted above, often unique.

Case Studies

The following case vignettes are designed to stimulate discussion and to facilitate various ideas for intervention. There is a vignette related to each area of practice (micro-, mezzo-, and macro-). When reading, and subsequently discussing, these vignettes, it is important to remember definition of the presenting problem; issues that may underlie the presenting problem; the role of the client and the clinician; the supportive and nonsupportive environments of the client; the interactions between the gay and the nongay communities; the role of institutional, individual, and internal homophobia; and the application of the empowerment perspective.

The Niece

Betty Jo, known as "B.J.," is the only heir to a nationally known costume jewelry fortune. She inherited her wealth when her mother died in 1965. Prior to her mother's death, B.J. had been her caretaker, living with her and ensuring that her mother's final years were comfortable. Having never married, B.J., although a law-school graduate who could have practiced law, was never able to be a lawyer because of the prevailing sexism of the 1930s. Before her retirement, at age 65, in 1970 she was employed as a supervisor in the U.S. Postal Service. She had worked for the post office since the 1930s. Since her mother's death, B.J. has lived in the same home with Madge, a woman with whom she began a monogamous lesbian relationship in 1935.

Madge, ten years younger than B.J., was born in 1915. Like B.J., Madge was an only child who found it necessary to care for her elderly mother, thus preventing a nursing home placement. Madge, too, had a graduate degree. Hers was in pharmacology. She earned her living as a professional pharmacologist at the local medical school. Madge's mother died in 1963, two years prior to BJ's. After the death of both of their mothers, the two women moved into a shared home that B.J. bought in her name alone. The relationship, while having some problems along the way, has survived well and the two always appeared happy.

The two women were well known in the nongay community in which they lived as they were avid patrons of the arts and B.J. was a large contributor to various local charities. But they never acknowledged their sexual orientation to anyone outside the relationship until after the women's movement and the gay liberation activities of the 1970s. By the mid 1980s, B.J. and Madge had become an institution in the gay community of the city in which they lived. Active in all aspects of the women's community they added their support to the lesbian resource center, the gay library offerings, and attended all-woman dances at the local Quaker meeting house. They had little to do with men and preferred the company of women. Because they were the only two women their age who openly acknowledged their sexual orientation, B.J. and Madge found that most of their close friends were younger than they.

Their families of origin were small. Madge had no living relatives while B.J. periodically entertained a distant cousin, Ralph, who lived in town. Also, in order to escape the harsh winters, B.J. would leave Madge at home and travel to Miami to stay with her only grandniece, Ella, for eight weeks. Madge hated the winters, too, but having no where to go and never being invited to Miami, stayed at home and fed the wild birds.

Ralph was financially extremely well off, having made his fortune in baby food. Ella, the only close relative B.J. had, was less financially secure than either Ralph or B.J. Interestingly, Ella had reappeared in B.J.'s life around 1987, saying she missed her family and wanted to get reacquainted. Over Madge's protests, B.J. accepted this reason and took Ella in. The annual trips to Miami began a couple of years later. Neither B.J. nor Madge have ever spoken of their sexual orientation with either Ralph or Ella and when the relatives come to call no mention is ever made of the fact that they are far more than just good friends.

Although Madge was ten years younger than B.J., her health was deteriorating at a more rapid rate and she found it increasingly more and more difficult to live without B.J. in the house. When B.J.'s annual trip to Miami in 1994 was planned Madge begged B.J. not to go because she was afraid to stay in the house alone. Concerned about Madge's well-being, B.J. called Ella and explained the situation. This prompted Ella to fly north to see B.J. After a week of discussion between Ella, B.J., and, at times, Madge, it was agreed that Madge was no longer capable of caring for herself and that she needed to be placed in a nursing home. This would allow B.J. the opportunity to sell the house and to move to Miami permanently, thus avoiding the nasty winter weather of the northeast and having a safe place in which to grow older. In a moment of stoicism, and feeling extremely hurt and confused, Madge agreed to the move. B.J., now almost totally deaf, and never one to share any personal emotions, helped Madge pack some personal belongings and sadly watched while Ella made the nursing home placement.

Madge, who has some financial security, is a private pay patient and found a nursing home placement quickly. She moved into the Stauffer Rest Home a week ago. As always Madge dresses in men's shirts and trousers, has short gray hair, a twinkle in her eye, and looks like a stereotypic "old dyke." She is mentally alert although she has physical problems that she realizes necessitate her placement. She speaks warmly of BJ, but has not had any contact with her since Ella placed her last week.

As you are the new social worker on Madge's floor, you are aware of the nursing home's nonsupportive policies and practices related to lesbians and gays. In fact, one of the nurses and several of the nurse's aides have already informed you about your new arrival by sharing some "old lady dyke" and "old faggot" jokes with you. You have been in new employee training for the past week and are on your way to meet with Madge.

Creating the Senior Center

Elrod, or "Roddy" to his friends, and Washington-Carver, "W.C.," had been intimately involved with each other off and on for the past twenty years. They did not live together or even live in the same town, but saw each other regularly. Now in his mid-sixties, Roddy had grown up in a small rural town and had been raised as a Southern Baptist. He still had his faith and went to Sunday church and Sunday school and prayer meetings on Wednesday night. His political views were ultra conservative and he had, in his youth, been an active member of the KKK. He had been married to Bess for more than thirty years and the couple had four children, now adults, all living on their own. The couple still lived in the house in which Roddy grew up. Although he privately thought of himself as gay, this was not known to his wife, children, friends, or members of his church. He rationalized his ongoing liaisons with gay men as being acceptable and had, years ago, stopped having any sexual relations with Bess. He was becoming less and less comfortable with his outwardly heterosexual lifestyle as he believed he was living a lie. While visiting an urban center more than 100 miles from their down-state locale, he and W.C. had become actively involved in the gay men's center.

W.C., an African American who had never married and who had had a series of gay relationships throughout his life, was seriously considering settling down now that he had passed his seventieth birthday. He lived fairly close to the town in which Roddy and Bess lived, but in another district. He had found considerable comfort with the involvement at the gay men's center and was eager to replicate their services closer to home. He had discussed this dream with Roddy who, although somewhat initially unnerved by the idea, had agreed that an organization that provided services to all gay men, but especially older gay men, was greatly needed in their mostly rural community. Both men knew of many older men in the surrounding countryside that were gay and thought creating some kind of senior center for them would be an excellent idea.

Because they realize they face many up-hill battles, they have called on you as the executive director of Senior Action in a Gay Environment to visit their area and provide some tips. You just pulled into the local café where Roddy and W.C. are having coffee waiting for your arrival. The café is full of the local regulars from several of the nearby towns.

The Office of Aging Executive Director

As the executive director for Louisiana's Office on Aging you are in a powerful position to influence public policy related to aging in Louisiana. As a governor's appointee you serve at the pleasure of the governor and are asked to draft, implement, and assess public policy related to aging as it evolves from the federal level. You are also responsible for the efficient planning and operation of the regional offices on aging, the more local area agencies on aging, and the delivery of services from local service providers. You live in a state that does not endorse same-sex relationships or behavior, but one major city in the state, New Orleans, has enacted several safe-guards for same-sex couples, including domestic partnership benefits for city employees and domestic partnership registration for Orleans Parish couples.

Current policies at the state, regional, and local levels regarding services to older persons, while not specifically prohibiting specialized services for older lesbians and gay men, do not define the need for such services. You have recently been contacted by Louisiana Electorate of Gays and Lesbians (LEGAL), a statewide organization supporting gay rights and the New Orleans-based Mayor's Advisory Council on Lesbian, Gay, Bisexual, and Transgender Issues (MAC) about ensuring adequate and appropriate services for older Louisianans who are lesbian, gay, bisexual, or transgender.

The governor, who recently supported a conservative candidate in a hotly contested political campaign where the winner won largely due to the gay vote, has not been known to support gay rights, but is more and more impressed with the political clout of this minority group.

The representatives from LEGAL and the MAC are scheduled to meet with you, your regional directors, and directors of the area agencies on aging in ten minutes. What will you tell them?

This chapter has focused on the empowerment perspective as it relates to older lesbians and gays. Definitions of aging were explored in terms of chronological, psychological, functional, and social aging, and elders were defined in terms of their fractiousness, friskiness, frailness, or fragility. What is known about older gays and lesbians was detailed using existing research data, and stereotypes and myths about older gays were explored. Common issues including relationships, historical cohorts, and coming out were discussed and problems related to health and legal dilemmas noted. Utilization of the empowerment approach was explored at the micro-, mezzo-, and macro-levels, the empowerment model was applied using a macro-level example, and case examples in each of these areas were presented.

7

Social Work, Politics, and Empowerment: Past and Current Stands and Possible Future Trends

Progressive social workers strive to alter oppressive institutions, systems, beliefs, and practices fundamentally by initiating social changes targeted at these public issues. They also work directly with individuals to help them heal their wounds, to educate them about their life choices and strategies, and to assist them as they determine their futures. Bombyk 1995, 1933.

The previous chapters have explored historical social and political issues related to lesbian and gay persons, the development of the empowerment perspective, and how empowerment constructs provide a useful framework when working with gays and lesbians across the life span. This final chapter explores how professional social work has responded to issues related to lesbian women and gay men, examines current professional standards and policies, explores research trends related to lesbian and gay issues, and discusses what future trends the profession may take in regard to empowering a minority that continues to be disenfranchised. Throughout the discussion it is important to remember that social workers are not immune to political influences. Thus, how the profession itself has resolved to meet the challenges created by the many views of the philosophical and political continuum reflects past, current, and future ideologies and trends.

Social Work's Response to the Queer Community

Social work as a profession is nearing its centennial. And when the celebrations to commemorate over one hundred years of social work begin, how many will be brave enough to publicly acknowledge that many of the founding mothers of the profession were lesbian (Goodman 1980)? Based on existing documentation, there is little doubt that Jane Addams, Mary Rozet Smith, and Ellen Gates Starr were lesbian, as were Lillian Wald and Bertha Reynolds (Goodman 1980). But the profession has been reluctant if not defiant in its failure to publicly acknowledge that many social workers and many of its most famous leaders, thinkers, and activists were not heterosexual. Does this imply that the profession does not want to embrace the lesbian and gay community and its members, or is it that professional social workers are ashamed of its roots? Or does it simply imply that social work is a profession that values personal privacy and sees little point in flaunting the sexual orientation of its members? Depending on one's philosophy there are various answers. And yet the profession has taken a public stand on the issues related to gays and lesbians. This stand is reflected in NASW's written policies and CSWE's accreditation requirements.

To have a better conceptual understanding of professional social work's position in relationship to philosophical and political influences, the basic purpose of social work as a profession must be explored. This section of the chapter will examine the purposes and values of social work and analyze the place of social work along the philosophical and political continuum that was detailed in chapter 2. How these fundamental purposes and values are applied to the empowerment perspective will conclude the chapter.

Bertha Reynolds, who helped define the social work profession, first viewed social work as "an individual approach to human beings in trouble" (Reynolds 1934:5). Her early thinking about working with people demonstrated an egalitarian approach where there was an air of democracy between the client and the professional, where the client had a right to decide whether or not he or she wanted treatment, and if treatment was sought, how much treatment was needed (Reynolds 1934, 1935). In her later writing on professional social work she not only refined this idea of empowerment but also expanded her thoughts about the profession. In her 1942 book, *Learning and Teaching in the Practice of Social Work*, she conceptualizes social work as occurring within a historical context where relationships exist between "other living forces" (p. 3) as well as between persons and their environments. Social work is seen as a problem-solving activity that involves people interacting within unique situations—person-in-situation. Social work is action-oriented, concerned with social functioning, is scientifically oriented, and has a focus on individual behavior as well as social change. People are seen as dynamic forces within their own social situations, and social work professionals must be able to have an understanding of people in a variety of different social settings. There is a dynamic balance between individuals and societal forces outside individuals. Social workers need to be able to negotiate between individual client needs and their abilities to succeed in meeting those needs in the context of existing social pressures and realities. To accomplish this, social work includes services related to individuals, groups, and community organization (Reynolds 1942).

Expanding on Reynolds's views, Harriet Bartlett (1970) conceptualized social work as having a central focus on social functioning and an orientation to people involved in various social situations. These two major foci were carried out through a specific body of values and body of knowledge that involved an interventive repertoire, knowledge of the characteristics of social situations, an ability to assess social situations, and an ability to appropriately determine interventive strategies. Philosophically, social work as a profession has been defined as a humanitarian, change-oriented endeavor committed to an understanding of the person in a social situation, the improvement of an individual's societal functioning, and the provision of adequate services for those who are vulnerable, living in poverty, or oppressed.

The primary purpose of social work is to enhance human well-being. First, it is conceptualized as a helping, person-oriented profession concerned for the individual. And, second, it is seen as being concerned with the social functioning of people within community settings (see figure 7.1) (Bartlett 1970; *Encyclopedia of Social Work*, 1977; NASW 1998; Reynolds 1942). There is an interplay between the philosophical ideas of working to "change people" and working to "change systems" that has been part of social work's philosophical history since the beginning of the profession. While the Charity Organization Societies' "friendly visitors" sought to change people to adapt to their environments, the settlement house workers as advocates sought to change social systems to better meet the needs of the community.

As the cornerstone of the profession, this focus on social functioning assumes that the social worker must be alert to persons involved in various life situations and the balance between the demands of the social environment and the individual's ability to cope with these demands. The primary orientation of social work toward persons in social situations is a characteristic that permeates the entire profession and is operationalized in two forms—an attitude toward and a relationship with people (conceptualized as social work values), and an approach toward knowl-

FIGURE 7.1
Conceptual Model of Social Work

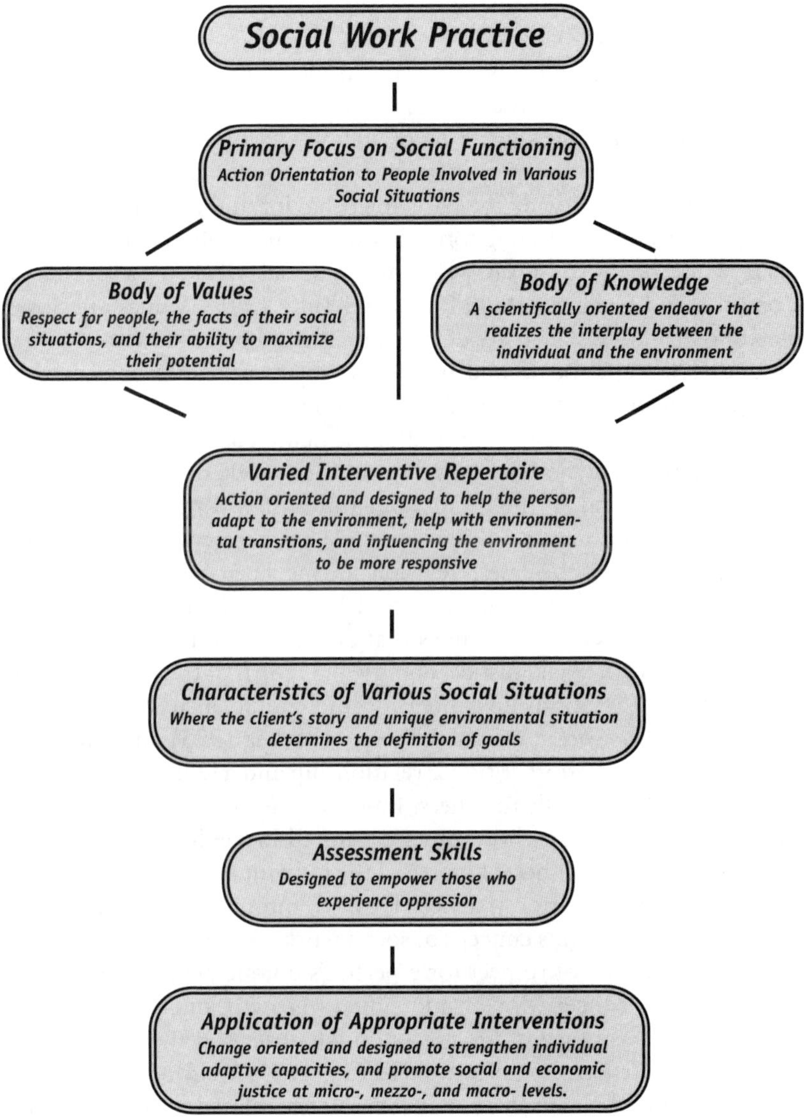

Social Work Practice

Primary Focus on Social Functioning
Action Orientation to People Involved in Various
Social Situations

Body of Values
Respect for people, the facts of their social
situations, and their ability to maximize
their potential

Body of Knowledge
A scientifically oriented endeavor that
realizes the interplay between the
individual and the environment

Varied Interventive Repertoire
Action oriented and designed to help the person
adapt to the environment, help with environmental transitions, and influencing the environment
to be more responsive

Characteristics of Various Social Situations
Where the client's story and unique environmental situation
determines the definition of goals

Assessment Skills
Designed to empower those who
experience oppression

Application of Appropriate Interventions
Change oriented and designed to strengthen individual
adaptive capacities, and promote social and economic
justice at micro-, mezzo-, and macro- levels.

edge of social situations in terms of their impact on and meaning for the persons involved (conceptualized as social work knowledge) (Bartlett 1970; Reynolds 1942).

The profession's philosophical stance along the continuum is best understood within the context of its value base. Generally, the term "values" is characterized as something of attributed or relative worth. When applied to a society, values are seen as beliefs of "the desirable" that are unproven but that provide the basis for behavior and actions. Values are conceptualized as the driving force that directs not only the profession of social work but also those who choose social work as a profession (Compton and Galaway 1994; Lloyd and Tully 1996). Values are closely related to attitudes, which are defined as a mental position with regard to a fact or a state of being and opinions, which are views or judgments about a particular matter (Lloyd and Tully 1996).

Values guide the profession and are articulated through the NASW Code of Ethics. The first attempt to establish a code of ethics was made by Mary Richmond in the 1950s, but the NASW Code of Ethics was adopted in 1960 (Reamer 1987). That code has been continuously monitored and updated, the latest revision having been adopted in August 1996 and put into effect in January 1997 (NASW 1998). The Code defines six core social work values that are central to the mission of the profession: service, social justice, dignity and worth of the person, importance of human relationships, integrity, and competence (NASW 1998). To these six, *The Social Work Dictionary* (Barker 1995) adds the confidentiality of the client/practitioner relationship and a willingness to transmit knowledge and skills to others. Embedded in these value stances are the two central values, whose roots are found in the history of the profession—belief in the inherent worth of the individual and the individual's right to self-determination (Bartlett 1970; Compton and Galaway 1994; Reynolds 1935). So, this concept of social work values is generally understood as an attitude of respect for a person's unique personal worth and individuality, a concern for an individual's growth and self-determination, and an acceptance of the person in whatever social situation he or she is found (Bartlett 1970; Reynolds 1934, 1935, 1942).

In keeping with the professional value stance related to the uniqueness of the individual and a person's right to self-determination, the current Code of Ethics states that, "social workers should not practice, condone, facilitate, or collaborate with any form of discrimination on the basis of race, ethnicity, national origin, color, sex, sexual orientation, age, marital status, political belief, religion, or mental or physical disability" (NASW, Code of Ethics, 4.02 1996). This value of nondiscrimination can be seen in the following early NASW policy statement related to homosexuality that was written in 1977:

> The National Association of Social Workers realizes that homosexuality has existed under varying circumstances throughout recorded history and in most cultures. A substantial number of women and men in American society are identified with a lifestyle that includes homosexual behavior. Homosexuality may properly be considered a preference, orientation, or propensity for certain kinds of lifestyles. Millions of women and men whose sexual orientation includes homosexuality are subject to severe social, psychological, economic, and legal discrimination because of their sexual orientation.
>
> NASW views discrimination and prejudice directed against any minority as inimical to the mental health of not only the affected minority, but of the society as a whole. The Association deplores and will work to combat archaic laws, discriminatory employment practices, and other forms of discrimination which serve to impose something less than equal status upon homosexuality oriented members of the human family. It is the objective of the social work profession not only to bring health and welfare services closer to people, but also help alter the unequal policies and practices of health and welfare institutions.
>
> NASW affirms the right of all persons to define and express their own sexuality. In choosing their own lifestyle, all persons are to be encouraged to develop their potential to the fullest extent possible as long as they do not infringe upon the rights of others.   (NASW 1981)

While NASW's Code of Ethics and policy statements seem to have a decidedly less than conservative tone, a careful reading reveals that social workers have a mandate (like the ACLU) to ensure that all individuals, irrespective of philosophical position, have access to appropriate services. And, while the profession's goal is to effect social change associated with issues related to social injustice, poverty, unemployment, and oppression, the goals of the profession are accomplished through providing individuals access to whatever information is necessary to help them achieve their maximum potential—goals accepted by the most conservative and the most liberal.

Although some will disagree, NASW's Code of Ethics, by definition, must be equally applied not only to the most radically conservative member of Aryan Nations, but also to the most flamboyant activist member of the Lesbian Avengers. The ethical balance is achieved through ensuring that, while protecting and ensuring the rights of one person or group, the rights of another individual or group are not abused. This is an awkward perch. And yet, if we as social workers truly embrace the Code of Ethics, then the rights of each individual are of importance. It is because of its mandate of respecting the person's unique individuality, personal growth, and self-determination, and of accepting the individual in a social situation, that NASW and social workers, by definition, must be placed in the middle of the philosophical and political continuum—accountable to all.

The other nationally recognized professional organization that monitors the professional educational development of social workers is the Council on Social Work Education (CSWE). As the organization responsible for the accreditation of baccalaureate and master's level degree programs in social work in the United States, CSWE's standards play an important role in the professional development of social work professionals. CSWE states that the purpose of professional social work is the alleviation of oppression and poverty and the enhancement of the human family through the improvement of social functioning, the development of needed social services, and the empowerment of at-risk groups (CSWE 1994).

CSWE identifies the purpose of social work education as being the preparation of effective, competent, and committed practitioners who are interested in providing services to the disenfranchised. The assumption made by CSWE is that social work is a profession based on certain values, skills, and knowledge grounded in a historical and philosophical base. In order to become competent with the knowledge, values, and skills necessary to be a professional social worker, one needs education (CSWE 1994). Through two primary policy documents, the Curriculum Policy Statement (there are two of these, one for baccalaureate level programs and one for master's level programs) and the Accreditation Standards, by which programs in social work education are evaluated for accreditation, CSWE defines curriculum content for BSW and MSW level programs.

The Accreditation Standards (for both the baccalaureate and master's levels) echo the importance of diversity as each program must demonstrate understanding of and respect for diversity. This is explicated in the following accreditation standard:

Evaluative Standard 3: Nondiscrimination and Human Diversity 3.0. The program must make specific, continuous efforts to provide a learning context in which understanding and respect for diversity (including age, color, disability, ethnicity, gender, national origin, race, religion, and sexual orientation) are practiced.   (CSWE 1997:1)

Exactly how this standard is to be met is left to the discretion of the program. Programs in social work education are as diverse as the philosophical and political continuum. Some are more conservative than others and some have more difficulty than others with issues of lesbian and gay content (Tully 1994). Because the Council on Social Work Education must balance the educational demands of its most conservative and liberal programs with the knowledge, skills, and values of the evolving profession, CSWE finds itself in a centrist position—not willing to cave in to the demands of the more conservative programs who say that teaching content related to homosexuality is against their beliefs, and not willing to agree with the more liberal programs that positive content related to gays and lesbians must be evident at all programmatic levels.

What has occurred is a somewhat awkward compromise in which CSWE mandates the inclusion of gay and lesbian content in all programs. However, that content is poorly monitored by site visitors and there are no checks and balances in place to ensure that students in all programs are being provided an educational context that promotes understanding of and respect for lesbians and gays. During the late 1990s within CSWE there was still debate between BSW and MSW programs in church-related conservative schools and other, more liberal, schools over what content related to lesbians and gays is appropriate, how it should be implemented, or even if it should be taught. This debate is one of long standing and represents the varying degrees of thought found in social work education. This diversity is also found throughout the profession.

Social work's professionals, while sharing a common base, find that the base is broad enough to include a wide array of philosophical views. In fact, such diversity is considered an attribute. So, there are radical gay and lesbian social workers, just as there are nongay social workers that are members of the religious right. There are lesbian and gay social workers who are members of the religious right and there are nongay social workers who are members of PFLAG and HRC. There are homophobic social workers, just as there are racist social workers. What the profession allows for is a tremendous amount of diversity and the beginning dialogue that must occur if the human family is to thrive. As our profession provides a forum for this dialogue, social workers are not immune from the society in which they exist, and that society has a long way to go before there is not conflict based on religion, sex, sexual orientation, color, ethnicity, race, national origin, disability, age, or political belief.

In sum, past and present professional practices support the rights of gay and lesbian persons and require that content related to them be included in both the baccalaureate and master's levels curricula. NASW has issued policies that denounce discrimination against and the use of reparative therapy on lesbians and gays, and yet some social workers remain homophobic and believers in a curative approach to the evil of homosexuality. Although these views seem impossibly divergent and unable to be connected at any level, perhaps one way that these schisms can begin to be brought closer together is through an understanding of how the scientific community deals with lesbian and gay issues and finally, the use of the empowerment perspective with this population.

Research Trends

The opening section of this chapter focused on how social work has responded to issues related to lesbian women and gay men and current standards and policies related to this population. Just as social work practitioners must have an understanding of those concepts, so too, must they consider how the scientific community has approached same-sex relationships. This section provides a perspective on research trends associated with homosexuality.

Research on lesbians and gays, while scant in the early part of the century, has been a topic of serious inquiry since the 1950s and can be divided into roughly four major areas. First were the etiological studies. This phase was followed by research into psychological functioning, and by studies related to social functioning and life span development inquiry. The 1990s have brought research related to professional intervention with gays and lesbians to the forefront and with it, the application of the empowerment perspective.

Etiological Studies

The etiological research phase of homosexual research focused on why homosexuals were homosexual by exploring the causes of what was then thought of as the homosexual disease (Tully 1995). Conducted almost exclusively by men, the studies of the etiology of lesbianism (Bell, Weinberg, and Hammersmith 1981; Gundlach and Riess 1967; Kaye et al. 1967; Kenyon 1968, 1969; Poole 1970; Siegelman 1974; Swanson et al.

1972; Thompson 1971; Thompson, McCandless, and Strickland 1971) have proven to be neither conclusive nor universally agreed upon. The etiological studies of the causes of male homosexuality (Bell and Weinberg 1978; Saghir and Robins 1973) are equally inconclusive and contradictory. Interestingly though, at least one of the etiological studies (Bell, Weinberg, and Hammersmith 1981) concluded, like LeVay (1991, 1996) and others (Bailey et al. 1991; DeCecco and Elia 1993) that perhaps homosexuality was more innate than learned.

Psychological Functioning

The next wave of gay and lesbian research sought to determine what psychological differences existed between heterosexuals and homosexuals and whether or not homosexuality was pathological. Studies related to the psychological functioning of gay men revealed that gay men may be less well-adjusted than their heterosexual counterparts during adolescence (Prytula, Wellford, and DeMonbreun 1979), and that homosexual men are perhaps more hostile and less guilty than straight men (Rizzo et al. 1981). But the researchers agreed such seeming psychological dysfunction was due to the issues confronted by gay adolescents and adults as a result of living in a hostile environment that did not accept the homosexual lifestyle. Williams (1981) found his gay male sample to have more emotional reactivity to stressful social stimuli and Ross (1978) found that if a gay man perceived society as hostile then the hostility would become internalized, leading to a nonacceptance of the homosexuality, lowered self-esteem, and psychological maladjustment.

To counter such negative data, evidence exists that gay men who have a commitment to a homosexual lifestyle and accept their sexual orientation have good self-concept, are well-adjusted psychologically, are more tolerant of difference, and have less anxiety and depression than heterosexual men (Bell and Wienberg 1978; Corbett, Troiden, and Dodder 1977; Hammersmith and Weinberg 1973; Jacobs and Tedford 1980; Ross 1973; Schofield 1965; Watters 1986). Further, ample data exist that demonstrate there are few differences between homosexual and heterosexual men. Although gay men may have fathers who are less nurturing and may be psychologically distant from their fathers (Mallen 1983; Townes, Ferguson, and Gillam 1976), data indicate gay men are similar to heterosexual men in appearance and demeanor (McDonald and Moore 1978) and not necessarily close to their mothers (Mallen 1983). Ross, Paulsen, and Stalstrom (1988) demonstrated that gay men scored within normal limits on such tests as the MMPI, Rorschach, and Adjective Checklist and concluded that homosexual men were no more psychologically dysfunctional than heterosexual men were. While there may be more alcoholism in a homosexual population, there has been no research data that links homosexuality with mental illness (Cabaj 1988; Saghir and Robins 1973; Watters 1986).

Some studies explored the sexual continuum by examining gay men, transgender men, and bisexuals. Data tend to demonstrate that while transgender men may have lower self-esteem and a poorer self-image than gay men, gay men in general are similar to lesbians and heterosexual men in relationship to self-acceptance and psychosomatic symptoms (Duffy and Rusbutt 1985/86; Roback et al. 1977). Saghir and Robins (1973) found that gay men do not usually cross-dress or have cross-gender childhood behaviors nor are they psychologically impaired. Bisexual men and transgender men seem to live on the fringes of both the heterosexual and homosexual worlds and may struggle with issues of identity (Brownfain 1985; Bullough, Bullough, and Elias 1997; Coleman 1985; Hansen and Evans 1985). Gay men perceive their homosexuality as an important part of their relationships with others (Jacobs and Tedford 1980), tend to recognize their sexual orientation in early childhood or adolescence (Telljohann and Price 1993), and like other populations, are extremely heterogeneous (Harry 1990). Like their heterosexual counterparts, homosexual men who are institutionalized or in treatment for psychological problems are less happy and well-adjusted than those who are not (Schofield 1965). Some men differentiate between same-sex sexual behaviors and identification as a homosexual (Weinberg 1978), thereby distinguishing between "doing" homosexual acts and "being" gay.

Research on the psychological functioning of lesbians tended to show that while lesbians seemed to have different personality characteristics than nonlesbians (Freedman 1967; Hassell and Smith 1975; Hopkins 1969; Ohlson and Wilson 1974; Thompson, McCandless, and Strickland 1971; Wilson and Greene 1971), lesbians seemed to be psychologically healthy, and psychodynamically similar to their heterosexual counterparts (Armon 1960; Freedman 1967; Hopkins 1969; Miranda and Storms 1989; Ohlson and Wilson 1974; Siegelman 1972; Wilson and Greene 1971).

When, in 1973, the American Psychiatric Association (APA) removed homosexuality from its diagnostic manual of mental disorders, the focus of research on homosexuality shifted from homosexuality as an illness to homosexuality as a more or less normal condition for at least some of the population. Lesbians and gays became more involved as researchers of homosexuality and formulated various models of identity development inherent in the development of a homosexual lifestyle (Cass 1979; Chan 1989; Chapman and Brannock; Kahn 1991; Klein, Sepekoff, and Wolf 1985; Lewis 1984; Reiter 1989; Sophie 1985/86). The psychological functioning phase of homosexual research tended to demonstrate that gay men and lesbian women are as psychologically healthy as heterosexuals are, and that homosexual behavior is not pathological.

Social Functioning and Life-Span Development

Since research data seemed to indicate that the causes for homosexuality were not clear and that homosexuals were as psychologically healthy as the rest of the population, the next phase of research focused on how lesbians and gays managed to function as a disenfranchised minority group in a heterosexual culture. Often qualitative, these studies tended to demonstrate, from the samples obtained, that lesbians are well-educated professionals involved in long-term, monogamous relationships, who function adequately in spite of what many perceived as a homophobic society that causes them stress (Albro and Tully 1979; Belote and Joesting 1976; Bullough and Bullough 1977; Chafetz et al. 1976; Cotten 1975; Gagnon and Simon 1973; Gundlach 1967; Lewis 1980; Mendola, 1980; Ponse 1978; Saghir and Robins 1969; Tanner 1978). Similar studies of gay men demonstrate them to be heterogeneous, usually well-educated, psychologically healthy, professionals in long-term monogamous or non-monogamous relationships, who, like lesbians, bisexuals, and transgender individuals, survive in an often hostile society (Hammersmith and Weinberg 1973; Jacobs and Tedford 1980; Kurdek and Schmitt 1985/86; Mallen 1983; McDonald and Moore 1978; Prytula, Wellford, and DeMonbreun 1979; Rizzo et al. 1981; Ross 1978; Ross, Paulsen, and Stalstrom 1988; Telljohann and Price 1993; Watters 1986; Weinberg 1978; Williams 1981).

These early studies of societal functioning were the basis of studies related to the diversity of gay and lesbian life that followed in the 1980s and continued into the 1990s. While the early studies had focused on fairly homogeneous white samples of individuals, research on cultural and ethnic diversity issues, disability, family structure, lesbian and gay parenting, suicide of gay and lesbian youth, bisexuality, and domestic partnership are now common (Carrier 1989; Chan 1989; Coleman, 1989; Kulkin and Percle 1997; Loiacano 1989; Lott-Whitehead and Tully

1993; Lukes and Land 1990; Wooden, Kawasaki, and Mayeda 1983; Rofes 1983). In addition to conducting research related to cultural diversity, social scientists also began to focus their attention on studying lesbians and gays across the life span. So, studies related to puberty and adolescence became popular (Hersch 1991; Hetrick and Martin 1987; Rofes 1983; Savin-Williams 1989b; Schneider 1989), as did studies related to middle age (Hetherington, Hillerbrand, and Etringer 1989; Hetherington and Orzek 1989; Tully 1989; Zak 1991) and aging (Berger 1996; Cruikshank 1990; Friend 1990; Galassi 1991; Poor 1982). Finally, research related to a still understudied phenomenon, bisexuality, began to appear (Berkey, Perelman-Hall, and Kurdek 1990; Nichols 1988; Shuster 1987; Zinik 1985) in what had been the "homosexual" journals. With an emphasis on the heterogeneous nature of nonheterosexuals, researchers seem to have confirmed that homosexuality in fact exists in every socioeconomic level of society and is a cross-cultural phenomenon.

Professional Intervention

Given the prevalence of homosexuality and the nature of institutionalized homophobia that causes mainstream society to marginalize and despise them, gays and lesbians may be at risk of internalizing this hatred or finding themselves unable to function effectively or navigate in their particular setting. The most recent wave of research in the area of lesbians and gays explores the wide array of social service interventions available to and utilized by some of the lesbian/gay/bisexual population. What distinguishes the current clinical research from clinical research conducted from the 1950s through the 1970s is that, rather than focus on homosexuality as an illness, researchers of the 1980s and 1990s focus on helping the lesbian or gay person lead a psychologically healthy life. With an emphasis on health, the focus of therapeutic intervention is on assessment, general issues of psychological health, codependency, monogamy, battering, substance abuse, internalized homophobia, coming out, and other issues associated with being a member of a generally despised and oppressed minority group that is not generally protected by law (Anderson and Henderson 1985; Faltz 1988; Finnegan and McNally 1988; Garnets et al. 1991; Glaus 1989; Hidalgo, Peterson, and Woodman 1985; Morrow and Hawxhurst 1989; Renzetti 1992, 1995; Rothblum 1988; Shernoff and Scott 1988; Smalley 1987; Woodman 1992).

A related area of research, developed in the 1980s and 1990s, examines the sexual orientation of therapists in relationship with the sexual orientation of the clients with whom they are working. Whether, for example, white heterosexual therapists can work with African-American lesbian women (Schwartz 1988) or whether any heterosexual therapist can work effectively with any homosexual client (Markowitz 1991) are typical research questions of the era. Also being questioned is whether or not the lesbian or gay therapist who may know her or his clients in social settings because the gay community is small can ethically provide intervention (Buhrke 1988; Woodman, Tully, and Barranti 1995). While gay and lesbian clients may prefer homosexual therapists (McDermott, Tyndall, and Lichtenberg 1989), would they be better served by those outside the gay or lesbian culture (Woodman, Tully, and Barranti 1995).

In sum, since the 1950s research on lesbians, gays, and bisexuals generally has evolved from examining sexual deviancy as pathology to exploration of it as an alternative lifestyle. Further, an emerging trend is to study the vast amount of difference in the homosexual and bisexual world to ensure that adequate and appropriate therapeutic services are provided by adequately trained professionals no matter what their particular sexual orientation.

Research and Philosophy: Before and After Stonewall

Philosophy and research are intricately interwoven insofar as the theoretical or conceptual frameworks that support traditional scientific research reflect the prevailing social and philosophical thought of that era. Gay and lesbian studies are no exception. The etiological and homosexuality as illness studies, conducted primarily in the 1950s, 1960s, and early part of the 1970s, tended to examine homosexuals and homosexuality using the lens of the medical model. This approach to research was mirrored in the therapeutic community, too, as therapists seemed more intent on curing homosexuality than accepting it as a viable alternative lifestyle (Bieber 1962; Nicolosi 1991; Socarides 1962). Given the influence of Freudian theory, the view of the American Psychiatric Association, reparative therapy, and prevailing social and political conservatism during the time, it is not surprising that homosexuality was treated as a pathology.

Interestingly, the Stonewall Inn riot of June 28, 1969, moved gay men and lesbian women into a new phase. From that moment in time, lesbians and gays were no longer willing to be viewed as a voiceless minority—Stonewall defined the empowerment of gays and lesbians and moved the lesbian and gay rights movement into the postmodern era. For the first time, gay men, lesbian women, and Puerto Rican and African-American transvestites stood up to those in power and began to define for themselves what it meant to be a member of a disenfranchised minority (Morales 1996). The Stonewall riot seems to embody the principles of the empowerment viewpoint, and these principles have become embedded in the struggle for equality faced by sexual minorities.

Foucault's ideas can clearly be seen in the historical evolution of the views toward homosexuality during this century. The early studies and treatment of gays and lesbians demonstrated the lack of power held by those who were not heterosexual. Power was vested in the knowledge held by those in the medical profession who were responsible for curing deviancy. Society defined homosexuality and, in doing so, legitimized what would come to be defined as institutional homophobia. Stonewall changed the locus of control. Suddenly, what had been an intimidated, frightened minority found its voice and with it began the journey, yet far from complete, toward equality for lesbians, gays, bisexuals, and transgender individuals.

In taking a stand against the New York City police, those who were in the Stonewall Inn that night in June 1969 demonstrated that power and knowledge are of utmost importance to the individual, that those in disenfranchised positions want to be empowered, and that individuals and communities have internalized power that can be discovered and utilized in oppressive situations. What has evolved since 1969 in the area of human rights for gays and lesbians includes: the 1973 decision by the American Psychiatric Association to declassify homosexuality as an illness in its manual of psychological disorders (Marcus 1992); the 1978, 1987, and 1993 gay rights marches on Washington; the passage of nondiscrimination ordinances or policies in many U.S. companies, cities, and counties; the legalization of homosexuality between consenting adults in eleven states; the election of openly lesbian or gay local, state, and federal officials; the creation of gay, lesbian, bisexual, and transgender advisory boards to local, state, and federal agencies; the passage of laws to protect sexual minorities from hate crimes; and, perhaps, the legalization of gay or lesbian marriage (NGLTF 1997).

To counter this homocentric perspective since the 1973 APA decision, there has been an increase in those providing reparative therapy in an attempt to cure homosexuals (Lloyd and Tully 1996); several counties and states have tried and succeeded in repealing human rights protections for lesbians and gays; churches deny the ordination of homosexuals; federal law does not protect sexual minorities; employers can still discriminate on the basis of sexual orientation (NGLTF 1997); and, as graphically demonstrated by Clinton's "Don't Ask, Don't Tell" policy related to the armed services, and Jerry Falwell's condemnation and loss of corporate sponsorship of television performer Ellen DeGeneres for coming out, institutional homophobia still exists (Martin and Miller 1997). So, while some strides have been made in the movement for human rights of lesbians and gays, much more needs to be accomplished. To help ensure true equality, as opposed to what Vaid (1995) has defined as "virtual equality," or the mere appearance of equality that many gays and lesbians currently seem to enjoy, it is important to comprehend exactly how the empowerment perspective can be applied to social work with lesbians and gays. In sum, the philosophical views associated with lesbians and gays continue to evolve.

The Empowerment Perspective, Social Work, and Lesbians and Gays

If one believes that professional social work has a mandate to serve those in need irrespective of their philosophical or political position, the empowerment perspective would seem a logical and pragmatic approach. As detailed in chapter 3, the empowerment perspective assumes that power over one's destiny is good and should be achieved; that those in disenfranchised positions should be empowered; that oppression is damaging and should be challenged; that people, communities, and societies have intrinsic power that can be discovered and applied to oppressive situations; and that social workers have the ability to tap and release internalized power. Empowerment is that process whereby those persons or groups who are defined to be without power are enabled, through a collaborative process using personal narratives, to increase the skills necessary for acquiring and controlling resources necessary for effective and satisfying personal, interpersonal, and political societal functioning. What must be added to this is that empowerment of one group cannot be at the peril of another. For example, let us use the religious right's views about curing homosexuality through the use of reparative therapy.

The issue of whether or not homosexuality is a curable disease has two distinct sides. Those on the right side of the philosophical and political continuum believe homosexuality is a disease of unknown etiology that can be cured through prayer and reparative therapy. Those on the left side of the continuum believe homosexuality is one variation on a sexual continuum where one end is represented by total heterosexuality, the other end by total homosexuality, and the middle comprises sexuality that is not completely heterosexual or homosexual. Those on the right point to testimonies by ex-homosexuals who claim to have overcome their disease through prayer and reparative therapy. Those on the left counter these assertions with ex-ex-homosexuals who, through reparative therapy and religious conversions, have been unable to be changed from homosexuality to heterosexuality because sexuality, they believe, is immutable.

Both sides cite research that supports their claims. The religious right and the liberal left both use biblical scriptures to support their arguments. The American Psychiatric Association has discredited reparative therapy as dangerous and causing more harm than good (Leland and Miller 1998). The NASW's National Committee on Lesbian and Gay Issues has denounced reparative (or conversion) therapies as nothing more than shaming, coercion, or brainwashing (National Committee on Lesbian and Gay Issues 1992). The Christian Coalition endorses reparative therapies as an effective method of helping those who wish to become spiritually and psychically whole by embracing the "natural" or "normal" sexual orientation of heterosexuality and turning away from destructive homosexual behaviors (CCW 1998a).

Those on the right, in what they call a loving spirit, embrace the sinner, but not the sin, and therefore are not accepting of what they have defined as immoral, sinful, and sick. Those on the left have defined the concept of homosexuality as merely a way different than heterosexuality of sexual expression and their tolerance is expressed through a willingness to accept difference. There are but a few points of agreement between the right and left. Both sides tend to agree that gay men and lesbians are a disenfranchised minority that is creating social issues involving what American citizens tend to hold in high esteem—namely, the family. While the Christian right wants to turn all homosexuals into heterosexuals, the liberal left argues for equality for all persons, including lesbians and gays.

All social work professionals do not view the issue of reparative therapy in the same way. How they perceive its utility or inappropriateness depends on their personal and philosophical value base and their own ethical application of the profession's Code of Ethics. While professional ethics demands a concern for the person in environment, a commitment to empowering those who experience oppression, and collaborative efforts with others to change oppressive structures and environments, these can be accomplished in a variety of ways and are dependent on one's personal values.

For example, as a born-again Christian social worker you deeply believe homosexuality to be a sin and a curable illness. Your client is a young adult male who identifies himself as being a devout Southern Baptist, once saved by Billy Graham and gay, who says he desperately wants to become straight because he believes himself to be a sinner who is less than whole. Do you encourage him to become involved in reparative therapy?

The empowerment approach would encourage the therapist to allow the young man to become involved in the therapeutic process by narrating his own story. The therapist's response should be to strengthen adaptive potentials and be honest about social and economic justice throughout the therapeutic process. Thus, the social worker in the example has a responsibility to become involved in the dialogue as an equal partner in the process. But, by doing so, the social worker must be honest about the realities and lack of success with reparative therapeutic approaches and the risks associated with such a treatment approach. By empowering the client to assess both sides of the situation, the decision to pursue or not to pursue reparative therapy becomes the client's.

On the other side, assume you are a liberal-thinking free spirit who fervently believes that all persons should be able to practice whatever kind of sexual activities they enjoy as long as no one is hurt and it occurs between consenting adults. The same devoutly religious young man meets with you stating his strong desire to change his sexual orientation because he views it as sinful, immoral, and an illness. Do you have him become active with the gay and lesbian community center so he can be around "normal" gays?

The pragmatic approach using the empowerment perspective is the same one as was used by the more conservative therapist. The ongoing dialogue emerges from the narrative of the client and guides the process. What is it that the client wishes to do and are these needs based on a total understanding of all of the variables associated with the issue? Does the client truly understand the ramifications of her or his actions or inactions and has she or he thought about the unanticipated consequences of those actions? The role of the social worker is to act as a collaborator, to point out possible pitfalls that may occur if one road is taken and another ignored.

To continue with the example of the Southern Baptist young man who indicated an initial desire to change his sexuality. Questions for the social worker to explore might include what prompted the client's current view, what is the problem, what does he wish to do about it, what resources (strengths) does he possess, and what does he know about possible solutions. As with most presenting situations, the underlying problem(s) may or may not be as easily defined as it first seems. Through the ongoing dialogue between the client and social worker possible solutions are weighed and accepted or discarded as the client becomes empowered to make meaningful decisions based on the current state of knowledge.

Having a working knowledge of the lesbian and gay community becomes an essential task for all social workers, of whatever philosophical or political ideology, because at some point in their professional careers they will be working with persons who are not heterosexual. So, to engage in a meaningful dialogue with gays and lesbians, social workers need to have knowledge of the gay community, but also have an in-depth awareness of the current views of the nongay community in relation to the gay community. For example, a recent cover of *Newsweek* pictured John and Anne Paulk, the ex-gays who are active with Exodus ministries, with the lead article entitled "Gay for Life? Going Straight: The Uproar Over Sexual Conversion" (*Newsweek*, August 17, 1998). (The terrorist bombing attack on two U.S. embassies in Africa, where more than 250 persons were killed, was relegated to a 2-in.-sq. insert on the cover.) The debate has stirred national interest and has escalated since 1997. The political link between the religious right, the presidential campaign in 2000, and an issue the religious right thinks will garner votes, political allies, and win elections cannot be overlooked. While conservatives are trying to empower gays and lesbians by becoming nongay, liberals are trying to empower them to gain equal rights as members of the human family whose sexual orientation is in the minority. While some on the left side of the continuum are convinced that it is merely a matter of time before equal rights are provided to lesbians and gays (ACT UP 1998; GLAAD 1998b; GLSEN 1998; HRC 1997; NGLTF 1998a), those on the right are just as positive that the sanctity of the heterosexual family will prevail and that gays and lesbians, while an inevitable part of society, will never enjoy the rights automatically provided to nongays (ALPHA 1998; CCW 1998b; FRC 1998a; Ku Klux Klan 1998). It is a curious battle.

The debate of the late 1990s about lesbians and gays is part of a historical journey begun centuries ago. Just as the empowerment perspective has evolved into what it is in the late 1990s, so, too, has the issue of homosexuality. The empowerment perspective, as one of many approaches to the practice of social work, is not static but rather a dynamic way of working with individuals, families, groups, communities, and organizational structures. As such, it will change and reflect current thinking and ways of knowing and doing. The same is true with the concept of same-sex relationships. To dare to imagine in the late 1960s that in the late 1990s

Newsweek would have on its cover, in the same year, both a lesbian couple who were having a child and an ex-homosexual husband and wife, would have been beyond reality. As liberal as the 1960s were and as progressive as social work in the 1960s perceived itself to be, the very idea of a book devoted to the empowerment of gays and lesbians would not have been acceptable. As powerful as the religious right seemed in the mid 1990s, by 1999 some of its members were beginning to discuss the possibility that the dramatic conservative change they had envisioned by the millennium was not to be and that a new era of more liberal beliefs was emerging.

Philosophical beliefs and politics tend to swing as if on a pendulum—the conservatism of the 1940s and 1950s yielded to the liberalism of the 1960s that faded with a move to the political right in the 1980s and 1990s. If the pendulum swing continues, the next five to ten years may bring another era characterized by more liberal than conservative values. But, liberal and conservative philosophical and political beliefs tend to create a dynamic balance that does not allow one view or another to dominate for extended periods of time. Assuming a more liberal view emerges at the beginning of the next century, no doubt there will be increased legal and social protections for lesbians and gays (as well as for other previously disenfranchised minorities). Same-sex couples will be allowed to legally marry, civil rights for gays and lesbians will be seen in the workplace, same-sex couples will be allowed to openly jointly adopt children, and military witch hunts for lesbians and gays will be a thing of the past. Discrimination on the basis of sexual orientation will vanish, the church will ordain gay and lesbian priests and ministers, the media will embrace same-sex protagonists in film and on television, and elected officials will include numbers of gays and lesbians. Such changes are possible if not inevitable and social work can play a role in creating all of these.

Change occurs either by revolution or evolution. For gays and lesbians the revolutionary activity of the Stonewall riots has yielded to a process of change by evolutionary means. Change is happening, lesbians and gays are being empowered to be whoever and whatever they want to be and are capable of becoming. The empowerment approach is one way to encourage the dialogue and help create this sociopolitical change. Social work professionals need to be leaders, advocates, and proponents of this change process. Will empowering any disenfranchised group that the religious right condemns be easy? The answer is "No," but for all social workers (irrespective of their personal beliefs) it is vital that all disenfranchised populations be permitted the opportunity to succeed, thus fulfilling the professional philosophy. This road can be made easier through use of the empowerment perspective. It is a challenging opportunity to become active at the micro-, mezzo-, or macro-level of social work practice. Social work's basic philosophical values and beliefs compel us to take action.

Now is the time to do so.

References

ACLU (American Civil Liberties Union). 1997. Guardian of liberty: American Civil Liberties Union [On-line]. Available: http://www.aclu.org/library/pbp1.html.

ACT UP. 1998. Documents [On-line]. Available: http://www.actupny.org/documents/documents.html.

ACT UP New York. 1998. Homepage [On-line]. Available: http://www.actupny.org/.

Adam, B. D. 1987. *The Rise of a Gay and Lesbian Movement.* Boston: Twayne.

Adelman, M. 1980. *Adjustment to Aging and Styles of Being Gay: A Study of Elderly Gay Men and Lesbians.* Ph.D. dissertation, Wright Institute, Berkeley.

Adleman, J. 1995. We never promised you a role model. In K. Jay, ed., *Dyke Life: From Growing Up to Growing Old, A Celebration of the Lesbian Experience,* pp. 77–94. New York: Basic Books.

AHD. 1985. *American Heritage Dictionary.* Boston: Houghton Mifflin.

AHD. 1992. *American Heritage Dictionary of the English Language.* New York: Houghton Mifflin.

Albro, J. C. and C. T. Tully. 1979. A study of lesbian lifestyles in the homosexual micro-culture and the heterosexual macro-culture. *Journal of Homosexuality* 4(4): 331–344.

ALPHA. 1998. ALPHA introduction [On-line]. Available: http://www.alpha.org/whatalpha/what.is.alpha.html.

alt.culture. 1998. Queer nation [On-line]. Available: http://www.pathfinder.com/altculture/qentries/Q/queerxnati.

Altman. D. 1982. *The Homosexualization of America.* Boston: Beacon Press.

Alverez, L. 1998. House backs ban on gay bias. *Times-Picayune,* August 6, p. A-6.

American Civil Liberties Union, *see* ACLU.

American Heritage Dictionary, see *AHD* 1985.

American Heritage Dictionary of the English Language, see AHD 1992.

American Psychiatric Association, *see* APA.

Anderson, C. L. 1981/82. Males as sexual assault victims: Multiple levels of trauma. *Journal of Homosexuality* 7(2/3): 145–162.

Anderson. G. 1998. Providing services to elderly people with HIV. In D. M. Aronstein and B. J. Thompson, eds., *HIV and Social Work: A Practitioners Guide*, pp. 443–450. New York: Harrington Park Press.

Annual Demographic Survey. 1997. March Supplement [On-line]. Available: http://ferret.bls.census.gov/macro/031997/hhlnc/3–001.htm.

Anthony, B. D. 1981/82. Lesbian client—lesbian therapist: Opportunities and challenges in working together. *Journal of Homosexuality* 7(2/3): 45–57.

APA (American Psychiatric Association). 1994. Gay and lesbian issues [On-line]. Available: http://www.thebody.com/apa/apafacts.html.

Appignanesi, R. and C. Garratt. 1995. *Introducing Postmodernism.* New York: Totem Books.

Appleby, G. A. and J. W. Anastas. 1998. *Not Just a Passing Phase: Social Work with Gay, Lesbian, and Bisexual People.* New York: Columbia University Press.

Armon, V. 1960. Some personality variables in overt female homosexuality. *Journal of Projective Technique of Personality Assessment* 24(3): 292–309.

Aronstein, D. M. and B. J. Thompson, eds. 1998. *HIV and Social Work: A Practitioners Guide.* New York: Harrington Park Press.

Atchley, R. 1977. *The Social Forces in Later Life.* 2nd ed. Belmont, Calif.: Wadsworth.

Attey, P. 1998. HRC Release, August 6: Hefley Amendment Defeated (252–176) [On- line].available: phil.attey@mail.hrcusa.org.

Bailey, J. M., R. C. Pillard, M. C. Neale, and Y. Agyei. 1991. Heredity factors influence sexual orientation in women. *Archives of General Psychiatry* 50(3): 217–223.

Barker, R. L. 1995. *The Social Work Dictionary.* 3rd ed. Washington, D.C.: NASW Press.

Bartlett, H. M. 1970. *The Common Base of Social Work Practice.* Washington, D.C.: NASW.

Bayer, R. 1981. *Homosexuality and American Psychiatry: The Politics of Diagnosis.* New York: Basic Books.

Beckett, J. O. and R. L. Schneider. 1992. Older women. In R. L. Schneider and N. P. Kropf, eds., *Gerontological Social Work: Knowledge, Service Settings, and Special Populations*, pp. 323–358. Chicago: Nelson Hall.

Bell, A. P. and M. S. Weinberg. 1978. *Homosexuality: A Study of Diversity Among Men and Women.* New York: Simon and Schuster.

Bell, A. P., M. S. Weinberg, and S. K. Hammersmith. 1981. *Sexual Preference.* Bloomington: Indiana University Press.

Belote, D. and J. Joesting. 1976. Demographic and self-report characteristics of lesbians. *Psychological Reports* 39: 621–622.

Benecke, M. 1998. Gay discharges are up 67%. *Times-Picayune*, April 7, p. A-5.

Berger, R. M. 1980. Psychological adaptation of the older homosexual male. *Journal of Homosexuality* 5(3): 161–175.

Berger, R. M. 1982. The unseen minority: Older gays and lesbians. *Social Work* 27(3): 236–242.

Berger, R. M. 1983. What is a homosexual? A definitional model. *Social Work* 28(2): 132–135.

Berger, R. M. 1996. *Gay and Gray: The Older Homosexual Man.* 2nd ed. New York: Harrington Park Press.

Berger, R. M. and J. J. Kelly. 1995. Gay men: Overview. In R. L. Edwards, ed., *Encyclopedia of Social Work.* 19th ed., vol. 2, pp. 1064–1075. Washington, D.C.: NASW Press.

Berke, R. L. 1998. Chasing the polls on gay rights. *New York Times,* August 2, section 4:3.

Berkey, B. R., T. Perelman-Hall, and L. A. Kurdek. 1990. The multidimensional scale of sexuality. *Journal of Homosexuality* 11(1/2): 67–87.

Berrill, K. T. 1992. Anti-gay violence and victimization in the United States: An overview. In G. M. Herek and K. T. Berrill, eds., *Hate Crimes: Confronting Violence Against Lesbians and Gay Men,* pp. 19–45. Newbury Park, Calif.: Sage.

Berzon, B. 1988. *Permanent Partners: Building Gay and Lesbian Relationships that Last.* New York: E. P. Dutton.

Besen, W. 1998. August 7. House passes anti-gay adoption amendment [On-line]. available: wayne.besen@mail.hrcusa.org.

Bieber, I. 1965. Clinical aspects of male homosexuality. In J. Marmor, *Sexual Inversion: The Multiple Roots of Homosexuality,* pp. 248–267. New York: Basic Books.

Bieber, I., H. J. Dain, P. R. Dince, M. G. Drellich, H. G. Grand, R. H. Gundlach, M. W. Kremer, A. H. Rifkin, C. B. Wilbur, and T. B. Bieber. 1962. *Homosexuality: A Psychoanalytic Study.* New York: Basic Books.

Birch, E. 1998. Maine repeal: Wake-up call to fair-minded majority. *The Federal Report* (March/April): 1.

Blau, P., ed. 1975. *Approaches to the Study of Social Structure.* New York: Free Press.

Bohn, T. 1983/84. Homophobic violence: Implications for social work. *Journal of Social Work and Human Sexuality* 2(2/3): 91–112.

Bombyk, M. 1995. Progressive social work. In R. L. Edwards, ed., *Encyclopedia of Social Work.* 19th ed., vol. 3, pp. 1933–1942. Washington D.C.: NASW Press.

Bond, B. K. 1998. Recruitment Request Letter. Washington, D.C.: Gay and Lesbian Victory Fund.

Bonfitto, V. F. 1997. The formation of a gay and lesbian identity and community in the Connecticut River Valley of Western Massachusetts, 1900–1970. *Journal of Homosexuality* 33(1): 69–96.

Boswell, J. 1980. *Christianity, Social Tolerance, and Homosexuality: Gay People in Western Europe from the Beginning of the Christian Era to the Fourteenth Century.* Chicago: University of Chicago Press.

Boswell, J. 1994. *Same-sex Unions in Premodern Europe*. New York: Villard Books.

Bowers v. Hardwick, 106 S. Ct. 2841 (1986).

Boxer, A. M. and Cohler, B. J. 1989. The life course of gay and lesbian youth: An immodest proposal for the study of lives. *Journal of Homosexuality* 17(3/4): 315–355.

Boyer, D. 1989. Male prostitution and homosexual identity. *Journal of Homosexuality* 17(1/2): 151–184.

Brady, S. and W. J. Busse. 1994. The gay identity questionnaire: A brief measure. *Journal of Homosexuality* 26(4): 1–22.

Brooten, B. J. 1996. *Love Between Women: Early Christian Responses to Female Homoeroticism*. Chicago: University of Chigago Press.

Browning, C. 1987. Therapeutic issues and intervention strategies with young adult lesbian clients: A developmental approach. *Journal of Homosexuality* 14(1/2): 45–52.

Bullough, B., V. L. Bullough, and J. Ellias, eds. 1997. *Gender Bending*. New York: Prometheus Books,

Bullough, V. L. 1976. *Sexual Variance in Society and History*. New York: Wiley.

Bullough, V. L. 1979. *Homosexuality: A History*. New York: New American Library.

Bullough, V. L. and B. Bullough. 1977. Lesbianism in the 1920s and 1930s: A Newfound Study. *Signs* 2(4): 895–904.

Bullough, V. L. and B. Bullough. 1995. *Sexual Attitudes: Myths and Realities*. Amherst, N.Y.: Prometheus Books.

Butler, B. 1990. *Ceremonies of the Heart*. Seattle: Seal Press.

Cabaj, R. P. 1988. Homosexuality and neurosis: Considerations for psychotherapy. *Journal of Homosexuality*, 15(1/2): 13–23.

Canning, P. 1998, August 5. Landmark congressional briefing to address sexual orientation and Human rights [On-line]. available: canning@ainbow.net.au.

Carrier, J. M. 1989. Gay liberation and coming out in Mexico. *Journal of Homosexuality*, 17(3/4): 225–252.

Cass, V. 1979. Homosexual identity formulation: A theoretical model. *Journal of Homosexuality*, 4(3): 219–235.

Cass, V. 1984. Homosexual identity: A concept in need of definition. *Journal of Homosexuality*, 9(2/3): 105–125.

Causby, V., Lockhart, L., White, B., and Greene, K. 1995. Fusion and conflict resolution in lesbian relationships. *Journal of Gay and Lesbian Social Services*, 3(1): 67–82.

CCE *(Concise Columbia Encyclopedia)*. 1995. New York: Columbia University Press.

CCW (Christian Coalition Worldwide). 1996. News releases [On-line]. Available: http://www.cc.org/publications/ccnews.html.

CCW. 1997. News releases [On-line]. Available: http://www.cc.org/publications/ccnews.html.

CCW. 1998a. Christian coalition joins other groups with message of hope for homosexuals [On-line]. Available: http://www.cc.org/publications/ccnews. html.

CCW. 1998b. Homepage [On-line]. Available: http://www.cc.org/about.html.

CCW. 1998c. News releases [On-line]. Available: http://www.cc.org/publications/ccnews.html.

Chafetz, J., P. Sampson, P. Beck, J. West, and B. Jones. 1976. *Who's Queer: A Study of Homo and Heterosexual Women.* Sarasota, Fla.: Omni Press.

Chan, C. S. 1989. Issues of identity development among Asian-American lesbians and gay men. *Journal of Counseling and Development* 68(1): 16–20.

Chapman, B. E. and J. C. Brannock. 1987. Proposed model of lesbian identity development: An empirical examination. *Journal of Homosexuality* 14(3/4): 69–80.

Cherry, K. and J. Mitulski. 1990. Committed couples in the community. *Christian Century* 107(7): 218–220.

Child Welfare League of America, *see* CWLA.

Christian Answers. 1998. What did the Bible say about same-sex marriages? [On-line]. Available: http://www.christiananswers.net.

Christian Anti-Homosexual Website. 1998. Homepage [On-line]. Available: http://www.antiomosexual.com.

Christian Coalition Worldwide, *see* CCW.

Clark, J. M., J. C. Brown, and L. M. Hochstein. 1990. Institutionalized religion and gay/lesbian oppression. In F. W. Bozett and M. B. Sussman, eds., *Homosexuality and Family Relationships*, pp. 265–284. New York: Haworth Press.

Clunis, D. M. and G. D. Green. *Lesbian Couples.* Seattle: Seal Press.

Coleman, E. 1989. The development of male prostitution among gay and bisexual adolescents. *Journal of Homosexuality* 17(1/2): 131–149.

Coleman, E. 1981/82. Developmental stages of the coming-out process. *Journal of Homosexuality* 7(2/3): 31–43.

Coleman, E. and G. Remafedi. 1989. Gay, lesbian, and bisexual adolescents: A critical challenge to counselors. *Journal of Counseling and Development* 68(1): 36–40.

Compton, B. R. and B. Galaway. 1994. *Social Work Processes.* 5th ed. Pacific Grove, Calif.: Brooks/Cole.

Compton's Encyclopedia Online. 1997. Ku Klux Klan [On-line]. Available: http://comptons2.aol.com/encyclopedia/articles/02660_A.html.

Concise Columbia Encyclopedia, see CCE.

Conlin, D. and J. Smith. 1981/82. Group psychotherapy for gay men. *Journal of Homosexuality* 7(2/3): 105–112.

Corbett, S. L., R. R. Troiden, and R, A. Dodder. 1977. Tolerance as a correlate of experience with stigma: The case of the homosexual. *Journal of Homosexuality* 3(1): 3–13.

Cornell University Empowerment Group. 1989. *Networking Bulletin* 1(October): 1–2.

Cotten, W. L. 1975. Social and sexual relationships of lesbians. *Journal of Sex Research* 11: 139–148.

Council on Social Work Education, *see* CSWE.

Cox, S. and C. Gallois. 1996. Gay and lesbian development: A social identity perspective. *Journal of Homosexuality* 30(4): 1–30.

Cramer, D. and A. J. Roach. 1988. Coming out to mom and dad: A study of gay males and their relationships with their parents. *Journal of Homosexuality* 15(3/4): 79–91.

Criminal Justice Information Services. 1995. Hate crime—1995 [On-line]. Available: http://www.fbi.gov/ucr/hatecm.htm.

Cropper, C. M. 1998. Baptist group ousts church for welcoming gay people. *New York Times*, March 1, p. A 20.

Cruikshank, M. 1990. Lavender and gray: A brief survey of lesbian and gay aging studies. *Journal of Homosexuality* 20(3/4): 77–87.

CSWE (Council on Social Work Education). 1994. *Handbook on Accreditation Standards and Procedures*. Alexandria, Va: Council on Social Work Education.

CSWE. 1997. Commission on accreditation revisions to evaluative standards, effective July 1, 1998 [On-line]. Available: http://www.cswe.org.

Cummerton, J. M. 1982. Homophobia and social work practice with lesbians. In A. Weick and S. T. Vandiver, eds., *Women, Power, and Change*, pp. 104–113. Washington, D.C.: NASW.

CWLA (Child Welfare League of America). 1991. *Serving Gay and Lesbian Youths: The Role of Child Welfare Agencies*. Washington D.C.: CWLA.

DC Lesbian Avengers. 1998. Homepage [On-line]. Available: http://www.well. com/user/barmitag/dcavengers.htm.

De Cecco, J. P. and J. P. Elia, eds. 1993. If you seduce a straight person, can you make them gay? Issues in biological essentialism versus social constructivism in gay and lesbian identities [Special Issue]. *Journal of Homosexuality*, 24(3).

Decker, B. 1983/84. Counseling gay and lesbian couples. *Journal of Social Work and Human Sexuality* 2(2/3): 39–52.

DeCrescenzo, T. A. 1983/84. Homophobia: A study of attitudes of mental health professionals toward homosexuality. *Journal of Social Work and Human Sexuality* 2(2/3): 115–136.

DeCrescenzo, T. and C. McGill. 1978. Homophobia: A Study of Mental Health Professionals Attitudes Toward Homosexuality. Manuscript. Los Angeles: University of Southern California School of Social Work.

Deisher, R. W. 1989. Adolescent homosexuality: Preface. *Journal of Homosexuality* 17(1/2): xiii-xv.

DeLombard, J. 1995. Who cares? Lesbians as caregivers. In K. Jay, ed., *Dyke Life: From Growing Up to Growing Old, A Celebration of the Lesbian Experience*, pp. 344–361. New York: Basic Books.

De Mar, G. 1998. What's wrong with the Christian Coalition? [On-line]. Available: http://www.inetresults.com/ustp_va/notcc.html.

D'Emilio, J. and E. B. Freedman. 1988. *Intimate Matters: A History of Sexuality in America*. New York: Harper and Row.

de Sausser, F. 1996. Course in general linguistics. In L. Cahoone, ed., *From Mod-*

ernism to Postmodernism: An Anthology, pp. 360–379. Cambridge, Mass.: Blackwell.

Dickens, D. R. and A. Fontana. 1994. Postmodernism in the social sciences. In D. R. Dickens and A. Fontana, eds., *Postmodernism and Social Inquiry*, pp. 1–22. New York: Guilford Press.

Domestic violence: The facts. 1998. In *A Handbook to STOP Violence* [On-line]. Available: http://www.famvi.com/dv_facts.htm.

Duberman, M. 1991. *Cures: A Gay Man's Odyssey*. New York: Dutton.

Duffy, S.M. and C. E. Rusbutt. 1985/86. Satisfaction and commitment in heterosexual and homosexual relationships. *Journal of Homosexuality* 12(2): 1–23.

du Mas, F. M. 1979. *Gay Is Not Good*. Nashville: Thomas Nelson.

Dunker, B. 1987. Aging lesbians: Observations and speculations. In the Boston Lesbian Psychologies Collective, eds., *Lesbian Psychologies: Explorations and Challenges*, pp. 73–82. Urbana: University of Illinois Press.

Durkheim, E. 1936. *The Rules of Sociological Method*. Chicago: University of Chicago Press.

Durkheim, E. 1951. *Suicide*. Glencoe, Ill.: Free Press.

Dynes, W. R. and S. Donaldson, eds. 1992a. *Studies in Homosexuality*: vol. 1: *Homosexuality in the Ancient World*. New York: Garland.

Dynes, W. R. and S. Donaldson, eds. 1992b. *Studies in Homosexuality*: vol. 2: *Ethnographic Studies of Homosexuality*. New York: Garland.

Dynes, W. R. and W. Johansson. 1990. Homosexual. In W. R. Dynes, ed., *Encyclopedia of Homosexuality*, pp. 555–556. New York: Garland.

Eliason, M. J. 1996. Identity formation for lesbian, bisexual, and gay persons: Beyond a "minoritizing" view. *Journal of Homosexuality* 30(3): 31–58.

Einhorn, J. 1998. GLAAD and GLSEN disturbed by senate legislation promoting internet censorship [On-line]. Available: http://ww.glstn.org/pages/sections/library/news/9807-6.article.

Ethics and Religious Liberty Commission of the Southern Baptist Convention. 1998. Homosexuality: Current homosexual issues [On-line]. Available: http://www.erlc.com/homosexuality/homosexuality/htm.

Ettore, E. 1980. *Lesbians, Women, and Society*. London: Routledge.

Exodus International. 1998. Exodus international homepage [On-line]. Available: http://www.messiah.edu/hpages/facstacc/chase/h/exodus.

Faces of hate crimes. 1998. [On-line]. Available: http://www.civilrights.org/lcef/hcpc/face.html#4.

Faderman, L. 1981. *Surpassing the Love of Men: Romantic Friendships and Love Between Women from the Renaissance to the Present*. New York: William Morrow.

Faderman, L. 1991. *Odd Girls and Twilight Lovers*. New York: Columbia University Press.

Family Research Council, *see* FRC.

Fassinger, R. E. and B. A. Miller. 1996. Validation of an inclusive model of sexual identity formation on a sample of gay men. *Journal of Homosexuality* 32(2): 53–78.

Feldman, D. A. 1989. Gay youth and AIDS. *Journal of Homosexuality* 17(1/2): 185–193.

Fisher, D. D. 1991. *An Introduction to Consructivisim for Social Workers*. New York: Praeger.

Ford, C. S., and F. A. Beach. 1951. *Patterns of Sexual Behavior*. New York: Harper and Brothers.

Forrister, D. K. 1992. The integration of lesbian and gay content in direct practice courses. In N. J. Woodman, ed., *Lesbian and Gay Lifestyles: A Guide for Counseling and Education*, pp. 51–65. New York: Irvington.

Foucault, M. 1996. Nietzsche, genealogy, history. In L. Cahoone, ed., *From Modernism to Postmodernism: An Anthology*, pp. 360–379. Cambridge, Mass.: Blackwell.

Foucault, M. 1996. Truth and power. In L. Cahoone, ed., *From Modernism to Postmodernism: An Anthology*, pp. 379–381. Cambridge, Mass.: Blackwell.

Francher, J. S. and J. Henkin. 1973. The menopausal queen: Adjustment to aging and the male homosexual. *Journal of Orthopsychiatry*, 43(4): 670–674..

FRC (Family Research Council). 1998a. Issues in depth [On-line]. Available: http://www.frc.org/frc/issues.

FRC. 1998b. Issues in depth: Homosexual culture [On-line]. Available: http://www.frc.org/frc/issues/homosexualmain.html.

Freedman, M. 1967. Homosexuality Among Women and Psychological Adjustment. Ph.D. dissertation, Case Western Reserve University, Cleveland.

Friend, R. A. 1980. Gayaging: Adjustment and the older gay male. *Alternative Lifestyles* 3: 231–248.

Friend, R. A. 1989. Older lesbian and gay people: Responding to homophobia. *Marriage and Family Review* 14(3/4): 241–263.

Friend, R. A. 1990. Older lesbians and gay people: A theory of successful aging. *Journal of Homosexuality* 20(3/4): 99–118.

Fritz, M. 1988. Hope for the politically homeless. *Fresno Bee*, September 4. [On-line]. Available: http://www.self-gov.org/hope.html.

Gagnon, J. H. and W. Simon. 1973. *Sexual Conduct*. Chicago: Aldine.

Galassi, F. S. 1991. A life-review workshop for gay and lesbian elders. *Journal of Gerontological Social Work* 16(1/2): 75–86.

Gans, H. J. 1982. *The Urban Villagers: Group and Class in the Life of Italian-Americans*. Rev. ed. New York: Free Press.

Gant, L. M. 1998. Essential facts every social worker needs to know. In D. M. Aronstein and B. J. Thompson, eds., *HIV and Social Work: A Practitioner's Guide*, pp. 3–25. New York: Harrington Park Press.

Garnets, L., S. D. Cochran, J. Goodchild, and A. Peplau. 1991. Issues in psychotherapy with lesbians and gay men: A survey of psychologists. *American Psychologist* 46(9): 964–972.

Gay and Lesbian Alliance Against Defamation, *see* GLAAD.

Gay and Lesbian Association of Retiring Persons. 1998. Vision Statement [On-line]. Avaialble: http://www.gaylesbianretiring.org/vision.htm.

Gay, Lesbian, and Straight Education Network, *see* GLSEN.

Gelman, D. 1993. Homoeroticism in the ranks. *Newsweek*, July 23, pp. 28–29.

Germain, C. B. 1979. Introduction: Ecology and social work. In C. B. Germain, ed., *Social Work Practice: People and Environments*, pp. 1–22. New York: Columbia University Press.

Germain, C. B. and A. Gitterman. 1980. *The Life Model of Social Work Practice*. New York: Columbia University Press.

Gerstel, C. J., A. J. Feraios, and G. Herdt. 1989. Widening circles: Ethnographic profile of a youth group. *Journal of Homosexuality* 17(1/2): 75–92.

Gibbs, E. D. 1989. Psychosocial development of children raised by lesbian mothers: A review of research. *Women and Therapy* 8(1/2): 65–75.

Gingrich, N. 1998. SpeakerNews [On-line]. Available: http://speakernews.gov/.

Gitterman, A., ed. 1991. *Handbook of Social Work Practice with Vulnerable Populations*. New York: Columbia University Press.

GLAAD (Gay and Lesbian Alliance Against Defamation). 1998a. GLAAD accomplishments [On- line]. Available: http://www.glaad.org/glaad/accomplishments.html.

GLAAD. 1998b. GLAAD history [On-line]. Available: http://www.glaad.org/glaad/history.html.

GLAAD. 1998c. Media release archive [On-line]. Available: http://www.glaad.org/glaad/projects.html.

GLSEN (Gay, Lesbian, and Straight Education Network). 1998. About GLSEN [On-line]. Available: http://www.glstn.org/pages/sections/about.

Gochros H. L. 1983/84. Teaching social workers to meet the needs of the homosexually oriented. *Journal of Social Work and Human Sexuality* 2(2/3): 137–156.

Goldberg, C. 1966. Shunning the "he" and "she" they fight for respect. *New York Times*, September 8, Section 1:10.

Gonsiorek, J. C. 1981/82a. Introduction: Present and future directions in gay/lesbian mental health. *Journal of Homosexuality* 7(2/3): 5–7.

Gonsiorek, J. C. 1981/82b. The use of diagnostic concepts in working with gay and lesbian populations. *Journal of Homosexuality* 7(2/3): 9–20.

Gonsiorek, J. C., ed. 1982. *Homosexuality and Psychotherapy: A Practitioner's Handbook of Affirmative Models*. New York: Haworth Press.

Goodman, B. 1977. *The Lesbian: A Celebration of Difference*. New York: Out and Out Books.

Goodman, B. 1980 *"Where Will You Be?" The Professional Oppression of Gay People: A Lesbian Feminist Perspective*. New York: Out and Out Books.

Goodman, B. 1985. Out of the therapeutic closet. In H. Hidalgo, T. Peterson, and N. J. Woodman, eds., *Lesbian and Gay Issues: A Resource Manual for Social Workers*, pp. 140–147. Silver Spring, Md.: NASW.

Goodman, E. 1998. Reframing anti-gay rhetoric. *New Orleans Times-Picayune*, July 24, p. B-7.

Gottman, J. S. 1989. Children of gay and lesbian parents. *Marriage and Family Review* 14(3/4): 177–196.

Grace, J. 1992. Affirming gay and lesbian adulthood. In N. J. Woodman, ed., *Les-

bian and Gay Lifestyles: A Guide for Counseling and Education, pp. 33–50. New York: Irvington.

Gray, J. 1992. *Men Are from Mars, Women Are from Venus: A Practical Guide for Improving Communication and Getting What You Want in Relationships.* New York: Harper Collins.

Greenberg, D. F. 1988. *The Construction of Homosexuality.* Chicago: University of Chicago Press.

Greer, D. 1995. Log cabin republicans gives Spechter campaign returned Dole contribution [On-line]. available: lccnj@aol.com.

Grigg, W. N. 1994. The lavender revolution: Undermining America's traditional values. *The New American* [On-line]. Available: http://jbs.org/ta/1994/vol10 no02.htm.

Grossman, A. H. 1997. Growing up with a "spoiled identity:" Lesbian, gay, and bisexual youth at risk. *Journal of Gay and Lesbian Social Services* 6(3): 45–56.

Grube, J. Natives and settlers: An ethnographic note on early interaction of older homosexual men with younger gay liberationists. *Journal of Homosexuality* 20(3/4): 119–135.

Gundlach, R. H. 1967. Research project report. *The Ladder* 11: 2–9.

Gundlach, R. H. and B. F. Riess. 1967. Birth order and sex of siblings in a sample of lesbians and non-lesbians. *Psychological Reports* 20: 61–62.

Gunter, P. L. 1992. Social work with non-traditional families. In N. J. Woodman, ed., *Lesbian and Gay Lifestyles: A Guide for Counseling and Education,* pp. 87–109. New York: Irvington.

Gusfield, J. R. 1978. *Community.* Oxford, England: Blackwell.

Gutierrez, L. M. 1990. Working with women of color: An empowerment perspective. *Social Work* 35(2): 149–153

Hamilton, G. 1951. *Theory and Practice of Social Case Work.* 2nd ed. New York: Columbia University Press.

Hammersmith, S. K. and M. S. Weinberg. 1973. Homosexual identity: Commitment, adjustment, and significant others. *Sociometry* 36(1): 56–79.

Hanley-Hackenbruk, P. 1989. Psychotherapy and the "coming out" process. *Journal of Gay and Lesbian Psychotherapy* 1(1): 21–39.

Harry, J. 1990. A probability sample of gay males. *Journal of Homosexuality* 19(1): 89–104.

Harry, J. and W. B. DeVall. 1978. *The Social Organization of Gay Males.* New York: Praeger.

Hartman, A. 1996. Social policy as a context for lesbian and gay families. In J. Laird and R. J. Green, eds., *Lesbians and Gays in Couples and Families: A Handbook for Therapists,* pp. 69–85. San Francisco: Josey-Bass.

Hartman, A. and J. Laird. 1983. *Family-Centered Social Work Practice.* New York: Free Press.

Hassell, A. and E. W. Smith. 1975. Female homosexuals' concept of self, men, and women. *Journal of Personality Assessment* 42: 83–90.

Hate crime statistics. 1996. [On-line]. Available: http://www.civilrights.org/lcef/hcpc/stats/table1.htm.

Hate crimes: A definition. 1994. [On-line]. Available: http://www.civilrights.org/lcef/hcpc/define.html.

Hatterer, L. J. 1970. *Changing Homosexuality in the Male: Treatment for Men Troubled by Homosexuality.* New York: McGraw Hill.

Herek, G. M. 1991. Stigma, prejudice, and violence against lesbians and gay men. In J. C. Gonsiorek and J. D. Weinrich, eds., *Homosexuality: Research Implications for* Public Policy, pp. 60–80. Newbury Park, Calif.: Sage.

Herdt, G. 1989. Introduction: Gay and lesbian youth, emergent identities, and cultural scenes at home and abroad. *Journal of Homosexuality* 17(1/2): 1–42.

Heritage. 1998. Ex-homosexuals ministry denounces violence aimed at homosexuals [On-line]. Available: http://www.fni.com/heritage/June97/homomin.html.

Hersch, P. 1991. Secret lives. *Networker* (January/February): 37–43.

Hetherington, C., E. Hillerbrand, and B. Etringer. 1989. Career counseling with gay men: Issues and recommendations for research. *Journal of Counseling and Development* 7(8): 452–454.

Hetherington, C. and A. Orzek. 1989. Career counseling and life planning with lesbian women. *Journal of Counseling and Development* 68(1): 52–57.

Hetrick, E. S. and A. D. Martin. 1987. Developmental issues and their resolution for gay and lesbian adolescents. *Journal of Homosexuality* 14(1/2): 25–43.

Hidalgo, H., T. L. Peterson, and N. J. Woodman. 1985. *Lesbian and Gay Issues: A Resource Manual for Social Workers.* Silver Spring, Md.: NASW.

Holland, J. 1998. August 4. Clinton order on gay rights is likely safe. *Times-Picayune*, August 4, p. A-5.

Hooker, E. 1965. Male homosexuals and their "worlds." In J. Marmor, ed., *Sexual Inversion: The Multible Roots of Homosexuality*, pp. 83–107. New York: Basic Books.

Hooyman, N. and H. A. Kiyak. 1996. *Social Gerontology: A Multidisciplinary Perspective.* 4th ed. Boston: Allyn and Bacon.

Hopkins, J. H. 1969. The lesbian personality. *British Journal of Psychiatry* 115: 1433–1436.

Houser, W. 1990. AIDS. In W. R. Dynes, ed., *Encyclopedia of Homosexuality*, vol 1, pp. 29–32). New York: Garland.

HRC (Human Rights Campaign). 1995a. Human Rights Campaign political action committee (PAC) [On-line]. Available: http://www.hrc.org/hrc/pac/index.html.

HRC. 1995b. HRC news 1995 [On-line]. Available: http://www.hrc.org/hrc-news/1995.html.

HRC. 1996. HRC News 1996 [On-line]. Available: http://www.hrc.org/hrc-news/1996.html.

HRC. 1997. Annual report [On-line]. Available: http://www.hrc.org/anrept1.html.

HRC. 1998a. Human Rights Campaign's mission [On-line]. Available: http://www.hrc.org/hrc/mission.html.

HRC. 1998b. HRC news [On-line]. Available: http://www.hrc.org/hrc/hrcnews/index.html.

Humphreys, N. A. and J. K. Quam. 1998. Middle-aged and old gay, lesbian, and bisexual adults. In G. A. Appleby and J. W. Anastas, eds., *Not Just a Passing Phase: Social Work with Gay, Lesbian, and Bisexual People*, pp. 245–267. New York: Columbia University Press.

Hunter, J. 1995. At the crossroads: Lesbian youth. In K. Jay, ed., *Dyke Life: A Celebration of the Lesbian Experience*, pp. 50–60. New York: Basic Books.

Icard, L. 1985/86. Black gay men and conflicting social identities: Sexual orientation versus racial identity. *Journal of Social Work and Human Sexuality* 4(1/2): 83–93.

In Case You Missed It. 1998. Interesting stories and quotes [On-line]. Available: http://www.rnc.org/news/misc/index.html.

Information About the Queer Nation. 1998. Homepage [On-line]. Available: http://www.cmu.edu/people/mjw/queer/mainpage.html.

Isay, R. A. 1989. *Being Homosexual: Gay Men and Their Development*. New York: Farrar, Straus, and Giroux.

In the LOOP. 1998. Newsletter topics [On-line]. Available: http://www.rnc.org/news/loop/index.html.

Jacobs, A. J. 1991. Family law. In R. Achtenberg and M. Newcombe, eds., *Sexual Orientation and the Law*, pp. 1.92.4–1.92.10. New York: Clark, Boardman, and Callaghan.

Jacobs, J. A. and W. H. Tedford. 1980. Factors affecting the self-esteem of the homosexual individual. *Journal of Homosexuality* 5(4): 373–382.

Jay, K., ed. 1995. *Dyke Life: From Growing Up to Growing Old a Celebration of Difference*. New York: Basic Books.

Jay, K. and A. Young. 1977. *The Gay Report*. New York: Summit Books.

Johansson, W. 1990. Tribade. In W. R. Dynes, ed., *Encyclopedia of Homosexuality*, pp. 1325–1326. New York: Garland.

John Birch Society. 1998. Pending legislation [On-line]. Available: http://www.jbs.org.

Kahn, M. J. 1991. Factors affecting the coming out process for lesbians. *Journal of Homosexuality* 21(3): 47–70.

Kahn S. 1995. Community organization. In R. L. Edwards, ed., *Encyclopedia of Social Work*. 19th ed., vol. 1, pp. 569–576. Washington, D.C.: NASW Press.

Kaplan, S. and S. Saperstien. 1985. Lesbian and gay adolescents. In N. Woodman, ed., *Lesbian and Gay Issues: A Resource Manual for Social Workers*, pp. 17–20. Silver Spring, Md.: NASW.

Karger, H. J. and D. Stoesz. 1998. *American Social Policy*. 3rd ed. New York: Longman.

Kates, S. M. 1998. *Twenty-Million New Customers: Understanding Gay Men's Consumer Behavior*. New York: Harrington Park Press.

Katz, J. 1976. *Gay American History: Lesbians and Gay Men in the USA*. New York: Thomas Y. Crowell.

Kaufman, G. and L. Raphael. 1996. *Coming Out of Shame: Transforming Gay and Lesbian Lives*. New York: Doubleday.

Kay, H. E., B. Stoll, J. Clare, M. R. Eleston, B. S. Gershwin, P. Gershwin, L. S.

Kogan, C. Torda, and C. B. Wilbur. 1967. Homosexuality in women. *Archives of General Psychiatry* 17(5): 626–634.

Kehoe, M. 1986a. Lesbians over 65: A triply invisible minority. *Journal of Homosexuality* 12(3/4): 139–152.

Kehoe, M. 1986b. A portrait of the older lesbian. *Journal of Homosexuality* 12(3/4): 157–161.

Kehoe, M. 1988. Lesbians over 60 speak for themselves. [Special Issue] *Journal of Homosexuality* 16(3/4).

Kelly, J. 1977. The aging male homosexual: Myth and reality. *The Gerontologist* 17(4): 328–332.

Kennedy, E. L. and M. D. Davis. 1993. *Boots of Leather, Slippers of Gold: The History of a Lesbian Community*. New York: Penguin Books.

Kenyon, F. E. 1968. Studies in female homosexuality: Psychological test results. *Journal of Consulting Clinical Psychology* 32: 510–513.

Kenyon, F. E. 1969. Studies in female homosexuality IV: Social and psychiatric aspects. *British Journal of Psychiatry* 114: 1337–1350.

Kim, E. K. 1998. Political funeral [On-line]. Available: http://www.actupny.org/reports/stevemichael.html.

Kimmel, D. C. 1977. Psychotherapy and the older gay man. *Psychotherapy: Theory, Research and Practice* 14(4): 386–393.

Kimmel, D. C. 1979. Adjustments to aging among gay men. In B. Berson and R. Leighton, eds., *Positively Gay*, pp. 146–158. Millbrae, Calif.: Celestial Arts.

Kinsey, A. C., W. Pomeroy, and C. Martin. 1948. *Sexual Behavior in the Human Male*. Philadelphia: W. B. Saunders.

Kinsey, A. C., W. Pomeroy, C. Martin, and P. H. Gebhard. 1953. *Sexual Behavior in the Human Female*. Philadelphia: W. B. Saunders.

Klein, F., B. Sepekoff, and T. Wolf. 1985. Sexual orientation: A multi-variable dynamic process. *Journal of Homosexuality* 11(1/2): 35–49.

Knight, R. H. 1995. New NIH study indicates homosexuality is learned [On-line]. Available: http://www.frc.org/frc/insight/is95flhs.html.

Knights of the Ku Klux Klan. 1998. An introduction to the Knights of the Ku Klux Klan [On-line]. Available: http://www.kukluxklan.org/introduc.htm.

Kooden, H. 1997. Sucessful aging in the middle-aged gay man: A contribution to developmental theory. *Journal of Gay and Lesbian Social Services* 6(3): 21–43.

Ku Klux Klan. 1998. FAQ about the KKK [On-line]. Available: http://www.kkk.com/klanfaq.htm.

Kulkin, H. and G. Percle. (in press). Suicide among gay and lesbian adolescents and young adults. *Journal of Homosexuality*.

Kurdek, L. A. and J. P. Schmitt. 1985/86. Relationship quality of gay men in closed or open relationships. *Journal of Homosexuality* 12(1/2): 85–99.

Laird, J. and R. J. Green. 1995. Lesbians and gays in couples and families. *Journal of Feminist Family Therapy* 7(3/4): 3–13.

Laird, J. and R. J. Green, eds. 1996. *Lesbians and Gays in Couples and Families: Handbook for Therapists*. San Francisco: Jossey-Bass.

Laner, M. R. 1979. Growing older female: Heterosexual and homosexual. *Journal of Homosexuality* 4(3): 267–275.

LCR (Log Cabin Republicans). 1998. About LCR [On-line]. Available: http://www.lcr.org/index2/htm.

Lee, J. A. 1987. What can homosexual aging studies contribute to theories of aging? *Journal of Homosexuality*, 13(4): 43–71.

Lee, J. A. B. 1994. *The Empowerment Approach to Social Work Practice.* New York: Columbia University Press.

Leland, J. and M. Miller. 1998. Can gay's convert? *Newsweek*, August 17, pp. 47–52.

Lenna, H. R. 1992. The outsiders: Group work with young homosexuals. In N. Woodman, ed., *Lesbian and Gay Lifestyles: A Guide for Counseling and Education*, pp. 67–89. New York: Irvington.

Lesbian Avengers Handbook. 1998. Action outline [On-line]. Available: http://www.lesbian.org/chicago.avengers/avengerhandbook.html.

Lesbian Mothers Support Society. 1998. *A Guide to Lesbian Baby Making.* http://www.lesbian.org/lesbian-moms/guide.html.

LeVay, S. 1991. A difference in hypothalamic structure between heterosexual and homosexual men. *Science* 253: 1034–1037.

LeVay, S. 1996. *Queer Science: The Use and Abuse of Research Into Homosexuality.* Cambridge, Mass.: MIT Press.

Lewis, L. A. 1984. The coming-out process for lesbians: Integrating a stable identity. *Social Work* 29(5): 464–469.

Lewis, M. I. 1980. The history of female sexuality in the United States. In M. Kirkpatrick, ed., *Women's Sexual Development*, pp. 19–38. New York: Plenum Press.

Levy, E. 1992. Strengthening the coping resources of lesbian families. *Journal of Contemporary Human Services* 73(1): 23–31.

Liu, P. and C. S. Chan. 1996. Lesbian, gay, and bisexual Asian Americans and their families. In J. Laird and R. Green, eds., *Lesbians and Gays in Couples and Families: A Handbook for Therapists*, pp. 137–152. San Francisco: Jossey-Bass.

Living on the Edge. 1998. [On-line]. Available: http://www.antihomosexual.com/livingonedge.htm.

Lloyd, G. A. 1995. HIV/AIDS: Overview. In R. L. Edwards, ed., *Encyclopedia of Social Work*. 19th ed., vol 2, pp. 1257–1290. Washington, D.C.: NASW Press.

Lloyd, G. A. and C. T. Tully. 1996. ReparativeTherapy: Useful Intervention of Cruel Hoax? Unpublished paper presented at Council on Social Work Education Annual Program Meeting, Cleveland.

Log Cabin Republicans, *see* LCR.

Loiacano, D. K. 1989. Gay identity among black Americans: Racism, homophobia, and the need for validation. *Journal of Counseling and Development* 68(1): 21–25.

Lorraine, T. E. 1990. *Gender, Identity, and the Production of Meaning.* Boulder: Westview Press.

Lott, T. 1998. Senate Republicans' five-pronged agenda will empower families, businesses, local communities [On-line]. Available: http://www.senate.gov/src/agenda98.

Lott-Whitehead, L. and C. T. Tully. 1993. The families of lesbian mothers. *Smith College Studies in Social Work* 63: 265–280.

Lousiana Electorate of Gays and Lesbians. 1998. http://www.legal.org.

Louisiana Lesbian and Gay Political Action Caucus 1998. *LAGPAC Lagniappe* 2(1): 1–8.

Lucco, A. J. 1987. Planned retirement housing preferences of older homosexuals. *Journal of Homosexuality* 14(3/4): 35–56.

Lukes, C. A. and H. Land. 1990. Biculturality and homosexuality *Social Work*, 35(2): 155–161.

Macdonald, B. and C. Rich. 1983. *Look Me in the Eye: Old Women, Aging, and Ageism*. San Francisco: Spinsters, Ink.

Maginnis, R. L. 1995a. The APA sustains homosexual agenda [On-line]. Available: http://www.frc.org/frc/insight/is95a7hs.html.

Maginnis, R. L. 1995b. Clinton administration scuttles first court test of military's homosexual law [On-line]. Available: http://www.frc.org/frc/insight/is95d1hm.html.

Mallen, C. A. 1983. Sex role stereotypes, gender identity, and parental relationships in male homosexuals and heterosexuals. *Journal of Homosexuality* 9(1): 55–74.

Mallon, G. P. 1998. Knowledge for practice with gay and lesbian persons. In G. P. Mallon, ed., *Foundations of Social Work Practice with Lesbian and Gay Persons*, pp. 1–30. New York: Harrington Park Press.

Mallon, G. P., ed. 1998. *Foundations of Social Work Practice with Lesbian and Gay Persons*. New York: Harrington Park Press.

Mallon, G. P. (in press). *Let's Get this Straight: Issues of Sexual Orientation in Child Welfare*. New York: Columbia University Press.

Manniche, L. 1987. *Sexual Life in Ancient Egypt*. London: KPI Ltd.

Manniche, L. 1992. "Some aspects of ancient Egyptian sexual life." In W. R. Dynes and S. Donalson, eds., *Studies in Homosexuality*: vol. 1: *Homosexuality in the Ancient World*, pp. 327–339. New York: Garland.

Marantha Newswatch. 1997. Top stories: Coming out of homosexual day [On-line]. Available:http://www.vector.wantree.com.au/˜7Echristip/news/newswatch/15oct97.html.

Marciano, Teresa D. 1991. *Wider Families: New Traditional Family Forms*. Binghamton, N.Y.: Haworth Press.

Marcus, E. 1992. *Making History: The Struggle of Gay and Lesbian Equal Rights (1945–1990)*. New York: Harper Collins.

Marin, R. and S. Miller. 1997. Ellen steps out. *Newsweek*, April 14, pp. 65–67.

Martin, A. D. and E. S. Hetrick. 1988. The stigmatization of the gay and lesbian adolescent. *Journal of Homosexuality* 15(1/2): 163–183.

Martindale, D. 1981. *The Nature and Types of Sociological Theory*. Boston: Houghton Mifflin.

Massey, S. G. and S. C. Ouellette. 1996. Heterosexual bias in the identity self-portraits of gay men, lesbians, and bisexuals. *Journal of Homosexuality* 32(1): 57–76.

McAllister, D. 1998. Can a gay person go to heaven? [On-line]. Available: http://www.christiananswers.net.

McCandlish, B. M. 1981/82. Therapeutic issues with lesbian couples. *Journal of Homosexuality* 7(2/3): 71–78.

McClellen, D. 1998. Second-parent adoption in lesbian families: Legalizing the reality of the child. Paper presented at Council on Social Work Education Annual Program Meeting, Orlando.

McDermott, D., L. Tyndall, and J. W. Lichtenberg. 1989. Factors related to counselor performance among gyas and lesbians. *Journal of Counseling and Development* 68: 31–35.

McDonald, G. J. 1982. Individual differences in the coming-out process for gay men: Implications for theoretical models. *Journal of Homosexuality* 8(1): 47–60.

McDonald, G. J. and R. J. Moore. 1978. Sex-role self-concepts of homosexual men and their attitudes toward both women and male homosexuality. *Journal of Homosexuality* 4(1): 3–14.

McKinlay, T., J. Kelly, and J. Patterson, J. 1977. Teaching assertiveness skills to a passive homosexual adolescent: An illustrative case study. *Journal of Homosexuality* 3(2): 163–170.

McWhirter, D. P. and A. W. Mattison. 1981/82. Psychotherapy for gay males. *Journal of Homosexuality* 7(2/3): 791.

McWhirter, D. P. and A. W. Mattison. 1984. *The Male Couple*. Englewood Cliffs, N.J.: Prentice Hall.

Meenaghan, T. M., R. O. Washington, and R. M. Ryan. 1982. *Macro Practice in the Human Services: An Introduction to Planning, Administration, Evaluation, and Community Organizing Components of Practice*. New York: Free Press.

Mendola, M. 1980. *The Mendola Report: A New Look at Gay Couples*. New York: Crown.

Messing, A. E., R. Schoenberg, and R. K. Stephens. 1983/84. Confronting homophobia in health care settings: Guidelines for social work practice. *Journal of Social Work and Human Sexuality* 2(2/3): 65–74.

Middleman, R. 1985. Interaction and experience in groups: Doing as life-learning. In C. Germain, ed., *Advances in Clinical Social Work Practice*, pp. 159–170. Silver Spring, Md.: NASW.

Miller, M. 1998. The right: Going to war over gays. *Newsweek*, July 27, p. 27.

Mills, K. I. 1997. Gay rights civil rights: Head of LCCR reflects on shared goals and responsibilities. *HRC Quarterly* (Winter): 6–7.

Minnigerode, F. A. 1976. Age-status labeling in homosexual men. *Journal of Homosexuality* 1(3): 273–276.

Minnigerode, F. A. and M. D. Adelman. 1978. Elderly homosexual women and men: Report on a pilot study. *Family Coordinator* 27(4): 451–456.

Minton, H. L. 1986. Femininity in men and masculinity in women: American psychiatry and psychology portray homosexuality in the 1930s. *Journal of Homosexuality* 13(1): 1–21.

Minton, H. L. and G. J. McDonald. 1984. Homosexual identity formations a developmentalprocess. *Journal of Homosexuality* 9(2/3): 91–104.

Miranda, J. and M. Storms. 1989. Psychological adjustment in lesbians and gay men. *Journal of Counseling and Development* 68(1): 41–45.

Mondimore, F. M. 1996. *A Natural History of Homosexuality*. Baltimore: Johns Hopkins University Press.

Mondros, J. B. and S. M. Wilson. 1994. *Organizing for Power and Empowerment*. New York: Columbia University Press.

Morales, E. S. 1989. Ethnic minority families and minority gays and lesbians. *Marriage and Family Review* 14(3/4): 217–239.

Morris, J. F. 1997. Lesbian coming out as a multidimensional process. *Journal of Homosexuality* 33(2): 1–22.

Morrow, D. F. 1993. Social work with gay and lesbian adolescents. *Social Work* 38(6): 655–660.

Morrow, S. L. and D. M. Hawxhurst. 1989. Lesbian partner abuse: Implications for practice. *Journal of Counseling and Development* 68(1): 58–62.

Moses, A. E. and R. O. Hawkins. 1982. *Counseling Lesbian Women and Gay Men: A Life-Issues Approach*. St. Louis: C. V. Mosby.

Moss, Z. 1970. It hurts being alive and obsolete: The ageing woman. In R. Morgan, ed., *Sisterhood Is Powerful: An Anthology of Writings from the Women's Movement*, pp. 170–175. New York: Random House.

Murphy, B. C. Difference and diversity: Gay and lesbian couples. In M. Duberman, ed., *A Queer World*, pp. 345–357. New York: New York University Press.

Murray, S. O. 1979. The institutional elaboration of a quasi-ethnic community. *International Review of Modern Sociology* 9: 165–177.

NASW (National Association of Social Workers). 1981. Policy statement on gay men and lesbians. Washington, D.C.: NASW National Committee on Lesbians and Gay Issues.

NASW. 1996. Code of Ethics. Washington, D.C.: NASW Press.

NASW. 1998. Homepage [On-line]. Available: http://www.naswdc.org.

National Coalition of Anti-Violence Programs, *see* NCAVP.

National Committee on Lesbian and Gay Issues. February 23, 1992. Position statement regarding "reparative" or "conversion" therapies for lesbians and gay men. Washington, D.C.: NASW.

National Gay and Lesbian Task Force, *see* NGLTF.

National Opinion Research Center. 1989–1992. *General Social Survey*. Chicago: Author.

National Political Index. 1998. Contacting national political parties [On-line]. Available: http://www.politicalindex.com/sec8.htm.

NCAVP (National Coalition of Anti-Viollence Programs). 1998a. NCAVP Annual report: Assaults, injuries, and weapons [On-line]. Available: http://www.avp.org/assaults.html.

NCAVP. 1998b. NCAVP Annual report: HIV related violence [On-line]. Available: http://www.avp.org/hiv.html.

NCAVP. 1998c. NCAVP Annual report: introduction [On-line]. Available: http://www.avp.org/intro.html.

NCAVP. 1998d. NCAVP Annual report: Murders [On-line]. Available: http://www.avp.org/murders.html.

NCVAP. 1998e. NCAVP Annual report: Offences [On-line]. Available: http://www.avp.org/offenses.html.

NCAVP. 1998f. NCAVP Annual report: Offenders [On-line]. Available: http://www.avp.org/offenders.html.

NCAVP. 1998g. NCAVP Annual report: Reporting to law [On-line]. Available: http://www.avp.org/police.html.

NCVAP. 1998h. NCAVP Annual report: Summary [On-line]. Available: http://www.avp.org/summary.html.

NCAVP. 1998i. NCAVP Annual Report. Victims [On-line]. Available: http://www.avp.org/victims.html.

Nelson, J. B. 1981/82. Religious and moral issues in working with homosexual clients. *Journal of Homosexuality* 7(2/3): 163–175.

The New American. 1998. Back issues [On-line]. Available: http://www.jbs.org/bckissue.htm.

Newsweek. 1998. August 17, cover photograph.

NGLTF (National Gay and Lesbian Task Force). 1995. Press releases 1995 [On-line]. Available: http://www.ngltf.org/pr2.html.

NGLTF. 1996a. *1996 year end report*. Washington, D.C.: National Gay and Lesbian Task Force.

NGLTF. 1996b. Press releases [On-line]. Available: http://www.ngltf.org/pr96.html.

NGLTF. 1997. Press release: adoption [On-line]. Available: http://www.ngltf.org/press/adoption.html.

NGLTF. 1998a. Homepage [On-line]. Available: http://www.ngltf.org/main.html.

NGLTF. 1998b. News Notes. *Task Force Summary*: 7.

NGLTF. 1998c. Press releases [On-line]. Available:http://www.ngltf.org/pr.html.

Nichols, M. 1988. Bisexuality in women: Myths, realities, and implications for therapy. *Women and Therapy*, 7(2/3): 235–252.

Nicolosi, J. 1991. *Reparative Therapy of Male Homosexuality*. Northvale, N.J.: Jason Aronson.

Nolan, D. 1971. Classifying and analyzing politico-economic systems. *Individualist* (January): 20–26.

Ohlson, E. L and M. Wilson. 1974. Differentiating female homosexuals from female heterosexuals by use of the MMPI. *Journal of Sex Research* 10: 308–315.

Office of International Criminal Justice. 1998. OICJ online: Aryan nations [On-line]. Available: http://www.ascp.vic.edu/gangs/aryan/contacts.shtml.

Original Prime Timers Worldwide. 1998. Who are prime timers? [On-line]. Available: http://www.primetimers.org.

Parents, Familits, and Friends of Lesbians and Gays, *see* PFLAG.

Patterson, C. J. 1992. Children of gay and lesbian parents. *Child Development* 63: 1025–1042.

PAW (People for the American Way). 1998. Ralph Reed v. Pat Robertson: Christian Coalition director calls for civility and tolerance while his boss rips opponents and preaches extremism [On-line]. Available: http://www.theshop.net/tia-ok/2voices.htm.

Pence, E. and M. Paymar. 1993. The Duluth domestic abuse intervention project [On- line]. Available: http://www.infoxchange.net.au/wise/dvim/daip/htm.

People for the American Way, *see* PAW.

Perlman, H. H. 1957. *Social Casework: A Problem Solving Process*. Chicago: University of Chicago Press.

Perry, T. 1971. *The Lord is my Shepherd and He Knows I'm Gay*. West Hollywood, CA: Metropolitan Community Church.

Perry, T. 1998, June 24. Upstairs Fire Memorial. Memorial service presented at the Royal Sonesta Hotel, New Orleans.

Peterson, T. L. and J. H. Stewart. 1985. The lesbian or gay couple as a family: Principles for building satisfying relationships. In H. Hidalgo, T. L. Peterson, and N. J. Woodman, eds. *Lesbian and Gay Issues: A Resource Manual for Social Workers*, pp. 27–32. Silver Spring, Md.: NASW.

PFLAG (Parents, Families, and Friends of Lesbians and Gays. 1991. Policy statement: Statement to the radical right [On-line]. Available: http://www.pflag.org/press/policy/rright.html.

PFLAG. 1998a. How does PFLAG work? [On-line]. Available: http://www.pflag.org/works/works.html.

PFLAG. 1998b. National parents group calls for dialogue with right-wing groups in wake of continued ad campaign [On-line]. Available: http://www.pflag.org/press/releases/72498.html

PFLAG. 1998c. PFLAG responds to religious right's ad campaign [On-line]. Available: http://www.pflag.org/press/ad.html.

PFLAG. 1998d. Policy statements [On-line]. Available: http://www.pflag.org/press/policy.html.

PFLAG. 1998e. Project open mind [On-line]. Available: http://www.pflag.org/pom/pom2.html.

Pincus, A. and A. Minahan. 1973. *Social Work Practice: Model and Method*. Itasca, Ill.: Peacock.

Ponse, B. 1978. *Identities in the Lesbian World*. Westport, Conn.: Greenwood Press.

Poole, K. 1970. A Sociological Approach to the Etiology of Female Homosexuality and the Lesbian Social Scene. Ph.D. dissertation, University of Southern California, Los Angeles.

Poor, M. 1982. Older lesbians. In M. Cruikshank, ed., *Lesbian Studies: Present and Future*, pp. 165–173. New York: Feminist Press.

Pope, M. and R. Schulz. 1990. Sexual attitudes and behavior in midlife and aging homosexual ales. *Journal of Homosexuality* 20(3/4): 169–177.

Porter, A. 1998. Gay rights are undone [On-line]. Available: http://ellsworthamerican.com/archive/021298.html.

Porter-Chase, M. 1987. *Circles of Love: A Woman's Unity Ritual.* Cotati, Calif.: Samary Press.

Pratte, T. 1993. A comparative study of attitudes toward homosexuality: 1986 and 1991. *Journal of Homosexuality* 26(1): 77–83.

PRIDENET. 1998. [On-line]. Available: http://www.pridenet.com/senorg.htm.

Prytula, R. E., C. D. Wellford, and B. G. DeMonbreun. 1979. Body image and homosexuality. *Journal of Clinical Psychology* 35(3): 567–572.

Racial supremacy and neo-Nazi hate groups. 1998. [On-line]. Available: http://www.dc.state.fl.us/security/reports/gangs/racial.html

Raphael, S. and M. Robinson. 1981. Lesbians and gay men in later life. *Generations* 6(1): 16–18.

Raphael, S. and M. Robinson. 1980. The older lesbian's love relationships and friendship patterns. *Alternative Lifestyles* 3(2): 207–229.

Rappaport, J. 1981. In praise of paradox. *American Journal of Community Psychology* 9: 1–25.

Rappaport, J. 1986. In praise of paradox: A social policy of empowerment over prevention. In E. Seidman and J. Rappaport, eds., *Redefining Social Problems*, pp. 141–164. New York: Plenum Press.

Rappaport, J., T. M. Reiscl, and M. A. Zimmerman. 1992. Mutual help mechanisms in the empowerment of former mental patients. In D. Saleebey, ed., *The Strengths Perspective in Social Work Practice*, pp. 84–97. New York: Longman.

Reamer, F. G. 1987. Values and ethics. In A. Minehan, ed., *Encyclopedia of Social Work*, vol 2, pp. 801–808. Silver Spring, Md.: NASW.

Reisner, N. 1998. Christians run ads urging gay people to change lives. *Times-Picayune*, July 16, p. A-19.

Reiter, L. 1989. Sexual orientation, sexual identity, and the question of choice. *Clinical Social Work Journal* 17(2): 138–150.

Relkin, C. H. 1990. Stereotypes and myths of aging males. Manuscript. School of Social Work, University of Georgia, Athens..

Renzetti, C. M. 1992. *Violent Betrayal: Partner Abuse in Lesbian Relationships.* Newbury Park, Calif.: Sage.

Renzetti, C. M. 1995. Studying partner abuse in lesbian relationships: A case for the feminist participatory research model. *Journal of Gay and Lesbian Social Services*, 3(1): 29–42.

Reynolds, B. C. 1934 (reissued 1982). *Between Client and Community: A Study in Responsibility in Social Case Work.* Silver Spring, Md.: NASW Press.

Reynolds, B. C. 1935. Discussion by Bertha C. Reynolds. In Family Welfare Association of America, ed., *Diagnosis and Treatment Process in Family Social Work*, pp. 25–27. New York: Family Welfare Association of America.

Reynolds, B. C. 1942. *Learning and Teaching in the Practice of Social Work.* New York: Farrar and Rinehart.

Rifkin, I. and D. E. Anderson. 1996. Religious right's momentum slows [On-line]. Available: http://www.pioneerplanet.com/news/campaign96/pres/dox/031841.htm.

Rivera, R. R. 1991. Sexual orientation and the law. In J. C. Gonsiorek and J. D. Weinrich, eds., *Homosexuality: Research Implications for Public Policy*, pp. 81–100. Newbury Park, Calif.: Sage.

Rizzo, A. A., L. A. Fehr, P. M. McMahon, and E. L. Stamps. 1981. Mosher guilt scores and sexual preference. *Journal of Clinical Psychology* 37(4): 827–830.

Roback, H. B., D. S. Strassberg, E. McKee, and J. Cunningham. 1977. Self-concept and psychological differences between self-identified male transsexuals and male homosexuals. *Journal of Homosexuality* 3(1): 15–20.

Robinson, K. E. 1991. Gay youth support groups: An opportunity for social work intervention. *Social Work* 36(5): 458–459.

Robson, R. 1997. Convictions: Theorizing lesbians and criminal justice. In M. Duberman, ed., *A Queer World*, pp. 418–430. New York: New York University Press.

Rochlin, M. 1981/82. Sexual orientation of the therapist and therapeutic effectiveness with gay clients. *Journal of Homosexuality* 7(2/3): 21–29.

Rofes, E. R. 1983. *I Thought People Like That Killed Themselves: Lesbians, Gay Men, and Suicide*. San Francisco: Grey Fox.

Rogers, P. 1993. How many gays are there? *Newsweek*, February 15, p. 46.

Romesburg, D. 1998. Lesbian avengers response to ads [On-line]. Available: http://www.glaad.org/glaad/glaad-lines/980727/04.html.

Ross, M. W. 1978. The relationship of perceived societal hostility, conformity, and psychological adjustment in homosexual males. *Journal of Homosexuality* 4(2): 157–168.

Ross, M. W., J. A. Paulsen, and O. W. Stalstrom. 1988. Homosexuality and mental health: A cross-cultural review. *Journal of Homosexuality* 15(1/2): 131–152.

Ross, P. 1995. What's race got to do with it? In K. Jay, ed., *Dyke Life: From Growing Up to Growing Old a Celebration of Difference*, pp. 141–148. New York: Basic Books.

Rust, P. 1993. "Coming out" in the age of social constructionism: Sexual identity formation among lesbian and bisexual women. *Gender and Society* 7(1): 50–77.

Saghir, M. F. and E. Robins. 1969. Sexual behavior in the female homosexual. *Archives of General Psychiatry* 2: 147–154.

Saghir, M. F. and E. Robins. 1973. *Male and Female Homosexuality: A Comprehensive Investigation*. Baltimore: William and Wilken.

Saleebey, D. 1992. *The Strengths Perspective in Social Work Practice*. New York: Longman.

Salkind, S. 1998. Framing Maine: In wake of repeal, Maine activists consider next steps. *HRC Quarterly* (Spring): 8.

Savin-Williams, R. C. 1988. Parental influences on self-esteem of gay and lesbian youth: A reflected appraisals model. *Journal of Homosexuality* 17(1/2): 93–109.

Savin-Williams, R. C. 1989a. Coming out to parents and self-esteem among gay and lesbian youth. *Journal of Homosexuality* 18(1/2): 1–35.

Savin-Williams, R. C. 1989b. Gay and lesbian adolescents. *Marriage and Family Review* 14(3/4): 197–216.

Savin-Williams, R. C. 1990. Coming out. In W. R. Dynes, ed., *Encyclopedia of Homosxuality*, pp. 251–254. New York: Garland.

Savin-Williams, R. C. 1996. Self-labeling and disclosure among gay, lesbian, and bisexual youth. In J. Laird and R. J. Green, eds., *Lesbians and Gays in Couples and Families: A Handbook for Therapists*, pp. 153–182. San Francisco, Jossey-Bass.

Sawicki, J. 1991. *Disciplining Foucault: Feminism, Power, and the Body.* New York: Routledge.

Scanzoni, L. and V. R. Mollenkott. 1978. *Is the Homosexual My Neighbor? Another Christian View.* New York: Harper and Row.

Schneider, M. 1989. Sappho was a right-on adolescent: Growing up lesbian. *Journal of Homosexuality* 17(1/2): 111–130.

Schneider, R. L. and N. P. Kropf, eds. 1992. *Gerontological Social Work: Knowledge, Service Settings, and Special Populations.* Chicago: Nelson Hall.

Schofield, M. 1965. *Sociological Aspects of Homosexuality.* Boston: Little, Brown.

Schopler, J. H. and M. J. Galinski. 1995. Group practice overview. In R. L. Edwards, ed., *Encyclopedia of Social Work.* 19th ed., vol. 2, pp. 1129–1142. Washington, D.C.: NASW Press.

Senior Cyborgs. 1998. [On-line]. Available: http://www.online96.com/seniors/gay.htm.

Sergois, P. and J. Cody. 1985/86. Importance of physical attractiveness and social assertiveness skills in male homosexual dating behavior and partner selection. *Journal of Homosexuality* 12(2): 71–84.

Shapiro, C. H. 1980. Sexual learning: The short-changed adolescent male. *Social Work* 25(6): 489–493.

Shernoff, M. 1995. Gay men: Direct practice. In R. L. Edwards, ed., *Encyclopedia of Social Work.* 19th ed., vol. 2, pp. 1075–1085. Washington, D.C.: NASW Press.

Shernoff, M. 1998. Getting started: Basic skills for effective social work with people with HIV and AIDS. In D. M. Aronstein and B. J. Thompson, eds., *HIV and Social Work: A Practitioner's Guide*, pp. 27–49. New York: Harrington Park Press.

Shernoff, M. 1998. Individual practice with gay men. In G. P. Mallon, ed., *Foundations of Social Work Practice with Lesbian and Gay Persons*, pp. 77–103. New York: Harrington Park Press.

Shuster, R. 1987. Sexuality as a continuum: The bisexual identity. In The Boston Lesbian Psychology Collective, eds., *Lesbian Psychologies*, pp. 56–71. Urbana: University of Illinois Press.

Siegelman, M. 1972. Adjustment of homosexual and heterosexual women. *British Journal of Psychiatry* 120: 477–481.

Siegelman, M. 1974. Parental behavior of homosexual and heterosexual women. *British Journal of Psychiatry* 124: 14–21.

Silverstein, C. 1981. *Man to Man: Gay Couples in America.* New York: William Morris.

Silverstein, C., ed. 1991. *Gays, Lesbians, and Their Therapists: Studies in Psychotherapy*. New York: Norton.

Simon, B. L. 1994. *The Empowerment Tradition in American Social Work: A History*. New York: Columbia University Press.

Slavin, E. A. 1991. What makes a marriage legal? *Human Rights*, 18(1): 16–19.

Smith, J. 1988. Psychopathology, homosexuality, and homophobia. *Journal of Homosexuality* 15(1/2): 59–73.

Smith, J. R. and B. S. Smith. 1980. *Essentials of World History*. Rev. ed. Hauppauge N.Y.: Barron's Educational Series.

Socarides, C. 1978. *Homosexuality*. New York: Jason Aronson.

Soldo, B. J. 1980. *America's Elderly in the Early 1980s*. Washington, D.C.: Population Reference Bureau.

Solomon, B. B. 1976. *Black Empowerment: Social Work in Oppressed Communities*. New York: Columbia University Press.

Solomon, B. B. 1985. Community social work practice in oppressed communities. In S. H. Taylor and R. W. Roberts, eds., *Theory and Practice of Community Social Work*, pp. 217–57. New York: Columbia University Press.

Sophie, J. 1985/1986. A critical examination of stage theories of lesbian identity development. *Journal of Homosexuality* 12(2): 39–51.

Special Committee on Aging U.S. Senate. 1986. Older Americans Act. In *Developments in Aging: 1985*, vol. 1, pp. 308–323. Washington, D.C.: U.S. GPO.

SPLC (Southern Poverty Law Center). 1998. Active hate groups in the U.S. in 1997. *Intelligence Report* 89: 29–33.

Stachelberg, W. 1997. Position of strength: ENDA reintroduced with more cosponsors, momentum. *HRC Quarterly* (Summer): 12.

Stan, A. M. 1996. A Christian right smear campaign [On-line]. Available: http://mojones.com/mother_jones/mj96/stan2.html.

Steinhorn, A. 1998. Individual practice with lesbians. In G. P. Mallon, ed., *Foundations of Social Work Practice with Lesbian and Gay Persons*, pp. 105–129. New York: Harrington Park Press.

Steinhorn, A. I. 1985. Lesbian mothers. In H. Hidalgo, T. L. Peterson, and N. J. Woodman, eds., *Lesbian and Gay Issues: A Resource Manual for Social Workers*, pp. 33–37. Silver Spring, Md.: NASW.

Stephenson, J. 1981. *Women's Roots: Status and Achievements in Western Civilization*. Napa, Calif.: Diemer, Smith.

St. Pierre, T. 1998. Countdown in Hawaii: Situation in flux in the aloha state. *HRC Quarterly* (Spring): 9–11.

Streitmatter, R. 1995. *Unspeakable: The Rise of the Gay and Lesbian Press in America*. Boston: Faber and Faber.

Sullivan, A. 1998. They've changed, so they say. *New York Times*, July 26, Section 1:15.

Swanson, D. W., S. D. Loomis, R. Lukesh, R. Cornin, and J. A. Smith. 1972. Clinical features of the female homosexual patient: A comparison with the heterosexual patient. *Journal of Nervous and Mental Disease*, 155(2): 37–58.

Sweet, M. J. 1996. Counseling satisfaction among gay, lesbian, and bisexual college students. *Journal of Gay and Lesbian Social Services* 4(3): 35–49.

Swigonski, M. E. 1998. Social work, Judeo-Christian scripture, and lesbian/gay/bisexual/ transgendered empowerment. Paper presented at the Annual Program Meeting of the Council on Social Work Education, Orlando, Florida.

Talan, J. 1997. Psychologists censure gay "therapy." *Times Picayune*, August 15, p. A-8.

Talk Topics. 1998. News releases [On-line]. Available: http://www.rnc.org/news/talking/index.htm.

Tanner, D. M. 1978. *The Lesbian Couple.* Lexington, Mass.: D. C. Heath.

Tate, D. D. 1991. Homophobia among rural and urban social work students: A pilot study. *Human Services in the Rural Environment* 15(1): 16–18.

Telljohann, S. K. and J. H. Price. 1993. A qualitative examination of adolescent homosexuals' life experiences: Ramifications for secondary school personnel. *Journal of Homosexuality* 26(1): 41–56.

Terry, P. 1992. Relationship termination for lesbians and gays. In N. J. Woodman, ed., *Lesbian and Gay Lifestyles: A Guide for Counseling and Education*, pp. 111–122. New York: Irvington.

Thompson, N. L. 1971. *Family Background and Sexual Identity in Male and Female Homosexuals.* Ph.D. dissertation, Emory University, Atlanta.

Thompson, N. L., B. R. McCandless, and B. R. Strickland. 1971. Personal adjustment of male and female homosexuals. *Journal of Abnormal Psychology* 78: 237–240.

Townes, B. D., W. D. Ferguson, and S. Gillam. 1976. Differences in psychological sex, adjustment, and familial influences among homosexual and nonhomosexual populations. *Journal of Homosexuality* 1(3): 261–272.

Trattner Walter I. 1994. *From Poor Law to Welfare State: A History of Social Welfare in America.* New York: Free Press.

Trebilcot, J. 1994. *Dyke Ideas: Process, Politics, and Daily Life.* Albany: State University of New York Press.

Tremble, B., M. Schneider, and C. Appathurai. 1989. Growing up gay or lesbian in a multicultural context. *Journal of Homosexuality* 17(3/4): 253–267.

Treuthart, M. P. 1990. Adopting a more realistic definition of "family." *Gonzaga Law Review* 26(1): 91–124.

Trimble, D. 1994. Confronting responsibility: Men who batter their wives. In A. Gitterman and L. Shulman, eds., *Mutual Aid Groups, Vulnerable Populations, and the Life Cycle*, pp. 257–271. New York: Columbia University Press.

Troiden, R. R. 1989. The formation of homosexual identities. *Journal of Homosexuality* 17(1/2): 43–73.

Troiden, R. R. and E. Goode. 1980. Variables related to the acquisition of a gay identity. *Journal of Homosexuality* 5(4): 383–392.

Tully, C. T. 1983. *Social Support Systems of a Selected Sample of Older Women.* Ph.D. dissertation. Richmond: Virginia Commonwealth University.

Tully, C. T. 1989. Caregiving: What do midlife lesbians view as important? *Journal of Gay and Lesbian Psychotherapy* 1(1): 87–103.

Tully, C. T. 1994. Epilogue: Power and the social work profession. In R. Greene, ed., *Human Behavior Theory: A Diversity Framework*, pp. 235–243. Boston: Aldine de Gruyter.

Tully, C. T. 1995. In sickness and in health: Forty years of research on lesbians. *Journal of Gay and Lesbian Social Services* 3(1): 1–18.

Turn Left. 1998. Political glossary [On-line]. Available: http://www.cjnetworks. com/˜7Ecubsfan/glossary.html.

United States Code. Vol. 1. Title 5 Executive Order No. 10450 s 631.

Uribe, V. and K. M. Harbeck. 1991. Assessing the needs of lesbian, gay, and bisexual youth: The origins of PROJECT 10 and school based intervention. *Journal of Homosexuality*, 22(3/4): 9–28.

U.S. Census (U.S. Bureau of the Census). 1992. *1990 Census of the Population*: Vol. I: *Characteristics of the Population*. Washington, D.C.: U.S. GPO.

U.S. Census. 1995. Sixty-five plus in the United States. Statistical Brief [On- line]. Available: http://www.census.gov/ftb/pub/socdemo/www/agebrief.html.

U.S. Census. 1997. Households by type: March 1997 [On-line]. Available: http://www.bls.census.gov/cps/pub/1997/hhldtype.htm.

Vander Zanden, J. W. 1975. *Sociology*. 4th ed. New York: Wiley.

Vaid, U. 1995. *Virtual Equality: The Mainstreaming of Gay and Lesbian Liberation*. New York: Anchor Books.

Vergara, T. L. 1983/84. Meeting the needs of sexual minority youth: One program's response. *Journal of Social Eork and Human Sexuality* 2(2/3): 19–38.

Vickers, L. 1996. The second closet: Domestic violence in lesbian and gay relationships: A Western Austrailian Perspective [On-line]. Available: http://www.murdoch.edu.au/elaw/issues/v3n4/vickers.html.

Wahler, J. and S. G. Gabbay. 1997. Gay male aging: A review of the literature. *Journal of Gay and Lesbian Social Services* 6(3): 1–20.

Wait, H. 1995. Lesbians leaping out of the intergenerational context: Issues of aging in Australia. *Journal of Gay and Lesbian Social Services* 3(3): 109–127.

Walker, K. 1997. Couple's friendship, concern helped homosexual find Jesus [On-line]. Available: http://www.erlc.com/homosexuality/1997/714couples.htm.

Watters, A. T. 1986. Heterosexual bias in psychological research on lesbianism and male homosexuality (1979–1983), utilizing the bibliographic and taxonomic system of Morin (1977). *Journal of Homosexuality* 13(1):35–58.

Weick, A. 1992. Building a strengths perspective of social work. In D. Saleebey, ed., *The Strengths Perspective in Social Work Practice*, pp. 18–26. New York: Longman.

Weick, A. and S. T. Vandiver, eds. 1982. *Women, Power, and Change*. Washington, D.C.: NASW.

Weinberg, G. 1973. *Society and the Healthy Homosexual*. New York: Anchor Books.

Weinberg, M. S. 1970. Homosexual samples: Differences and similarities. *Journal of Sex Research* 6: 312–325.

Weinberg, M. S. and C. J. Williams. 1975. *Male Homosexualities: Their Problems and Adaptations*. New York: Penguin Book.

Weinberg, T. S. 1978. On "doing" and "being" gay: Sexual behavior and homosexual male self-identity. *Journal of Homosexuality* 4(2): 143–156.

Weiss, R. 1997. Psychologists debate attempts to convert gays. New Orleans *Times Picayune*, August 14, p. A-6.

Wetzel, J. W. 1982. Redefining concepts of mental health. In A. Weick and S. T. Vandiver, eds., *Women, Power, and Change*, pp. 3–16. Washington, D.C.: NASW.

White, M. 1989. The externalizing of the problem and the re-authoring of lives and relationships. In M. White, ed., *Selected Papers*, pp. 5–28. Adelaide, South Australia: Dulwich Centre Publications.

White, M. 1989. *Selected Papers*. Adelaide, South Australia: Dulwich Centrre Publications.

White, M. and D. Epston. 1990. *Narrative Means to Therapeutic Ends*. New York: Norton.

White Pride Worldwide. 1998. Homepage [On-line]. Available: http://www. wpww.com.

Wilbur, C. B. 1965. Clinical aspects of female homosexuality. In J. Marmor (Ed.), *Sexual Inversion: The Multiple Roots of Homosexuality*, pp. 268–281. New York: Basic Books.

Williams, S. G. 1981. Male homosexual responses to MMPI combined subscales of M_1 and M_2. *Psychological Reports*, 49(2): 606.

Wilson, A. K. 1991. Same-sex marriage: A review. *William Mitchell Law Review*, 17(2): 539–562.

Wilson, M. L. and Greene, R. L. 1971. Personality characteristics of female homosexuals. *Psychological Reports*, 28: 407–412.

WISE (Women's Issues and Social Empowerment). 1998a. Domestic violence information manual: The dynamics of domestic violence [On-line]. Available: http://www.infoxchange.net.au.wise/dvim/dvdynamics.htm.

WISE. 1998b. Domestic violence information manual: Forms of domestic violence [On-line]. Available: http://www.infoxchange.net.au.wise/dvim/dvabuse. htm.

WISE. 1998c. Domestic violence information manual: Interpreting the signs of domestic violence [On-line]. Available: http://www.infoxchange.net.au.wise/ dvim/dvsigns.htm.

WISE. 1998d. Domestic violence information manual: What is domestic violence [On-line]. Available: http://www.infoxchange.net.au.wise/dvim/dvim1.htm.

Wisniewski, J. J. and Toomey, B. G. 1987. Are social workers homophobic? *Social Work*, 32(5): 454–455.

Witt, L., S. Thomas, and E. Marcus, eds. 1995. *OUT in all Directions: The Almanac of Gay and Lesbian America*. New York: Warner Books.

Wolfe, A. 1998, February 8. The homosexual exception. *The New York Times Magazine*, Section 8: 46–47.

Women's Issues and Social Empowerment, *see* WISE.

Wooden, W., H. Kawasaki, and R. Mayeda. 1983. Lifestyles and identity maintenance among gay Japanese American males. *Alternative Lifestyles* 5(4): 236–
243.

Woodman, N. J. 1982. Social work with lesbian couples. In A. Weick and S. T.
Vandiver, eds., *Women, Power, and Change*, pp. 114–124. Washington, D.C.:
NASW.

Woodman, N. J. 1985. Introduction. In H. Hidalgo, T. L. Peterson, and N. J.
Woodman, eds., *Lesbian and Gay Issues: A Resource Manual for Social Workers*, p. 13. Silver Spring, Md.: NASW.

Woodman, N. J., ed. 1992. *Lesbian and Gay Lifestyles: A Guide for Counseling
and Education*. New York: Irvington.

Woodman, N. J. 1995. Lesbians: Direct practice. In R. L. Edwards, ed., *Encyclopedia of Social Work*. 19th ed., vol. 2, pp. 1597–1604). Washington, D.C.:
NASW Press.

Woodman, N. J. and H. R. Lenna. 1980. *Counseling with Gay Men and Women:
A Guide for Facilitating Positive Life-Styles*. San Francisco: Jossey-Bass.

Woodman, N. J., C. T. Tully, and C. C. Barranti. 1995. Research in lesbian communities: Ethical Dilemmas. *Journal of Gay and Lesbian Social Services* 3(1):
57–66.0

Woods, M. E. and F. Hollis. 1990. *Casework: A Psychosocial Therapy*. New
York: McGraw-Hill.

Zak,. P. D. 1991. AIDS and grieving: Middle adult crisis. *Social Work Perspectives*, 2(1): 46–50.

Zawitz, M. W. 1994. U.S. Department of Justice: Violence between intimates:
Domestic violence [On-line]. Available: http://www.ojp.usdoj.gov/pub/bjs/
ascii/vbi.txt.

Zehner, M. A. and J. Lewis. 1983/84. Homosexuality and alcoholism: Social and
developmental perspectives. *Journal of Social Work and Human Sexuality*
2(2/3): 75–89.

Zimmer, L. R. 1990. Family, marriage and the same-sex couple. *Cardoza Law
Review* 12: 681–706.

Index